To Norman Schneider
with every best with,
Sincerely,
Stanley R. Hopper
— Madison, 2/18/52

THE CRISIS OF FAITH.

THE CRISIS OF FAITH

By

Stanley Romaine Hopper

ABINGDON-COKESBURY PRESS

New York • *Nashville*

THE CRISIS OF FAITH
COPYRIGHT, MCMXLIV
By WHITMORE & STONE

Wartime Books

*Wartime shortage of pulp, manpower, and transportation has
produced a severe shortage of paper. In compliance with orders
of the War Production Board, wartime books are printed on
lighter-weight paper. This reduces thickness and weight. New
books have more words to the page and smaller margins. This reduces the number of pages without reducing reading content.*

*Thinner books save paper, critical copper, and other metals.
They help also to avoid wartime increases in book prices.
Wartime books appear to be smaller, but their content has not
been cut. They are complete. The only change is in appearance.*

K

PRINTED IN THE UNITED STATES OF AMERICA

In Memory of

CAPTAIN SAMUEL DUFF HOPPER

Soldier, Teacher, Pioneer
but to me
Father, Philosopher of Faith, and Friend

PREFACE

IT IS THE AIM OF THIS STUDY TO EXAMINE THE PRESENT CRISIS OF civilization from the standpoint of the Christian faith. The present situation witnesses to a profound contradiction in the spirit of man. We are enabled to see today those patterns of compromise which lie far back along the pathway we have come—patterns which serve to clarify a lurking ambiguity heretofore concealed. Superficially, man's most pressing problems appear to be political, social, and economic in character. Underneath, however, we know that something far more fundamental is at stake. This deeper issue is that of the ultimate goal and meaning for the life of man. For the issue at stake has to do with nothing less than our whole way of life and with the inmost spiritual demand of the soul. It is the question as to our nature and destiny. Indeed, it would appear that the confusion of recent times has reached such extremities that our thinking must almost inevitably recoil into Christian truth. Modern man has brought himself face to face with the redemptive problem—the old, old question: What must I and my world do to be saved?

In this it will readily be seen that there is a necessary correlation between a crisis of culture and our way of looking at the world, between what we do and what we believe. Any inquiry into the nature of these relationships falls within the field of practical philosophy. But it also falls within the realm of Christian anthropology and enforces thereby the primacy of faith in all our practical determinations.

We recognize, of course, that Christianity itself has been called in question. In proposing, therefore, a renewal of the Christian understanding of the nature of man and of his destiny as necessary to order and stability in our world, we do not suggest a simple retreat upon history. Harmony will not be restored by a mere reduplication of some previous historical synthesis. A new understanding is required, one that will do justice to whatever is permanently true in traditional standpoints, but which will at the same time take into account whatever is valid in the modern experiment. There is a sense, indeed, in which the crisis serves to clarify the real nature of Christian belief, even as Christianity provides the only true key for a full understanding of the crisis.

The first task of the study, therefore, will be to clarify the basic nature of our need. That being done, we shall be in a position to show how two fundamental principles may be united: the primacy of faith on the one hand, and the appeal to experience on the other.

Heretofore the appeal to experience has failed to be sufficiently Socratic. That is, in its attempt to be purely "scientific" it has avoided that Socratic "criticism of life" to which a thoroughgoing use of the principle should lead. On the other hand, the appeal to faith has suffered equally through dogmatic, legalistic, or authoritarian curtailments which have handicapped from the source all efforts to bring the faith into relation with a truly creative interpretation of life. The content of revelation and faith must be realized both creatively and evangelically just as the empirical appeal must consummate itself in a true Christian criticism of life. The Cross will be seen to be the meeting point of these appeals.

In such times it is inevitable that "prophecies, apocalypses, glances at and studies of the future" should appear. Since Spengler's *The Decline of the West* this prophetic role has been ventured by poets, philosophers, sociologists, political reformers, literary critics, and theologians. To all of these I am indebted. They are, to some extent, prophetic antennae reaching forward into what's-next-to-be in the world. One cannot fail to be impressed with the high seriousness of their works and with the way in which they have probed deeply into the inner problem of man's destiny. They are an integral part of the evidence I have tried to bring to bear upon the problem of the present crisis. I have incorporated many insights from these volumes, and those who wish to pursue them further will find in the footnotes a documentation of the most important sources. This will also mark the trail of my indebtedness, though it has been my aim to find my way between the thoughts of others rather than to reduplicate them.

It has also been necessary to treat of men, movements, and ideas more summarily than would be desirable from an ideal standpoint. The estimates of men, therefore, are not rounded estimates, and abridgements of historical movements and ideas run the risk of doing violence to many elements which must be regarded as secondary for this present purpose. My main thought has been to emphasize the factors which throw light on destiny and which help to clarify the means of Christian renewal.

One thing is sure. The age now agonizes after truth. The truth which it seeks with an intense wistfulness is a peculiar transfiguration of its failures and frustrations into hope and glory. But it does not understand this. It does not yet behold how great a glory was in Christ, or how "in him all things cohere."

S. R. H.

CONTENTS

11

Interlude

ALICE AND THE WHITE KNIGHT, *or* REACTION AND THE PHILOSOPHY OF HISTORY

Part Two

OUR HERITAGE OF FAITH

Man as image of God and the problem of the evil will. (iv) Christian
humanism. Its personal and universal character. Christian humanism versus
rationalism and legalism. Promethean character of other humanisms.
Christianity both humanizing and personalizing.

The journey to the self. (i) Problem of identity and the discovery of self-
transcendence. Hume. Definitions. The false infinite. (ii) The capacity for
self-transcendence as the primary mark of man. Augustine, Heraclitus,
Nietzsche, Kant. Man understood as spirit, as the capacity whereby the
self may relate itself. (iii) The alternatives of relating oneself: to the impersonal, to the fantastical, to the self, to the power to relate itself, to the
idea, to the world, to other persons, to God. (iv) Corollaries concerning
man. The paradox of man's search for himself. Man as viator. The levels
of experience. Man in relation to God's will. (v) Corollaries concerning
God. Discreteness of relationship. God and his Word. Christ the Teacher
and the Way.

True self-knowledge prerequisite to relationship to God. (i) Solutions proposed by Socrates, medieval mysticism, and Christianity. (ii) The Socratic
formula: sin as ignorance. Its latent rationalism. Objections to the view.
(iii) The mystical view: sin as privation of the good. The pattern of
ascent. The capacity for self-transcendence falsely hypostatized. Mode of
union metaphysical primarily. (iv) The Christian view: sin as evil will.
Pascal and the maieutic discipline toward faith. Augustine. Christ and the
true self-knowledge.

The Cross as the "crux" of the human situation and the unacknowledged
presupposition of Western culture. (i) The Cross as the revelation that the
human contradiction is grounded in the spirit. Presumption and anxiety,
limited knowledge and unlimited capacity, finitude and infinitude, contingency and potentiality, creaturehood and capacity for God. (ii) The
Cross as the revelation that the practical nature of truth is personal and
relational. The Cross as the true analogy of the human condition, thrusting
man out of the abstract and upon the infinite particular. (iii) The Cross as
the revelation that the inner forms of history are founded dialectically upon
the use of human freedom. Discrepancies between fate and destiny, necessity and possibility, faith and denial, spirit and law, history and *eschatos*.
(iv) The Cross a revelation of the way of victory. Apostasy, reversal, re-
capitulation. Beyond good and evil. The crisis of faith. (v) The Christian
task a redemptive and creative transfiguration of the world through the
power of the Spirit. Christ the source of peace and power.

Introduction

THE MIDNIGHT HOUR

CIVILIZATION HAS REACHED IN OUR TIME WHAT TIUTCHEV HAS CALLED the "hour of wordless longing," when man, "without home, or-phaned, alone, impotent, . . . sees and knows a fatal heritage." This heritage roots backward in our past, how far we scarcely know. It also roots in the modern soul, how deeply we are loath to say. But that this heritage is ours, and that we have reached at last a "midnight hour in which each one must unmask," is clear to all who are attentive to the world's bewilderment, its pain, its longing, its contention, and its impotence. This is a moment that we share; and, since we share it, there are few today who shun the issue of the soul's perplexity.

Civilization has come alarmingly near to a failure of nerve. The rise of forces powerful enough to overwhelm and nullify the bequest of centuries is the sobering fact of our time. We are ex-periencing a crisis of our total culture, a crisis which is also the most profound crisis of the spirit since the beginning of the Chris-tian era. In the terse but penetrating pronouncement of Léon Bloy, "Modern man has been brought to bay at the extremity of all things."

This means that we are faced today with a problem that is almost infinitely complex. Both inwardly and outwardly we are faced with the multiple contradictions inherent in our way of looking at the world—as though some deeply basic contradiction of the soul were reflected back upon it again and again from every conceivable angle by multiple mirrors. At the same time there are advantages which come with "crisis," when the foundations of an epoch are wearing out, when the structure itself is threatened, and when the supposed unity of a culture or civilization betrays

15

its inner contradictions and a fundamental error long persisted in reveals its inconsistencies. The moment of crisis may, on the one hand, be filled with fate; and the civilization, like many another before it, may succumb. But the moment of crisis may also be big with prophetic possibilities, not the least of which is the liberating perspective which it brings to bear upon ourselves and our world.

It is imperative, however, that we should seize upon whatever is prophetic in the present situation and hold it firmly, very much as Jacob held the angel at the ford of the Jabbok; for the man who has been brought to bay at the extremity of all things is a man like Jacob. In a profound sense, we wrestle through the dark night of these times with none other than God's angel. And what we seek is what Jacob sought—to know God's name. For until we know his name, we shall not rightly know our own.

i

In the period of crisis, then, two fundamental aspects of our human situation stand opposed: our *fatal heritage* and our *heritage of faith*. It would be convenient if we could ignore the first, or leap over it by a kind of acrobatic miracle. It would indeed be a miracle, tantamount to leaping over our own heads; for the very meaning of the crisis is that our heritage of faith has been called in question. Principles which men have long believed in are threatened fatally. That which enervates all moral action and which nullifies all simple programs for recovery and all propae-deutics for reform, is a backlying skepticism which cuts the ground from under each proposal. We cannot, therefore, in the first motion, counsel faith; it is the faith precisely which is in question. The doubt is there beforehand. It is a doubt, however, which conceals itself and hides in the depths of the human heart. Thence the deep depression of the world, which can hardly rouse itself to throw off the naïve tyrannies which threaten to destroy it.

In every historical development two contrary possibilities are present. They are based upon the fact of human freedom, which works upon the causal factors in our "limit situation." The judicious exercise of this freedom, and the successful fruition of man's just aims within the world, makes for *destiny*. The injudicious

16

use of human freedom, compounded demonically with the impersonal succession of effects upon causes, makes for *fate*. Between these tendencies the drama of existence plays.

The cause-and-effect factor is not in itself fatal. It is not evil. When we speak of natural law—a term which sums our naïve reckonings—we speak of something we have come to understand in part. We understand its nature from observation of its regularities. Even the child soon learns that it is dangerous to fall, that some things cut, that others burn. We depend upon these regularities, upon the recurrence or predictable sequence of causes and effects. We employ them to abet our aims. Through them we fashion destiny. But when we fall afoul of them, or when the spirit gets wedged between two regularities that act upon it as upper and nether millstones, grinding into powder something we had hoped for, we lapse into the antique dignity and call it "Fate."

The factor of fate, however, is a complex factor. As causality, it conditions us. As time, it pursues us. As mortality, it overtakes us, enforcing on us the final bounds of creaturehood. But we resent the limitations and defy the terms which fix our finitude. And when the instrument of human freedom is employed defiantly, it enters into a kind of demonic complicity with fate and gives to the causal recurrence a spirited—though antispiritual—dynamic of its own. In recent times this demonic consciousness has entered into the world more sharply than at any previous period. Yet, paradoxically, our loss of orientation toward religious meanings has left even the demonic consciousness strangely vitiated by the overwhelming hopelessness of struggle in an impersonal world. The little tyrannies usurp the thrones. No longer certain as to what the end of man is, or his destiny, we lapse from power and control and suffer ourselves to be carried along by the fatal momenta of our epoch's prior choosing. We are thus swept forward into the doom that has long been preparing.

That this has come to pass in our enlightened world has been, for some, an unexpected turn. It is a sharp reversal of the plot of modern history, a baffling denouement of reason, progress, and the rights of man. It is not merely an unexpected denouement, but one which discloses suddenly an inner impotence in modern man. The sense of threat, uneasiness, and frustration that men have felt is at once fateful and prophetic. It is fateful in the literal sense of being filled with fate. It is prophetic in the sense that we experience a new demand—the demand for a total revision of our postulates.

In becoming aware of this, our century has experienced already a preliminary psychological recoil. The recoil has been twofold. There has been the initial reluctance to confess the failure. There is now the second reluctance to make the new decision. The first experience is filled with fate; we chose to flee from it rather than to confront it. It overtook us, like the avenging Furies. The second experience takes away the illusion of our supposed security and brings the suffering of effort—of venturing far out in a new commitment. Crisis means that the fate from which we fled has overtaken us and that the premises we thought secure are broken. We are brought to bay. We therefore experience today the anxiety which comes with every fatal undoing.

The experience of this fatality is morally hypnotic. Our situation is like that of the chess player who is suddenly confronted with "Discovered check!" A piece that stood protectively between the player's king and his opponent's threatening piece is suddenly withdrawn, leaving the king exposed to threat upon its very life, the game. So with us, certain of our notions which have served to veil from us the threat upon our culture have been suddenly withdrawn. The myths of man's intrinsic goodness, of the indefinite progress of man, and of the self-sufficient reason, which formerly were interposed protectively between contemporary man —the little king—and the threat of cultural disaster, have been removed, discovering to modern man the universal crisis of his hopes and aims.

This fatal element in the crisis has been felt so universally as to have brought about in the first half of the twentieth century a kind of suffocation of the spirit. The nihilism of the Continental schools, the esoteric defeatism of modern poets, the rise of totalitarianisms in the politics of the world, and the baffled indifference of the people have all borne witness to this fateful element. It is only comparable to the classical nemesis which pursued man remorselessly whenever he defied the gods. In recent times this sense of an impending nemesis has been even more fateful; for it has been impersonal, mechanical, and sure.

> Whichever way we turn, we see
> Man captured by his liberty,
> The measurable taking charge
> Of him who measures. . . .
> . . . .
> That is no giant, god, or dwarf,
> But one odd human isomorph.[1]

Such a benumbing rebuff to human dignity brings with it, however, one positive element: it brings man into sharp conflict with the boundaries of the human situation and asserts these reflexively, but none the less positively, at the point where the false premises of a culture or a civilization recoil upon man in the crisis. This positive element is illustrated most happily in G. K. Chesterton's figure: When a man jumps off a cliff, he doesn't defy the law of gravitation; he merely illustrates it. Similarly, when a culture or a civilization jumps off a cliff, it doesn't defy the ontological conditions which sanction it, or the nature of man, or the nature of God, or the nature of man's destiny under God. It merely illustrates them. In short, at the point of crisis, our reasonings are thrust against the ultimate nature and meaning of things. The religious and metaphysical understanding of man is thus renewed.

From this it will be seen that a culture, or a civilization, which has gone wrong on first principles is fundamentally in dialectical conflict with itself. It is like a many-headed hydra, growing lustily at first and breeding many heads. At length, however, it goes mad through willful opposition of the heads, which tear and rend each other until it has destroyed itself. This action, when thus fatally determined, is a negative clarification of what was implicit from the beginning—of what was "in the nature of the beast."

[1] W. H. Auden, *The Double Man* (New York: Random House, 1941), pp. 57, 69.

INTRODUCTION

Today we see many vicious opposites tearing and rending each other and threatening to destroy what men have known and cherished as the "West."

The West confronts its own principles deflected upon it violently from the East. This presents to the Western consciousness a perspective that is entirely new, and for which there is no precise historical precedent. The cataclysmic conflict of forces throughout the world is the external evidence of a deep inner cleft within the spirit of modern man.

It is clear today, for example, that the conflict itself is not primarily a conflict of East with West. The conflict is one of ideologies, of ways of looking at man and the world. Defiant ideologies have arisen from within the framework of the Western world view and are a form of rebellion from within the civilization itself. This rebellion is founded on a hostility to principles hitherto widely acknowledged: principles of freedom, integrity, and the rights of man. It is a rebellion against the Christian and classical origins from which these principles of human dignity have been derived. And it has succeeded so well because the subtleties of compromise have so far attenuated the principles themselves that ethical clarity and moral discrimination can no longer be claimed for great masses of men.

This process of moral obfuscation, which over a period of time has blurred the premises from which our civilization stems, has received also the sanction of many of the most celebrated minds of recent times. It has entered deeply into the "stream of consciousness" which forms the patterns for those masses of men who do little thinking for themselves. It has unwittingly aided the forces of rebellion, while vitiating at the same time the energies of men who might have suppressed it. We have been overtaken in a period of moral weakness through our failure to keep our mentality criticized by the great practical wisdom of the ages. The cleft within the world is rooted in the spirit of modern man; it is now brought into the open. Yet at the same time these defections lie deeply concealed in the human heart.

There is something in the so-called "modern" attitude, with its postulate of the universal autonomy of the self-sufficient man, that is in its throes of death. Somewhat is finished. The strife of isms is, on its negative side, the strife of this illogicality, the fortuitous expression of specious aims. What was abortive in the "modern" attitude is being purged away. What was parochial in the notion of the "West" is being thrust aside by the enhanced perspective of a newer "global consciousness." Christianity itself is discovering how its alliances with successive philosophic systems in Western thought have circumscribed its true spirit and made it partisan to ancillary causes, governments, or institutions. This also is a negative disclosure.

We may distinguish, therefore, in every crisis two conflicting tendencies—the elements of fate and the elements of destiny. In crisis the opposition between the two is brought to a climax. A crisis is not itself the end: it is the moment of fevered suspension when everything hangs in doubt between life and death, between victory and defeat. At such a moment we must specify the fatal elements within our heritage; we must also bring to bear upon the modern consciousness the principles within our heritage which make for faith, for destiny.

ii

In order to bring about such a clarification of our heritage, we must distinguish at the outset two aspects of method which must be employed by anyone who wishes to get at the roots of the problem. There is, on the one hand, the subjective or polemical aspect, whereby the soul must be made to acknowledge its own complicity in the problem. For crisis here, as in an illness, implies the climax of struggle between life and death. The real question about a culture in crisis is the question as to whether sufficient vitality of spirit remains to bring about a new and compendious decision. On the other hand, there is the objective task of analysis, whereby we work backward along the way which we have come in order to determine the point or points in history where our civilization went wrong. To undertake one or the other of these inquiries is not difficult; but to combine them, as must be done in cultural analysis, seems to perch the soul somewhat hazardously upon the point of logical ambiguity between the objective pursuit and the subjective demand. Nevertheless, as Karl Jaspers has said so trenchantly, "He who wishes to find his way to the origin of the crisis must pass through the lost domain of truth, in order to revise it possessively; must traverse the domain of perplexity to reach decision concerning himself; must strip off the trappings of the masquerade, in order to disclose the genuine that lies beneath." [2] The difficulty in procedure arises from the fact that all three of these things must be done at the same time.

Clearly this is a Socratic task. It implies a criticism of life more stringent even than that of Socrates. As Socrates cross-questioned the Sophists out of their supposed fixed knowledge and into an awareness of their fundamental ignorance, so we must cross-question ourselves out of our present sophistries and into an awareness of the ground lines of the human situation. History offers an immediate point of appeal; for, given the common starting point of crisis which all men share, we are driven backward upon the antecedents of the crisis in order to throw light upon the present situation.

Heretofore our speculations on history and culture and civilization have not probed deeply. History has been a perusal of surfaces. The myth of "objectivity" has tyrannized over us so that we have not dared to bring history into relation with the moral sciences, let alone employ it as an instrument for philosophic knowledge. But today a new dimension is thrust upon us. It is the dimension of the human boundary, with certain limit-notions forcing us out of our temporal self-sufficiencies and back upon the eternal. We are obliged today to renew meaning and wisdom and to reconsider what it means to be human. We have an immediate appeal to what Jacques Maritain has called "the *concrete logic of the events of history.*" [3] History, as the context of human choosing, is a means of self-knowledge and acquires thereby philosophical significance.

As for "culture," we have been largely frightened at the term ever since Matthew Arnold defined it as "a knowledge of the uni-

[2] *Man in the Modern Age* (tr. E. and C. Paul; New York: Henry Holt & Co., 1933), pp. 89-90.
[3] *Scholasticism and Politics* (tr. ed. Mortimer J. Adler; New York: The Macmillan Co., 1940), p. 1.

versal order which seems to be intended and aimed at in the world, and which it is a man's happiness to go along with or his misery to go counter to." [4] The philosophers and the moralists and the scientists, by a kind of undeclared conspiracy, have closed the topic off within the realm of aesthetics, which realm, thanks to the romanticists, was already severed from relations with the world. What Matthew Arnold aimed at, however, was at bottom an old Socratic principle, that "a life without criticism," or reflection upon the meaning of life, "is unworthy of a man." [5] We discover now that the events of history themselves perform this Socratic function over a period of time by carrying out in the dialectic of life itself whatever is implicit in the epoch's basic attitude. History, however, can only perform this negatively, since history is, properly speaking, nothing on its own account. It is merely the record of human choosing. The record serves merely to bring to our notice the dialectical element in the total conflux of human choices, at the point where these choices make for man's happiness or misery in the world.

History is the construct of men's choices qualified by the nature of the world we live in. Culture also may be defined as the soul of an epoch writ large—the tangible ordeal of the soul's efforts to realize its destiny in the world. The products of culture appear at the point where man's creative aims secure their victories over empiric fact. We must not only overcome this empirical factor; we must work within it. We also presuppose men's prior workings in the world. We work within and work upon momenta already moving like the tides through past and present. Without diligence of mind and will we may easily be overborne by these tidal cataracts of time and place which sweep through generations to roar and thunder on tomorrow's world.

In times of crisis the spirit is oppressed with the sense that these impersonal tides of tendency have overborne our powers of control and compass us round with disaster. We experience the momentary panic in which we summon all our powers to stop the tide externally before it engulfs the world. Beyond this there

[4] *Culture and Anarchy* (New York: The Macmillan Co., 1908), p. 9.
[5] *Apology*, 38A.

lies the reconstructive task which must reach within and heal the aeon's despair.

The use of history, therefore, which concerns us today is that use which unites dialectically the event, the idea, and the interpretation of life behind and beyond these. This form of inquiry has been used increasingly in recent times. It makes possible what Wilhelm Dilthey called a "critique of historical reason." It provides philosophy itself with a kind of historical self-knowledge. It fixes upon the central problem of man's orientation in the world. It provides in the widest sense the materials necessary for what Jaspers terms an "elucidation of existence" (*"Existenzerhellung"*). More simply, it is that fundamental "criticism of life" necessary to all wisdom and worthiness; only it is pushed Socratically against our "limit situation" and against ourselves. In times of extreme crisis we are bent back upon the primary terms of our situation. We are at such a point today. The soul has been shaken to its roots. What complicates the issue is that in this moment of crisis when we stand "between the times," every cast-off notion rises to renew its relevance, and the faiths and passions which we thought were dead prove now that they were dormant only.

In such a time the task of criticism is a sober one. The critic must pare away the surfaces of pain and pride. He must enter into the declivity of an aeon's despair. He must reach as far as possible into the mystery of human destiny, which is, indeed, "a pit too deep for mortal eyes to plumb." His task, as Jeremiah said, must be to pluck up and to plant; for a crisis of a civilization is a curious collision between our temporal aims and the ultimate conditions. It is not a simple opposition. It frustrates our aims and sets our principles ajar. It forces upon us a fundamental dislocation of all that we have heretofore assumed or taken for granted. It puts everything in abeyance, which means simply that the epoch has been brought to the point of a new decision.

Western civilization has reached a parting of the ways; and men of faith are now engaged in renewing vitally our heritage of faith, since by it alone can we transform the fatality that now besets us into an occasion for a fresh beginning in the world.

Part One

OUR FATAL HERITAGE

*Behold man, without home,
orphaned, alone, impotent,
facing the dark abyss. . . .
And in this strange mysterious night
he sees and knows a fatal heritage.*
—TIUTCHEV

Chapter I

ASPECTS OF THE CRISIS

To THROW A NOOSE AROUND THE SOUL AT THE SURFACE OF ITS PAIN is not difficult, in view of the present struggle in the world which outwardly attests to it. In fact, we welcome some such encirclement if it clarifies the inner nature of the present conflict in the world and if it brings to light the constant nature of our need. Unhappily, so much has been said and written about "crisis" and our cultural collapse that we easily insulate ourselves against the critic's task. And justly so if in his estimates of "culture" and "humanity" and "civilization" and the "world" he gets no nearer to the individual than these general class terms. The objective task is an important one, and one that we are obligated to perform; but it must be polemically related to the inner problem of all who experience the crisis. We must, then, summarize initially the aspects of the crisis as the crisis itself bears upon the individual, forcing him inwardly upon his "midnight hour."

i

The "midnight hour" in which "all men must unmask" is an hour of impotence, solitariness, confusion of spirit—crisis. It is characterized by man's loss of inner confidence in himself and his private powers, by chaos of aesthetic aims, by wars and spoliations, by every apparatus of escape and diversion of spirit that can be contrived. We perceive a nervous eagerness on the part of each man to avoid those deeper silences in which the soul is forced into its inner emptiness and loss of meaning.

This loss of meaning is betrayed in all cultures by a pervasive anonymity, wherein each man's enterprise is swallowed up in a totality which does not care. The apotheosis of the totality, as in

27

collectivist economies, does not resolve the anonymity. The dignity of work, wherein each man once set the seal of his own creative genius and derived those satisfactions which come from having set the stamp of one's own powers on a thing of usefulness or beauty, loses its power to inspire or to console. Work itself is mechanized, or regimented, or depersonalized. Such distinctions as the worker earns or receives do not bring with them satisfactions for the soul. The worker merely proves to nameless powers that he is "useful." and so becomes a tool for some more massive enterprise.

Anonymity forbids any careful analysis. It is clearly, none the less, a result. Anonymity is the effect of some concealed process of devaluation which draws all personal meanings and satisfactions off into the abstract, and at the same time it draws off all spiritual implications into a purely secular or prudential calculus of advantage and disadvantage. Men are thus depersonalized and dehumanized. The results are clear. We can only surmise that, lying far back in the psychological conditioning which must have prepared the mind for this incredible surrender of its inherent dignity, is the failure of religion, or—and this is by no means the same thing—the failure of ourselves and those who have gone before us properly to understand and to apply the values and standards which our religious heritage contained.

In the moment of crisis, however, we experience initially as a failure of religion what may be at bottom a failure in ourselves. In a crisis we observe that the failure of religion is the mark of such a time. Its impotence is everywhere attested by the lapse of value into secularity and money power. Men must live for something, so they live for "business" and machines, which enterprises carry ova in themselves and fertilize themselves perpetually, producing eggs like spiders' eggs, each sac containing hundreds of little spiders which feed on one another until only the strongest survive to break the shell. And to what end? To prey on other insects!

Failure of religion is a prelude always to a deadly secularity. Secularity supposes temporality. It is a capitulation to the here and now, to practicality. In it a dimension has been lost, or obviated, or ignored. It signifies a fracture of the faith, a loss of conscious rapport with the ideal, a loss of the sense of the presence of God, a denial. It divorces man's act from the permanent implications of his action; or it gives to his act only temporal implications. Meaning is localized, having no ultimate justification. Greatness is diminished, having no unimpeachable significance. "Man, proud man, dressed in a little brief authority" falls prey to endless divagation and remorse.

Remorse, however, is only a symptom of a deeper pain. Man loses God: he falls a victim to the false gods, which betray him daily, giving stones instead of bread. "The most prostituted being," said Baudelaire, "is God"! Indeed it is true, in the sense that his integrity is violated by every idol man sets up. And man, as Baudelaire was also well aware, sets up many idols. "Man is a worshiping animal. . . . There are in every man, at every moment, two simultaneous postulations: one toward God, the other toward Satan. The invoking of God, or spirituality, is a desire to rise in degree; that of Satan, or animality, is a joy in descending."[1] Or, as Luther put it, *"Der Mensch hat immer Gott oder Abgott"*—"Man has always either God or an idol." But not to have God—that is, to have an idol—is, as Baudelaire has said, to descend toward animality. Yet man is also spirit; and to descend toward animality while being yet a spirit is to evoke not remorse but anguish and vexation, as the spirit is progressively cheated in the pursuit of its idolatries.

There is a certain inevitability about this progressive discovery that the chosen object or value is a false god. To make an idol of anything that is not absolute is to confer upon that thing an absolute significance. Such an idol cannot support the demands we make upon it. The whole order of significance is perverted. A "transvaluation of values" takes place in accordance with the

[1] *Journaux intimes*, "Mon coeur mis à nu," 45, 19.

new object of worship. All things are subject to the new evaluation. We deceive ourselves in thinking that the new value will serve as well as the old; and the new value deceives us because, at bottom, it is of no *value* at all. It is in retreat from value, which can be determined only by reference to the true Object—God. If the idol chosen is less than spirit, all values are materialized; if it is less than personal, all men are dehumanized. *Secularization* has been in our time the particular form of this devaluation.

Perhaps this dignifies too much our secularities. But, on the other hand, perhaps our "secularity" diminishes too much the basic nature of our choosing.

The special idol of our times has been the proletarian appeal to *facts* (the most factitious term of all)—dogmatically mistaking the tangible for the real and growing like a fungus on the corpse of a materialistic science. This is a science long since discredited. It served, nevertheless, to propagate a "method" that bedizened us for decades with a new supposition—the supposition that, given time, it would solve the problem of the essences of things, lay bare the secret sequence of events, and clarify all mysteries, according to the laws of strict causality and evolutionary progress. Its history has been rehearsed now many times, and it is simple.

Beginning with the newer dispensation (the new covenant) of the Copernican revolution, setting free the "moribund" intelligences of medieval minds (to speak from within the revolution), and conferring on the "modern" man a sense of liberation and emancipation from Church authorities and dogmas, it ushered in the "age of reason and of man." In the eighteenth century this science took on a role more hallowed still: it became Revealer, and the age was called the age of the Enlightenment. Thence came the "century of hope," the century in which science as "the new Messiah" offered men a new salvation—the salvation of indefinite progress, the bliss of material achievement, with comfort, goods, and conveniences for all. The twentieth century acknowledged this new Kingdom, projected its utopias, complied with all pragmatics, and sought to usher in the Kingdom for the masses. Accepting Marx as its latter-day prophet, it sought the rationalization of all mankind (as Lenin said, the "electrification" of Europe).

Today, the Science which is the religion of the intelligentsia possesses its theologies, known as the philosophies of Materialism and Mechanism. It is elaborating its morals, from physical eugenesis to intellectual mathesis and social praxis; it acknowledges the *ipse dixit;* it owns its disciplines of research, its asceticisms of self-abnegation, its sanctimonies, shrines, saints. Nay, it has its fanatics and devotees, apoplectic intolerants and mystic visionaries, formulating great myths of cosmogenesis and apocalyptic doom.[2]

There is an obvious distinction here between the religion of science and the scientist doing his proper work in his proper sphere. The tests of scientific knowledge do not include "an intellectual invulnerability to error" but rather "impersonality of judgment, caution in theory, social subordination of the individual . . . what is called respect for truth, where truth is conceived as subject to abstract formulation." What we have failed to recognize is that not all truth is subject to this latter condition, which failure makes for that false universalization whereby science passes over unwittingly into the spheres of philosophy and religion without acknowledging at the same time the new requirements and the new tests for knowledge which these new spheres demand. The result is that either philosophy and religion are reduced to the preclusive demands of science or science usurps the fields of the former and appears, as with the "intelligentsia," as a new religion.

This new religion fed upon the Darwinian myths. It was prolonged in a hundred pseudo sciences, including mechanistic psychologies, sociologies, economic "orders," and "realistic" arts. It dominated, and still dominates, the common mind more thoroughly than many people are aware. For it supplies not merely a faith but a world view, which is the presupposition of every culture. It is a way of looking at the world, a way of comprehending life and truth. It has penetrated even into religion and philosophy, wherever philosophy has sought to be objective "like

[2] H. B. Alexander, *God and Man's Destiny* (New York: Oxford University Press, 1936), pp. 8-9.

science" and wherever religion has emptied its own terms of their significance in order to be more "rational." Philosophy became another science, just a little more abstract, and retreated into its sphere of specialization. Science was invested with authority over fact; and religion was relegated to the vague, the otherworldly, the irrelevant. Thereby religion was severed from life. Today men have religious "interests" just as they have political interests or aesthetic interests. Religion has become a phase or aspect of their thought and life. But for that very reason they are not religious, since religion makes a total claim. Religion is immanent within, and determinative of, man's every act; it is the basis for man's way of looking at the world. To relegate religion to the fringe of interests, or to make it secondary in any way, is subtly to abandon it. Science, when invested with authority over fact, both begs the question as to fact and supplants religion—becomes, that is, metaphysically presumptuous and religiously naïve.

The point is of some importance; for, from the standpoint of practical philosophy, which is the sphere of all inquiry into culture, the seat of authority or the focal point of dogma is all-significant. The important thing is not, as Max Weber held, that "a disenchantment of the world is taking place" and that all men have wished to see reality without illusions[3]; it is rather that by inference from these and other like words and attitudes religion and philosophy *became* the realms of unreality and illusion. Philosophy capitulated, wishing to be "disinterested" like science; and, following the analogy of the scientific method, it retreated into its hermetic sphere of speculation, carefully sealed off from contact with the world. Religion compromised with anthropology and sociology and so maintained a quasi function in the world. The power which could bring so much to pass was the transfer of authority to "fact" and the propagated dogma of a "method." At all times in the world there are, as Chesterton remarked, two kinds of people: the conscious dogmatists and the unconscious dogmatists. A dogma is no less powerful if it is held unwittingly. In this case the concealed assumption was the belief that science was

[3] Werner Brock, *Contemporary German Philosophy* (Cambridge University Press, 1935), p. 8.

synonymous with truth and that the truth itself must be susceptible of rational analysis and formulation, the work, as Pascal
phrased it, of "the geometric mind"—"*l'esprit de géométrie.*"
Thus science, and those who complied with its new dogmas,
idolized the *fact* and raised this fragile serpent on a rod in Jericho,
demanding universal obeisance.

iii

The crisis of the new physics has intercepted all of this. Philosophy and theology are now recovering their rightful relationships
to the interpretation of life. The work of Continental religious
thinkers, both Protestant and Catholic; the "existential" philosophies; the "world-view" interests of Nietzsche, Dilthey, Spengler,
and others; the work of the Personalists in France and of the
Personalists and Critical Humanists in America—all these confirm the movement toward a "human" starting point. It is possible for the student of philosophical trends to say today that
"autonomous science can no longer claim to be what it imagined
itself: . . . the highest intellectual achievement in the whole history of the Western mind." [4]

The confidence that came with discovery, invention, and indus-
trial achievement has been lost—in part, no doubt, because the
world view on which it long depended has been shattered. "Something unknown is doing we don't know what," [5] says Eddington.
At the same time confidence is lost because the industries themselves, the machines, the techniques, have recoiled upon the little
master and have imposed the pace and rhythm of mechanical
perfection upon him.

Twentieth-century man, therefore, has suffered two uprootings
—the one from Christian dogma, the other from scientific dogma.
As for the second of these uprootings, the myth of relativity has
arisen to supplant it. But, practically speaking, little is gained. The
common man, who relaxed his faith in Christianity to acquiesce
in the new scientific dogma, has now lost his myth again. He
either vacillates between the ancient faith and fragments of his

[4] *Ibid.,* p. 52.
[5] *The Nature of the Physical World* (New York: The Macmillan Co., 1928), p. 291.

causal cosmos, once so systematic and airtight; or he lapses into relativity, for him a moral flux, which leaves him skeptical of all results and baffled by each claim upon his loyalty. He has become a "sociological" animal—the irony of which is, that he can become a *sociological* animal only in so far as he rises above what is purely animal in him to become human. But to be human implies spiritual relatedness to the Absolute. This relatedness to the Absolute—to the personal God of religion—is, however, just that which was compromised when he became sociological. Unless, therefore, sociological man grounds his understanding of man on something more ultimate than man, the most that sociology can hope to do for him is to ameliorate altruistically that fatal rationalization of mankind which, as Dostoevski saw, leads to the "one unanimous and harmonious ant heap"—the sociological *animal*.

Matthew Arnold found himself between two worlds:

> Wandering between two worlds, one dead,
> The other powerless to be born,
> With nowhere yet to rest my head,
> Like these, on earth I wait forlorn.

He saw the end of the ancient faith in Renaissance modernity. He also saw the impotence of scientific rationalism to issue into life. Now this causal competence of science itself has been shattered. Matthew Arnold's predicament is doubled in our time. The "block-and-tackle universe" has been displaced by relativity and flux: Newton has been overwhelmed by Einstein, with Darwin but an episode. Or, to follow out these implications to their furthest point, man stands today not only at the point where "three dreams cross" but at the extreme point of tension where all the world views—Christian, pagan, medieval, modern, positivist, Marxist—lay their claims upon him, where each is imperious and none is imperial, the ideal vanishing point of assured self-consciousness. Culture disintegrates for want of a consistent world view. Personalities are atomized. *Individuals*—what Emerson described as "infinitely repellant particles"—appear; and these are compromised, dissolved, in the endless mutations of the collectivist ideal.

All this, however, is a surface estimate. The idolatry of fact of which we speak, is but the outer aspect of an inner defection. The true idolatry throughout the period was none other than that divined by Blaise Pascal, who, reflecting on these tendencies within his own century, exclaimed: "One makes an idol of truth even!" The autonomous science was based upon the autonomous reason. The autonomous reason seeks everywhere to justify itself; and this it does by presupposing itself. As Midas transmuted into gold everything he touched, so the self-sufficient reason translates everything into an abstract universal or into an ideal mathematical unity. Whether truth be summed up in the universal cipherhood of abstract "unity" or dissipated in the sign of the infinite. the life is lost. Our poets ask:

> Where is the Life we have lost in living?
> Where is the wisdom we have lost in knowledge?
> Where is the knowledge we have lost in information?
> The cycles of Heaven in twenty centuries
> Bring us farther from God and nearer to the Dust.[6]

Clearly we have reached a strange impasse. The autonomy of reason, which was the special pride of the "age of reason and enlightenment," and which supplemented itself so adroitly with the nineteenth-century myth of "indefinite progress," has now, through the extension of its autonomy into the realms of government and politics and culture, nullified itself in the totalitarian subordination of all things to the state. The modern mind has thus in the name of its autonomy lost its autonomy. The modern mind, still clinging to its self-sufficiency upon the one hand, is on the other hand appalled at the successful regimentation of the several aspects of its practical life. It is caught between its own vicious extremes. It is *tantalized*. Like Tantalus in the ancient myth, it fain would pluck a fruit it cannot reach and drink the water which it cannot touch; and thus, dialectically frustrate, it hungers and thirsts after a righteousness it does not understand.

One thing is clear, however. The principle on which the present age was founded has run its course. The "return to freedom"

[6] T. S. Eliot, "Choruses from *The Rock*," *Collected Poems 1909-1935* (New York: Harcourt, Brace & Co., 1936), p. 179.

which we see about us in the world is a profound turning, though purchased at the price of a purgation in death and suffering. It is at once a philosophic challenge and a religious repentance, though awfully projected through the demonic martyrdom of nations. It is also clear that the return to freedom must imply a freedom more fundamental than that envisaged by the Renaissance. We must "pass through the lost domain of truth in order to revise it possessively."

One hope is offered by this turning. In traversing the "domain of perplexity in order to reach decision concerning himself" the modern man may be thrust once more upon philosophy, where he may again acquire a foothold on the real, and so renew creative satisfactions. For by reflection and the love of wisdom mankind ever is ennobled, and by their offices man's image is restored. By the path of wisdom and the real, mankind must return from waywardness and wandering. But "what is needed is a word which is not an empty word," [7] a word which issues into life and not abstraction. For the very source of our modernity has been that pride of intellect which has supposed that thought is self-sufficient and the exclusive instrument of the real. Philosophy itself, in its several rationalist forms, has erred; and to return upon it, without subjecting it to reformation on its own account, would be to renew the sources of our error. In short, since the Renaissance there have been not many philosophies but one philosophy with many variations;[8] and what reflection yields with us, as Kierkegaard has said, is a certain "virtuosity and good sense,"

[7] Karl Jaspers, *Man in the Modern Age*, p. 228.

[8] The measure of agreement on this point is today very wide: Karl Jaspers speaks of the philosophic schools of the modern period which, "despite the violently polemical atmosphere of their literature, were all fundamentally identical, although they bore various names, such as idealism, positivism, neo-Kantianism, criticism, phenomenology, objectivity." (*Man in the Modern Age*, p. 162.) T. E. Hulme remarked flatly that "all philosophy since the Renaissance is at bottom the *same* philosophy. The family resemblance is much greater than is generally supposed. The obvious diversity is only that of the various species of the same genus." (*Speculations* [New York: Harcourt, Brace & Co., 1924], p. 12.) Jacques Maritain goes further: "Whether they be neo-Kantians or neo-positivists, idealists, Bergsonians, logistics, pragmatists or neo-Spinozists, or neo-mysticists, one ancient sin works in the roots of all modern philosophies—the old error of *nominalism*." (*The Degrees of Knowledge* [New York: Charles Scribner's Sons, 1938], p. 1.)

which "consists in trying to get a judgement . . . without ever getting as far as action." [9]

Philosophical virtuosity is, from the moral standpoint, a sophistry, a means of avoiding the issue with dignity. It is a posture of the mind in which reflection covers over and masquerades our incapacity for moral choice. The purely academic thinker has always been a target for the ironies of satirists and moralists alike. An ironist like Heine might easily be moved to pay his disrespects to much contemporary speculation by a polite but formal overstatement of such theoretic aims. The thinker, he might say, perspicaciously assembles all the formidable apparatus of pedantry, deploys with academic detachment in the circumambient nomenclature of a pending cerebration, and concludes in a dignified article read at the Association or published in *Mind, a Journal of Philosophy* that what we must do is reason more systematically concerning reason: that is, pursue the *n*th refinement on the Neo-Kantian refinement of the epistemological impasse pommeled by Kant himself and stemming from Descartes: that is, think harder about thinking. What is apparent is the futility, in the present situation, of effort that, by postulation, issues only in reflection. For reflection—that is, the false reflection which systematically substitutes itself for and shuns the practical decision—is itself disease. It is the subtlest means by which our moral virtue has been enervated. Our incapacity for moral choice is nurtured by this ambiguity of reason and of doubt. It deprives our rectitude of standards by which to measure and of conviction wherewith to choose. Thus everywhere men sense the emptiness and the vacuity of moral aims. The mind itself, which once was postulated as the mark of man's essential dignity, has, through its own presumption, deprived man of his true dignity by reducing him to the "objective" and abstract. Nevertheless, the age is "intellectualist": it turns in circles on the surface of its own aberrant powers.

What we observe, then, in the modern period, is a situation strangely paradoxical. On the one hand we have a science which

[9] *The Present Age* (London: Oxford University Press, 1940), p. 3.

has idolized the fact, pressing everything into the objective and concrete; on the other we have had a philosophy reducing man to the abstract. Or, again, we have had a moral attitude affirming everywhere the autonomous individual; but we have produced a society reducing everywhere the individual to collectivity and anonymity. All of this has been done in the name of the autonomous reason.

iv

There are two rather remarkable documents which have appeared in recent years, the one in France and the other in the United States, the burden of whose argument is to show how our basic moral heritage has been sacrificed by precisely those persons in each society whose special province it is to preserve it. The first of these is *La trahison des clercs* (1927), [10] by Julien Benda, French critic and philosopher; the second is *The Irresponsibles* (1940), by the American poet and critic Archibald MacLeish.

Benda saw two things quite clearly. He saw that national loyalties were becoming the assertions of "one form of soul against other forms of soul," that political wars were fundamentally wars of cultures. He perceived further that these contending ideologies all pretended to be based upon science and "the strict observation of facts." Actually, however, they resulted from a loss of tradition. The time had compromised its Christian and classical heritage. Men were no longer concerned with the true image of men after the manner of the true humanists, the "great patricians of the mind" (Erasmus, Goethe, and others), but had allowed the *studia humanitatis* to be displaced by a "sentimental form of humanitarianism" which left the nation sapped by pacifisms, by secularity, and by "intellectual gregariousness." [11]

The second thing that Benda saw in this defection from the antique wisdom was that those who were responsible were the intellectuals—the "clerks"—the preachers and the scholars and

[10] English translation, *The Great Betrayal* (tr. Richard Aldington; London: G. Routledge & Sons, 1928).

[11] *La trahison des clercs* (Paris: Bernard Grasset, 1927), pp. 29, 33, 42, 98, 99, 226, 172, 152.

the men of letters who, by their turning from the heritage, had brought on France a "great betrayal." It is interesting to note that Benda chooses as an epigraph to Chapter III, in which he stirringly indicts the "clerks," these words from Bossuet: "I made him to be spiritual in the flesh; and now he has become carnal even in the spirit." [12] What he does not observe is that these precise words were used by Augustine in his *City of God* to show how "secret ruin precedes open ruin" and how the only enduring foundation for the cities of this world is that which is laid upon another—upon the City of God.[13] For Augustine's problem was the same as that of Benda, only the decay was more elaborate and the defection more profound.

Archibald MacLeish's *The Irresponsibles* is at once more damning and provocative, for it exploits a moral hesitation which has since become evident. What he sought to understand was the ironic fact that scholars in America, when confronted by an obvious barbaric threat in Europe, "made no effort to defend themselves or the world by which they lived," the puzzling fact that men of letters could remain indifferent and irresponsible when confronted by forces "cunning enough to destroy the entire authority of the inherited culture." He was forced to the conclusion that this curious indifference was due to the "destruction of intellectual responsibility" through the division of men of letters into "two castes, two cults—the scholars and the writers." Of these, the scholars had retreated into a "kind of academic narcissism," employed in learning for learning's sake, while the writers had become "refugees from consequences, exiles from the responsibilities of moral choice" through having learned from the physicist the skepticism of "detachment," "objectivity," the neuter pride, superior to judgment or ultimate beliefs.

It is the distinction of our time—perhaps unhappily its most memorable distinction—that it and it alone has provided the formula by which this overthrow could be achieved. . . . The men of thought, the men of learning in this country were deceived and rendered impotent by the best

[12] *Élévations*, VII, 3.
[13] *De civitate Dei* XIV. xv, xiii.

they knew. . . . And by that sublimation of the mind they prepared the mind's disaster.[14]

This is a serious indictment. Like that of Benda, it fixes on that Protean motion of the mind and will when confronted by embarrassments of time and place, of belief and order—on the sophistries of shape and disposition they assume, the protective coloring of ambiguous reflection, which is the mask by which the mind covers over moral impotence and skillfully escapes detection. This imposture could not be prolonged. It was inevitable that it would be unmasked. At this moment in our destiny it is being unmasked; but contemporary man meanwhile is baffled, left with all his hungers and his thirsts. His instincts and his appetites remain; but these, without the sense of moral sanctions, become vulgarities—the invoking "of Satan, or animality, . . . a joy of descending," a sordid apparatus of escape.

v

One thing stands out clearly from an indictment of this kind. It is the disquieting realization that Western civilization has reached a parting of the ways. The elements of compromise whereby its inconsistencies have been overlooked or loosely held together have in our time reached the point of fatal contradiction. This is at once a contradiction in our history and a contradiction in ourselves. It is the conflict which must arise between the Christian and classical presuppositions of our way of looking at the world as over against our attempts in these latter days to have the fruits which the presuppositions make possible while at the same time refusing the postulates and responsibilities that go with them.

The attempt to retain the fruits of Christianity without the beliefs which have been the source of those fruits is clearly contradictory and ironical. If it were not for the untold sufferings involved, such a predicament would be comical—like that of the man who, wishing to go in opposite directions at the same time, starts impulsively first one way and then the other without being

[14] *The Irresponsibles* (New York: Duell, Sloan & Pearce, 1940), pp. 17-18, 33-34.

able to decide for either. In history, however, this ambivalence becomes tragic, inasmuch as the prior causalities already rampant in the world lay hold on our hesitations and hurry us forward into complicity with the choices of compromise which already bulk large in the world. Those who do not choose for God become accessories of Caesar.

We try, of course, to obscure this contradiction as far as possible by turning our consciousness of self outward upon the world, avoiding the issue through a multiplicity of our actions and "interests," through amusements, through work. This is true also of nations. When a threat arises in the form of a new lust for power, our "civilized" minds will not credit it, for it runs counter to the common sense of mankind. Yet it is just this common sense which we have compromised, and which is subject, therefore, to just such perversions as the lust for power implies. The lust for power, incarnating itself in a few second-rate minds, overrides our hesitations for the simple reason that these impassioned souls are able to decide, for power and tyranny and oppression, whereas the balance of the world swings in indecisiveness, able neither to reject the evil nor to embrace the good.

Clearly, then, any preliminary indictment such as this which we have been drawing must have a focus in our history, as a record of results and causes, and in ourselves, as ironic victims and partial accessories before the facts. The betrayals in the world are never any more invidious than the possible betrayals in our own souls. The individual soul is the true analogue of destiny. In it resides our failure and our hope for new determinations in the world.

Somewhere in our history *a principle of enervation* has entered which fatally debilitates the whole—what Kierkegaard would call a "dialectical deceit" which "leaves everything standing" (churches, laws, customs, dignities, institutions, works, and cultures) but "cunningly empties [them] of their significance." Thus we preserve today the shell of Western civilization, the civilization founded on classical antiquity and Christianity. We have left the shell of these things standing while depriving them of their significance.

41

This principle of enervation goes back very far in our historical consciousness. We are like Descartes, who was perfectly
willing that God should exist as the tradition said that he did,
or that Christ should be the unique means of our redemption as
the Church proclaimed, but who wished on his own account to
take another starting point. He wished to start at a point where
these things might be true or not. For his purpose, his own means
of getting at the truth, they would not matter.

Or we are like Voltaire. Voltaire, that particular idol of our
vanity, whose wit was like our own—sharp enough to puncture
circumspect presumptions, superficial enough to make us think
that this was thinking! Tolerance and Reason! Let the Church
be the Church, let God be God, let the Scriptures be made use
of, so long as nothing contradicts our rationality—whereupon he
merrily unfrocked the clergy, lifted the veils from superstitions
and presumptions, exposed the heritage of faith to much marvel-
ous ridicule and much salutary criticism, and left us cultivating
gardens! In all of which we have rejoiced. But what satires Voltaire *might* have written had he recognized that he employed one
myth with which to flay another, that his own deism would shortly prove as empty as the emptiness his wit proscribed. Then indeed we might have had high comedy, and Lucian would have
had another chance to rise to Aristophanes.

Comedy, as Spencer said, is a great effort which suddenly encounters a void. Had Voltaire, with his greatly reasoned effort,
beheld the void of institutions which his age left standing when
their significance had been removed, and had he understood that
they were emptied with an emptiness—that is, had he understood
what he was doing, had he understood himself or his age—then
the century, and possibly our culture, would have been redeemed
with laughter. Instead, the little reason sparkled into wit, and the
wizened sage of Ferney shriveled into fame and cleverness. He
attacked Pascal, naturally enough. Pascal, like Molière a man of
comedy, was also a man of reason and of faith. The reason, said
he, does not suffice in order to be reasonable. In him Voltaire
discerned the enemy, the man who had already turned his own

42

weapon against him and whose triumph would imply that in the end the whole of Voltaire's genius would turn out to be an epigram upon the autonomous reason's emptiness—a subterfuge, a mask, a dialectical deceit, a shell.

But if so, if the pretense of our culture has doubled back upon itself, confronting thereby its emptiness, what then is the midnight hour? It is the hour in which the principle of enervation, having run its course, precipitates the crisis, revealing man, his culture, his civilization, his aims, for what they really are. It is the moment when the institutions that have been left standing are discovered to be empty. It is the moment when the intercepting piece is moved upon the chessboard, leaving our king, our fraudulent and wishful aims, exposed. We should consider a man a fool, said Pascal, who would run carelessly off a precipice after having placed some object in front of his eyes to prevent his seeing it. The midnight hour is the moment in which this object is removed from in front of our eyes leaving us barely poised upon the brink of the abyss. It is the moment when some simple child who waits to see the king pass by with his new and costly clothes, woven by the most proficient tailors, throws consternation into the body politic by exclaiming: "He isn't wearing any clothes!" It is the moment when some simple mind, with eyes of faith, says bluntly that the pride of modernity with which mankind has cloaked itself for nigh four hundred years is no cloak at all—is, in fact, nothing—and that our credulity has been imposed upon. It is the hour when man's history recoils, the hour when "not-being masquerading as life triumphs in the incomprehensible configurations of sophistry" [15] and *when the presence of internal sophistry is detected.* It is the moment when man is thrust inward upon his own nudity, when his history confronts nullity, when the question as to his own significance balances between life and death. It is the hour when the "dark gods" slowly converge upon our little patch of consciousness and we are forced to choose which god is God. As D. H. Lawrence said,

[15] Jaspers, *op. cit.,* p. 206.

43

I believe:

That I am I.

That my known self will never be more than a
little clearing in the forest.

That gods, strange gods, come forth from the
forest into the clearing of my known self,
and then go back.

That I must have the courage to let them come and
go.

That I will never let mankind put anything over
on me, but that I will always try to recognize and submit to the gods in me and the
gods in other men and women.[16]

But submission to these gods within us is a choice. "My great religion," Lawrence said again, "is a belief in the blood, the flesh,
as being wiser that the intellect. We can go wrong in our minds.
But what our blood feels, and believes, and says, is always
true." [17] In so blithe an inconsistency the sophistry of introverted
vanity completes itself. We will never permit mankind to put
anything over on us; the dark gods of the blood stream are more
trustworthy. The dark gods are at least our own, and we retain
a vestige of our dignity in knowing that if we are duped the
dupery is our own.

We may say, then, that the disclosure of crisis, this unmasking,
is an unmasking of a negative fatality, that it is fraught with ambiguities and that men who share in it (as who does not?) are
everywhere belabored with perplexities and contradictions.

> Things fall apart; the center cannot hold;
> Mere anarchy is loosed upon the world;
>
> .   .   .   .
>
> The best lack all conviction, while the worst
> Are full of passionate intensity.[18]

[16] Knud Merrild, *A Poet and Two Painters; A Memoir of D. H. Lawrence* (New
York: The Viking Press, 1939), p. 238.

[17] *The Letters of D. H. Lawrence* (ed. Aldous Huxley; New York: The Viking
Press, 1932), p. xiv.

[18] From "The Second Coming" in *The Collected Poems of W. B. Yeats*. By permission of The Macmillan Company, publishers.

The initial task, therefore, of the critic of culture is clear: he must specify the ambiguities, lay bare the impotence, and beat the bushes of uncertainty until the contradictions everywhere are fully flushed from hiding.

Chapter II

ANTECEDENTS OF THE CRISIS

MANY CRITICS IN RECENT YEARS HAVE TRIED TO ANALYZE THE PRINCI-
ple which enervates the culture of the West. They have traced its
antecedents backward through the years. They have contrived
theories of history to explain these antecedents. But none has
penetrated so directly to the root evil as did Sören Kierkegaard
when, writing over a hundred years ago on *The Present Age,* he
ascribed the principle which enervates our culture to a *silent
sorites*—a syllogism, or sophism, which leads by gradual steps
from truth to absurdity. Our world today exhibits everywhere
such a reduction—to the absurd, or to the ironic, or to the terrible
pathos of the present conflict.

The principle here involved is a sound one. In the realm of practical knowledge—which includes the spheres of culture and of
ethics—the test that must be brought to bear is the test of the reduction to the absurd. Truth as it is lived in history is not speculative, and it is not ideal: it is sternly actual. It is lived. For this
reason a reduction to the absurd *in fact* is more often than not a
reduction to tragedy and suffering.

The crisis of our time is "not of the hands, but of the heart,"
as Archibald MacLeish has said. It is "a failure of desire." [1]

It is also, however, a failure of the mind, of the intelligence. It
is a crisis of perversion arrived at through the malevolent despot-
ism of a set of pseudo categories which have tyrannized over and
coerced unwittingly our choices. Their coercive power has been
unbreakable because it has been concealed. It has been concealed
in the hidden premises of our period's assumptions—the initial
premises which we assume and never criticize.

[1] *A Time to Speak* (Boston: Houghton Mifflin Co., 1940), pp. 2f.

46

"We are all of us," wrote T. E. Hulme, "under the influence of a number of abstract ideas, of which we are as a matter of fact unconscious. We do not see them, but see other things *through* them." [2] The difficulty is that in so far as we see other things through them, we are not capable of occupying any other standpoint. It is only when these assumptions are reduced to the absurd, or when their implications are brought ironically or tragically to the point of their essential incompatibility, the point of crisis, that we are made aware of the concealed premises—quite as though the glasses that we wear should crack, or break, and focus our attention on the glasses instead of on the world which formerly we saw through them.

This shortsightedness is not uncommon in history. A religious standpoint will seem incredible to a "rationalist." An "empirical" standpoint will appear dwarfed and despicable to an intuitionalist. Each assumes that his assumptions are to be identified with "truth." We are led into an awareness of our antecedent and unconscious assumptions by disaster, by Socratic self-knowledge, or by reduction to the absurd. The latter is in many respects, the most decisive. Thus it is related of Cortes that, when he withdrew from Mexico, he left behind him an ass, which, being a strange animal to the natives, was at once taken into the village and worshiped as a god. This singular devotion, which seems absurd to us, was not considered so by them because of *their point of view,* which in no wise prohibited an animal's being venerated as a god. To have argued the point with them would have been to no purpose: the ass would nevertheless have been accounted a god. But inasmuch as the natives neglected to feed the poor animal it died, and thus declared (by the "concrete logic of events in history"!) its mortality. There was in this situation a silent sorites, so to speak, which effectually reduced false premises to the absurd.

This little episode need not be regarded as a parable of our present situation; but it will serve to illustrate, in an absurd fashion, what is nevertheless true of peoples: the fact that when

[2] *Speculations* (ed. Herbert Read; Harcourt, Brace & Co., 1924), p. 37.

historical momenta are frustrated suddenly, or when they are seen to have spent their force, we are oftentimes released from the tyranny of unrecognized assumptions. The assumptions lose their inevitability. They are brought out into the open. We are freed from their coerciveness, and we are less naïve. We have reached such a period in our time, and the perspective of history is an immediate means whereby we may grasp the meaning of the human situation. History becomes, as Savigny held, "the only true way to obtain a knowledge of our true condition."

The premises of the "modern" period stem from the Renaissance. The basic assumptions which have given rise to our passion for freedom, for reason, for investigation, for science, for modernity, were projected in that historical upheaval which Machiavelli called a *"ritorno al segno"*—a return to the original source of life. Today we are skeptical as to the real content of that "life," and as to the "originality" of the "source" and as to whether it was in fact a "return." We are far enough removed from that axis of initial choosing to have an ironic perspective upon it. Something was wonderfully right in it; but we realize today that something was wonderfully wrong in it. The assumptions on which that new enthusiasm was based have had time to work out in history the implications of their premises, by way of "the concrete logic of events in history." We occupy today the point of their tragic clarification. It is therefore easy to perceive that that which might have been a deliverance into faith and freedom in the Renaissance has passed by degrees from both of these until the hidden contradiction in its premises is explicated tragically in the crisis of this century. Coming as we do at the *end* of the series, the disclosure is not comforting. It performs for us, however, one great service: it releases us from the tyranny of the unconscious assumptions which heretofore we took for granted.

This is an important liberation. It is a movement of the critical consciousness altogether necessary to an understanding of the present crisis of culture.

i

The Renaissance was primarily an attitude. It was not a philosophy, not a principle, not a manifesto (though its descendants had their manifestoes, and have had them throughout the period and down to our own time). It was an attitude that has remained dominant and constant until recent times. "Spirits have awakened. It is good to be alive!" exclaimed von Hutten. "These men enjoyed," says Symonds, four hundred years later, "the first transcendent springtide of the modern world." "The Renaissance was the liberation of the reason from a dungeon, the double discovery of the outer and the inner world." [3] Or, as Emerson's brother observed to him, in accents reminiscent of von Hutten's enthusiasm, though at three and a half centuries' remove, "The nap is wearing off the world." Anatole France doubled the same cape when he spoke of "the great breath which passed over the whole world at that time, the warm breathing of the springtime of the mind."

There is no denying the validity of this mood. The Renaissance elation was a mark of a return to freedom. The hierarchical oppressiveness of Church and feudal system fell from the soul like darkness from light. Men occupied once more the point of immediate relationship with God, with truth, and with their fellow men. Men stood once more uncircumscribed, unprejudiced by cant—whether social, philosophical, or religious—and eager to confront themselves with chance and destiny. Nevertheless, the hope miscarried. The intrinsic soundness of its turn to freedom and unmediated truth led to contradictory fulfillments: heroism and default, genius and folly, faith and sophistry. Not only was this genius many-sided; it was also, unhappily, many-minded. It was prismatic; and truth, whose light it sought to meet in full immediacy, was broken into brilliant scintilla of partial apprehensions. In secondary minds these partial apprehensions passed easily to misconstructions, and the Renaissance-modern period has tried to retain the intrinsic validity of the mood together with what was partial and heretical in its grasp.

We must therefore view with suspicion all such statements as those just cited. They are filled with the overtones of the badly concealed assumptions of the first historians who, in order to demarcate the modern period from the Middle Ages, ventured to

[3] *Renaissance in Italy* (New York: Modern Library, 1935), I, 8, 9.

use those question-begging terms "Renaissance" and "Dark Ages." It is astonishing that our age, with its especial pride in being "scientific" and "disinterested" and "objective," should at the same time have basked so uncritically in the light of this reflex flattery. Such is the case, however; and the degree to which we have indulged it, by the reflex vanity of feeling sorry for the people who lived before the Renaissance, is not less astonishing. "It is pathetic," writes Symonds, "to think of the medieval students poring over a single ill-translated sentence of Porphyry, endeavouring to extract from its clauses whole systems of logical science, and torturing their brains about puzzles hardly less idle than the dilemma of Buridan's donkey." Or again: "The mental condition of the Middle Ages was one of ignorant prostration before the idols of the Church—dogma and authority and scholasticism." [4] We may allow for the element of truth in these statements; but we must note also the *attitude,* with its patronizing tone—meanwhile reflecting that in more recent times all such attitudes *as history* have been blown higher than a kite—or, not forgetting our sorites, have died like the venerated ass of Cortes—from an excess of propitiations and prostrations which could not be swallowed.

The following from Diderot is characteristic:

The Christian religion is, to my mind, the most atrocious in its dogmas; the most unintelligible, the most metaphysical, the most intertwisted and obscure, and consequently the most subject to divisions, sects, schisms, heresies; the most mischievous for the public tranquillity, the most dangerous to sovereigns by its hierarchic order, its persecutions, its disciplines; the most flat, the most dreary, the most Gothic, and the most gloomy in its ceremonies; the most puerile and unsociable in its morality, considered not in what is common to it with universal morality, but in what is peculiarly its own, and constitutes its evangelical, apostolical, and Christian morality, which is the most intolerant of all. Lutheranism, freed from some absurdities, is preferable to Catholicism; Protestantism to Lutheranism; Socinianism to Protestantism; Deism, with temples and ceremonies, to Socinianism. Since it is necessary that man, being superstitious by nature, should have a fetish, the simplest and most harmless will be the best fetish.

[4] *Ibid.,* I, 5 f.

This is the Renaissance *attitude* after the yeast of the new "discovery of man and of the world" (Michelet, Burckhardt, Symonds) had worked for two hundred years. In the nineteenth century it acquired a new enthusiasm from science and discovery and the evolutionary myth; and an interminable future of surprise and enchantment unrolled before it. It would

> . . . follow knowledge like a sinking star,
> Beyond the utmost bound of human thought,

as Tennyson's Ulysses said—which was a poetic equivalent for that motto of the Comtians: *Savoir afin de prévoir*—"to know in order to foresee."

The alliance which this attitude made with rationalism and with science is clear in the case of Comte. But its prevalence as a leaven through the lump of our modernity must be noted also in the poets and the prophets who gave voice to the same attitude. Pater is a case in point:

The Renaissance of the fifteenth century was, in many things, great rather by what it designed than by what it achieved. Much which it aspired to do, and did but imperfectly or mistakenly, was accomplished in what is called the *éclaircissement* of the eighteenth century or in our own generation.

Chesterton has chided the "Victorian historians" for always regarding history as a story that ended well—because it always ended with themselves!

Robert Bridges is even more specific:

> Science has pierced man's cloudy common sense,
> Dowered his homely vision with more expansive an embrace,
> And the rotten foundation of old superstition exposed.
> That trouble of Pascal, those vain paradoxes of Austin,
> Those Semitic parables of Paul, those tomes of Aquinas,
> All are thrown to the limbo of antediluvian idols.[5]

Shelley's paean of liberation remains, however, the most ecstatic of them all:

[5] From "Poems in Classical Prosody," in *Poetical Works of Robert Bridges* (Oxford University Press, 1914), p. 421.

The loathsome mask has fallen, the man remains,—
Sceptreless, free, uncircumscribed, but man:
Equal, unclassed, tribeless, and nationless,
Exempt from awe, worship, degree.[6]

Matthew Arnold, who looked more deeply into the problem than did Shelley, saw in this lyrical outburst of nineteenth century romanticism something abortive: he called it "premature." And in our midnight hour, where each one must unmask, it appears that Shelley's unmasking also was a mask.

This attitude is gone suddenly. The present crisis has dissolved whatever vestiges remained. Its naïveté is incredible to us. What was wishful in it has been stripped away by the reality of crisis in which we stand.

Modern man, the man of dignity, of reason, the Renaissance man of godlike aspirations, now witnesses a brutal humiliation. We witness wars of lust, which feed upon our loss of unity and loss of faith. Spengler's men of third-rate intelligence successfully pre-empt the place of statesmen—Plato's hoped-for philosophers as kings! They exploit our indecision. "We are now taking part," wrote Nicholas Berdyaev in 1919, "in the beginnings of the barbarization of Europe."[7] The reason for this capitulation to Caesarism he found in the fact that "man is tired to death and is ready to rest upon any kind of collectivism that may come."[8] Our wars convict us of our moral weakness. Nevertheless, they press the spirit to *decision,* and tend thus viciously to terminate our probationary balance between the times. They bring the basic terms of human destiny into the open—terms heretofore screened by sophistries of spirit. Greatness must today be wrested from that deadly paralysis of doubt with which the modern mind and will was stricken. Only by a gigantic effort of the common will, and by a reassertion of the values of mind and spirit, can this inner impotence be overcome. It is possible to say that at the present moment it is being overcome; but it is being overcome for the very reason that men have been brought into tragic collision with

[6] *Prometheus Unbound,* Act III, scene iv, ll. 501-4.
[7] *The End of Our Time* (tr. D. Attwater; London: Sheed & Ward, 1933), p. 57.
[8] *Ibid.,* p. 16.

the nature of things. We have changed our attitude: we have abandoned the Renaissance way of looking at things without, perhaps, being in the least aware of it.

The messiahship of science no longer serves to unite us. The view of science set forth above by Bridges, a poet, may be contrasted with that confessed by Archibald MacLeish, a poet:

> The conquest of the cosmos by Science. But it is no lordship. It gives mankind no position of honor. It is no more a conquest than the collection of rain is a conquest of rain. It is finding out How. You learn what you can do with electricity. A monkey learns what it can do with a nut.
>
> The great modern sickness of boredom has its roots there. We do not wish to be kings. We wish to know How. And we know. And we are bored. To death.[9]

This is one more witness to Berdyaev's "weariness that comes from knowledge alone." It is, however, a contrast at the surface of the attitudes.

Much more to the point would be a comparison between Ciriaco de Pizzicolli, born in 1404, and Jean Cocteau, born in 1891. Pizzicolli was a fanatic for learning, wandered perpetually, and in answer to inquiries as to whither he was bound replied, "I go to awake the dead!" Jean Cocteau, the French poet, reverses the mood in our time: "It is with sadness that we close the eyes of the dead: it is with sadness also that we must open the eyes of the living." [10]

This brings us round once more to the issue—the issue of which Tertullian spoke, that of man's nature under God, the question as to who are the living and who are the dead! But this issue is brought forth today in an altogether new manner. It is not so much sought for by us as it is thrust upon us. It is in terms of this issue that the attitude of the Renaissance must be specified.

ii

At bottom, the attitude of the Renaissance was an attitude toward man and his place in the cosmos. It differed from the

[9] *Op. cit.,* p. 157.
[10] *Le rappel à l'ordre* (5th ed.; Paris: Stock, 1920), p. 22.

medieval point of view precisely as the two periods differed in their conceptions of man. To the medievalist, man was a creature living in God's world under God's law. "A man's worth is what he is in the sight of God, no more, no less," said St. Francis. This understanding of man's worth under God implied a hierarchy of values resting upon absolute foundations. Bossuet's oft-cited formula—*"une foi, un roi, une loi"* ("one faith, one king, one law") —though coming decades later, retained the medieval sense of hierarchy. Pascal's "three rivers of fire" reflect the lust of power, the lust of the senses, and the lust of knowledge wherewith the medievalist summarized man's temptations to sin. For the medievalist, perfection was not centered in man; it was something to be apprehended, something *above* him, something supernatural. Man on the contrary, was imperfect and limited, a victim of "original sin." Participation in the perfect was possible to him, but it was not possible that he should himself *be* perfect.

T. E. Hulme drew a line of distinction between the medieval world view and the Renaissance at precisely these points. For the man of the Renaissance, original sin was not binding; and hence the problem of moral evil disappeared, the notion of sin was emptied, and that "bastard conception of *Personality*" appeared from which all values were expected to spring spontaneously.

The notion of original sin, when properly understood, is a profound notion. It is an attempt to state mythopoeically a fact common to all human experience which cannot be stated rationally or analytically. This fact is the inexplicable certainty which all men have of their actual falling short of the glory of God, and of the sense that they are somehow responsible for it, both individually and collectively. The sense in which I am "against God" is discovered also to be the sense in which the whole of humanity is against God. The notion of original sin must be understood against a prior fact—the fact of original freedom, which it implies. This is the initial freedom of each man to love God or not to love him, to obey him or not to obey him. Original sin is thus a negative assertion of our essential human dignity *under God*. The doctrine, in short, must be understood existentially and personally: every attempt to explain it *causally* reduces it to pharisaism and legalism. For the man of the Renaissance, the notion of perfection was surreptitiously introduced into man, no longer radically imperfect, and thus a foundation was laid for the myth of indefinite progress, the natural goodness of man, and the subjectivity of values. We aim today at the "integrated" personality rather than at the redeemed person.

At least three other terms of the rift with medievalism may be added.

The first is obvious: it was the deliberate turning from the "other world" to this world and to man in this world, a shift from a theocentric to an anthropocentric consciousness. This was a choice both of practical consequences (the relativity of ethics) and of metaphysical implication. It implied, metaphysically, a turning from "the Unseen to the seen," a capitulation to the world as a tangible reality in space and time. This turning to the world is of the greatest possible significance for an understanding of the new consciousness. For, subsequent philosophical idealisms to the contrary, the practical tangibility of the world is not disturbed throughout the period; nor is the tacit naturalism of the modern attitude disabused. "Time is money," said Benjamin Franklin in a characteristic utterance whose metaphysical implications are easily overlooked. Whatever gods there be, the natural world remains for the Renaissance-modern mind a primary datum of experience, the visible limit of our endeavors, and a sufficient theater for the unfolding of man's limitless powers. *Nature,* with all its resplendent wonders, was soon to be "discovered."

Here, however, we encounter an interesting paradox. Religious feeling, formerly directed to God and the angels, was transferred to nature. Nature was divinized. God, who had stood above the world, became God within the world: he was, indeed, identified with the world and with its processes. God ceased thereby to be a God of judgment. His rule over the world was accomodated to rule within the world. This was managed through a divinizing of the causal process. This process was given mystical signification in the notion of indefinite progress. Progress was always toward the good. Indefinite progress was tied in mystically and teleologically with that one "far-off divine event" toward which the whole creation now began to move.

This turning to the world carried with it a second corollary. It discovered to man his own infinite capacities. As the world was mystically endowed with indefinite progress and goodness, so man turned toward an unlimited future wherein he might unfold his limitless powers. This new self-confidence implied a rejection of something in the medieval view which was oppressive and, at bottom, destructive of the creative impulse. That something was the metaphysical foundation of the European world view, which contained all things in the aesthetic-mathematical unity of a Neo-Platonic and Aristotelian sphericity. This was, in the main, a product of Greek rationalism. It produced the static culture and hierarchical rigidity of the medieval period. Its virtue was order. Its fault was a metaphysical regimentation of the spirit.

Man's discovery of his limitless possibilities was at once bold and liberating. We know the pride which Renaissance humanists took in "many-sidedness." Leon Battista Alberti has often been celebrated for his having been musician, painter, sculptor, architect, scientist, Christian apologist, classical scholar, author of Italian and Latin treatises on art, morals, history, philosophy, and, furthermore, one who, with both feet together, could jump over a man's head.

The inner significance of this turning may be seen more clearly in Marlowe's Mortimer. Mortimer remarks just prior to his execution:

> Weep not for Mortimer,
> That scorns the world, and, as a traveller,
> Goes to discover countries yet unknown.

This is a foretaste of Tennyson's resolution

> To sail beyond the sunset, and the baths
> Of all the western stars.

There is, however, this difference: whereas Tennyson's Ulysses feels no restriction on his powers save that of age, Marlowe's Mortimer asserts his powers as a last defiance. He is overtaken in his ambitions, and he knows that all his infinite powers cannot overleap his finitude:

> Base Fortune, now I see, that in thy wheel
> There is a point, to which when men aspire,
> They tumble headlong down; that point I touched.

The Renaissance had fared better in its new-found powers had it recognized this point of fundamental limitation and held it firmly as it held its power to create.

Two more consequences follow. The Renaissance discovered *history,* which, since the ancient Hebrews and, in part, the ancient Greeks, had been forgotten. The notion of progress had at least this merit, that it threw the consciousness forward toward goals, though these were nebulous and mystical and never specified. The new world view was teleologically energized, whereas the medieval world was ontologically enclosed. The failure of the Renaissance was not in this teleological turning. This reinstated man as an existential factor in the real determination of the world's destiny. The failure lay, on the one hand, in the mystical, pantheistic divinizing of the world,[11] which gave to men no goals of value beyond their wish-projections, and in overlooking, on the other hand, the Hebrew-Christian teleology whereby the eternal and the temporal come together in the historical moment of the "fullness of time"—the eschatological

---

[11] The extent to which this divinizing of the world, of "Nature," came to dominate the "modern mind" is illustrated significantly by the tendency of nineteenth-century biographers, when describing Erasmus' journey over the Alps en route to England, to point out that he recorded not a single observation on the beauty of nature in the Alps—as though a radical deficiency in Erasmus were thus made clear. It does not occur to these historians that so scandalous an oversight might be accounted for by the fact that Erasmus was contemplating the writing of his *Praise of Folly,* or even more simply by the fact that Erasmus was raw-boned and did not sit comfortably on his mule. He is known to have complained of other conditions of travel in those times. But the likeliest explanation is that the Wordsworthian mood has enjoyed its period of dominance and that we have all of us been to some extent

> . . . well pleased to recognise
> In nature and the language of the sense,
> The anchor of [our] purest thoughts, the nurse,
> The guide, the guardian of [our] heart, and soul
> Of all [our] moral being.

conditioning of history. The Renaissance thus founded history on the indefinite protraction of the time series, whereby all meanings and events are in the end swallowed up by the infinite oblivion of time, precisely because there was no philosophical or religious means whereby the moments in time might become what Kierkegaard called "atoms of eternity."

The final point of turning was of equal importance, though less tangible than the foregoing. It was the accomodation of religious faith to a sort of specious neutrality, a skeptical suspension of decision on ultimate questions; an *attitude* such as Pascal remarked in Montaigne as a "nonchalance" toward salvation, a life "without fear and without repentance." It is this antecedent doubt concerning the absolute order that comprises the unrecognized *prius* which stands behind and is immanent within every subsequent formulation of truth, whether that truth be called skepticism, or rationalism, or deism, or romanticism, or (to include the capitulation of religion itself to the Renaissance attitude) humanitarianism. This was not a Christian reticence, as in the formula, "Lord, I believe; help thou mine unbelief!" It was a pagan reticence wherein man's "faith unfaithful kept him falsely true." It was a reticence adopted in pride and not in humility. Montaigne, for example, paid certain respects to the faith; but his preoccupation was with himself, which he studied with a kind of introverted classical enthusiasm—"Nothing that is human is alien to me!"—the whole of that which was human being ready to hand within his own ego.[12]

Renaissance man is thus turned inward upon himself. He must live from within his own resources, must rely on his reason,

---

[12] It may be worth while to observe, at this point, that to summarize these Renaissance attitudes under the term "humanism" is an error. The first "humanists" of the Renaissance were neither anti-Christian nor self-preoccupied in the sense just indicated. The observations of M. Maritain on this subject are, in this respect, useful, though they do not go to the heart of the problem. The fault, he writes (*L' Humanisme integral,* p. 35), with anthropocentric humanism is not in its being humanistic but in its being *anthropocentric.* This is also the vice of classical humanism in general: "This vice, in my judgment, concerns not so much what this humanism affirms, as what it negates, denies and divides. It is what we may call an *anthropocentric* conception of man and of culture." (*Scholasticism and Politics,* p. 2.)

or his instincts, or his "customs," or his "intuitions," or, more recently, his blood! The supernatural is ruled out by arbitrary fiat of the antecedent assumptions that (1) we cannot know whether it *is* or not; that (2) if it is, it is not what we thought it was (is to be found within us rather than above us); and (3) as long as we are uncertain about it, we would better occupy ourselves with what we have—that is, what we can be certain of —ourselves and the tangible world about us. This cuts man off both from faith and from metaphysics; or, more exactly, delivers him a victim to a naïve faith and a naïve metaphysic which are the more tyrannical just in proportion as he congratulates himself on being free of them. It opens the way for rationalism, skepticism, empiricism—the self-sufficiency of reason, the subjectivity of knowledge, and the investing of science with authority over "fact." The Renaissance-modern period is the dialectical unfolding of the implications of this attitude.

iii

This dialectical unfolding is fairly easy to trace, though the documentation of the same is endless and comprises the subject matter of a special discipline: what Matthew Arnold referred to indifferently as "criticism," or "criticism of life," but which, from the Christian standpoint, would have to be termed the "Christian criticism of life." [13]

Such summations differ superficially; but certain broad areas of agreement may be noted between critics of culture otherwise so different as Oswald Spengler and Nicholas Berdyaev, William Butler Yeats and Christopher Dawson, Jacques Maritain and Reinhold Niebuhr, Karl Jaspers and John MacMurray, Pitirim Sorokin and Emil Brunner. [14]

[13] Cf. the definitive exposition of these principles by Dean Lynn Harold Hough in his *The Christian Criticism of Life* (New York and Nashville: Abingdon-Cokesbury Press, 1941).

[14] Cf. Spengler, *The Decline of the West;* Berdyaev, *The End of Our Time;* Yeats, *Collected Poems* (also C. Brooks, *Modern Poetry and the Tradition*, pp. 177ff.); Dawson, *Enquiries into Religion and Culture*, pp. 67-116; Maritain, "Religion and Culture," *Essays in Order;* Reinhold Niebuhr, *The Nature and Destiny of Man;* Karl Jaspers, *Man in the Modern Age;* John MacMurray, *The Clue to History;* Pitirim Sorokin, *The Crisis of Our Age;* Emil Brunner, *Man in Revolt.*

M. Maritain, the greatest of the contemporary French Catho-
lics, seeing in modern culture a culture dominated by anthropocentrism, or "humanism dissociated from the Incarnation," divides the period from the Renaissance to the present into three
"moments," or degrees of unfolding. The first of these moments
is a "classical" moment—a moment of vigorous and rewarding
productivity, lavishly creating, out of the surplus sap still running in the vine though the root has been severed, a period of
"Christian naturalism" (!). The second moment begins when the
culture discovers that, being cut off from the "supernatural," it
must necessarily take sides against it, that is, must establish an
order based on nature—the moment of "rationalist optimism,
the *Bourgeois* moment of our culture." This is followed by the
third moment, in which this order based optimistically on nature recoils—a *revolutionary* moment, a moment of materialistic
pessimism, in which the spirit rebels against both natural law
and its Author, a moment such as we have witnessed in Russia
and elsewhere in the twentieth century. These "moments" unfold chronologically; but there is also a sense in which they
coexist, overlapping and mingling together in varying degrees.
Maritain concludes: "All these conceptions misunderstand human nature and ultimately conduce to claiming for human nature
the conditions of pure spirit, yet in the flesh itself and by the
exasperation of an absolutely material power." [15]

Peter Wust, a German Catholic theologian, sees three distinct
"phases" in the unfolding of the Renaissance. In the first phase
the supernatural idea of God grows dim and passes into eighteenth-century deism. The second phase is an interlude witness-
ing the development of German idealism. The third phase, in
which we find ourselves today, "evolves a positivist and historicist
humanism and ends with the total uprooting of man." [16]

Christopher Dawson, an English Catholic historian, beginning
with the same premise—man's turning away at the Renaissance
from "the eternal and the absolute to the world of nature and

[15] "Religion and Culture," *Essays in Order* (New York: The Macmillan Co., 1931),
p. 20.
[16] "Crisis in the West," *Essays in Order,* p. 109.

human experience"—classifies the unfolding somewhat differently. In philosophy, it moves from the "dogmatic rationalism" of Descartes and the "dogmatic empiricism" of Locke to the "radical scepticism" of Hume, and the "subjectivism of later German thought." The reason is thus stripped gradually of its prerogatives and culminates weakly in Vaihinger's "as if" philosophy. In science, the period of discovery and control of nature is followed by a growing sense of dependence upon its forces. Man "sinks back into nature" and falls prey to the mechanical system his own genius has devised. Similarly in the economic process, man's initial exploitation of the world and the acquisition of material wealth ends in the subjection of man to mechanization. In the political and social sphere, the throwing off of the medieval principle of hierarchy has culminated with us in the new absolutism, the "new bureaucratic state." Marxism is seen as "the culminating point of the modern tendency to explain that which is specifically human in terms of something else." [17]

In like manner Karl Jaspers, one of Germany's "existentialist" philosophers, distinguishes three great principles which in recent centuries have become dominant: rationalism, the subjectivity of the selfhood, and the conviction that the world is a tangible reality in space and time. These principles have been to a degree salutary. Now, however, we are experiencing a reversal of mood: skepticism, the despiritualization of the world, the "void man has made for himself." We have slowly become aware that we "are living in an epoch when the world is undergoing a change so vast as to be hardly comparable to any of the great changes of past millenniums." [18]

Perhaps the best statement of the dialectical unfolding of the Renaissance postulates is that of Nicholas Berdyaev, the distinguished theologian of the Greek Orthodox Church. He holds categorically that "the Renaissance was the starting-point of modern times; and the Reformation and the Enlightenment and the French Revolution and Positivism and Socialism and An-

[17] "Christianity and the New Age," *Essays in Order*, p. 165.
[18] *Man in the Modern Age*, p. 23.

61

archism are all part of its disintegration." The ground for this opinion resides in the fact of the division made by the Renaissance between man and his Christian and classical heritage: a "rift in the soul" which has become "the theme of modern history."

It is an unfolding of ideas and events wherein we see Humanism destroying itself by its own dialectic, for the putting up of man without God and against God, the denial of the divine image and likeness in himself, lead to his own negation and destruction; the affirming of paganism against Christianity means the denial and demolition of his sacred past. The image of man, the image of his body and soul, is the work of classical antiquity and of Christ. Modern Humanism[19] in breaking with Christianity departs from the ancient knowledge of what man is and changes his image.[20]

The Renaissance, in short, "uncovered the creative powers of man as a natural being, not a spiritual one"; the dialectical result of which is that he drains himself dry, and, like the branch cut off from the vine, he withers away spiritually by successive stages of impoverishment. "When he lost the spiritual centre of Being he lost his own at the same time. . . . Man ceased to be a spiritual organism, and so false centres were formed at the periphery of his life." [21]

Berdyaev speaks here, of course, as a Christian ontologist, as a good Alexandrian Neo-Platonist, in fact. He sees the world of becoming over against true Being. The historical implications of the Renaissance assumptions are inevitably bound up with their metaphysical implications. The Renaissance man's choice of himself and his world as over against the hierarchical primacy of Being was a choice of nonbeing, and hence destined to nullify itself. Thus the modern man, the man of the Renaissance, progressively empties himself—that is, to recover the language of Jaspers, he arrives ultimately at an hour when "not-being masquerading as life triumphs in the incomprehensible configurations of sophistry." [22]

[19] Berdyaev's use of the term "Humanism" is lax and is to be accepted only when qualified, as in the above paragraph, by the phrase "in breaking with Christianity."
[20] Op. cit., p. 29.
[21] Ibid., p. 17.
[22] Op. cit., p. 206.

iv

The return to Jaspers raises, however, a fundamental question. It will have been observed that the foregoing analyses, with the single exception of Jaspers, either are based upon or imply the medieval world view centered in ontology. This was that world view from which the Renaissance man broke away, thrusting the mind forward into a teleological consciousness, thus qualifying the rigidity of the medieval standpoint. The question may be raised, therefore, as to whether the projection of these appraisals against the background of medieval ontology is not an oversimplification of the problem. The Renaissance world view had presumably arisen out of the inadequacy of a static and ontologistic view of man and the world, a view which had already failed to meet the test of long-term adequacy for the spiritual needs of men. It is quite true that the Renaissance world view has failed to withstand the test also. It does not follow, however, that we must therefore react into the world view that preceded it. It merely follows that *the basic issue raised by the Renaissance is today renewed.* The Renaissance-modern world view has indeed been brought to a crisis. We are not obliged on that account to hold that its appeal to teleology as against the medieval ontology was wrong: it may just as easily mean that, through a misconception of its own insight, it appealed to the wrong teleology. It may have misconstrued its own destiny.

This issue is, of course, the entire question as to the nature of man and his destiny. This issue was precipitated by the Renaissance out of the necessity it was under to throw off the metaphysical oppressiveness of the medieval alliance between Christianity and pagan rationalism. This unstable blend suppressed the personal powers of men. It subordinated man's creative capacities to an aesthetic-rationalistic world view which turned all destiny inward upon an ideal, static circularity. This was a bequest of latter-day Greek speculation; and it was, indeed, Christianity itself which broke the bonds of this "ontologism" and restored to man the sense of his infinite dignity before God. Both St. Francis and Luther—the two men from whom the

Renaissance and the Reformation are sometimes said to have sprung—came from the monasteries. Each renewed the sense of individual responsibility before God. The failure of the Renaissance was not in this appeal. It was in the miscarriage of this appeal.

This is a very complex issue. In renewing it today we renew it because we have been driven upon it by being brought to bay at the extremity of all our experiments with life and destiny. We experience today both a recoil upon ourselves and a recoil upon our history. We are thrust upon ourselves in the momentary dereliction which the soul experiences when the principles which gave it confidence are suddenly disclosed as false and impotent. We are thrust upon our history when we seek to understand just how the crisis of our aims and principles has come to pass.

At the same time we recognize that the foregoing summations of the Renaissance turning are all true. There was the moment of exhilaration which the world felt when it put aside the yoke of external authority and appealed to the infinite worth of every man; the fault was not in this turning. But when it put aside the sense of responsibility and creaturehood, and the fact of sin, and introduced perfection into man; and when, through its new liberty, it made man the center of value and meaning and lost thereby the theocentric reference; and when it divinized the world and projected the infinite capacities of the soul upon a future mystically endowed with beauty, truth, and goodness, toward which we move with some wonderful inevitability; and when it grounded history and destiny thereon—in all of this the times in their fulfillment bear witness to some deep misunderstanding of the issue which its genius raised.

The failure of the Renaissance can be understood by pressing inwardly into that unrecognized *prius* of doubt which is its back-lying principle of enervation, and which, over a period of years, has emptied the Renaissance elation of its hopes and hardihood. But the failure of the Renaissance cannot be understood by projecting it against the metaphysics of the medieval world view. In that direction lies the sacrifice of moral dignity and freedom and the prophetic significance of human destiny under God. Underneath the defense of man's basic freedoms in the world today lies the search for an ultimate sanction, which can be found only in terms of Christian destiny, and not by re-absorption into metaphysics. Furthermore, medievalism was it-self vitiated by a principle of enervation not unlike the principle which step by step has emptied the Renaissance postulates of their significance. Medievalism also contained a silent sorites—of the intelligence. The Renaissance contained a silent sorites of the will.

The medieval world view was, like the unfortunate ass of Cortes, reduced to the absurd by the dialectical unfolding of its concealed premises. Erasmus had little difficulty in lampooning its faults:

Of such subtile trifles there are an infinite number, and others more subtile than these: of notions, relations, instants, formalities, quiddities, ecceities, which no one can perceive without Lynceus' eyes, that could look through a stone wall, and discover those things under the thickest dark-ness whatsoever. . . . One cannot hope to conceive these mysteries unless he has spent at least six and thirty years in the philosophical and super-celestial whims of Aristotle and the Schoolmen . . . or with Aristoteli-totical Thomas himself. . . . And while they play the Fool at this rate in their schools, they make account the Universal Church would otherwise perish, unless, as the Poets fancied of Atlas that he supported Heaven with his shoulders, they underprop't t'other with their syllogistic buttresses [conducting their proofs] as if Holy Writ were a nose of wax, to be fash-ioned and refashioned according to their pleasure.[23]

This does not signify very much. The merits of the better School-men are well established, and the basic flaw in the medieval sys-tem has yet to be disclosed. Also, the ass of Cortes is hardly a medieval figure. Buridan's donkey would do much better, for, when caught between two bales of hay and desiring each of them equally, it could not decide which to eat and starved to death. Similarly, the bringing of metaphysics into relationship with the religious removed God to the ideal realm of absolute Being (*Actus Purus*) and reduced the world to nonbeing, in such wise that man was caught between the two, contemplating the One

[23] *The Praise of Folly* (John Wilson tr.), *passim.*

and denying the other. This also was an attitude based on concealed assumptions, which we shall speak of farther on.

For the present, our initial task is to understand the failure of the Renaissance attitude. It is the crisis of this attitude which we now experience. It is not to be understood outwardly by appeal to history as such. It is to be understood inwardly by that approach to history which discloses the unfolding dialectic of the period's assumptions. Outwardly we work backward in our history to specify the antecedents of our crisis; inwardly these focal points of idea and decision become analogues of our own soul's inner life. Outwardly, by donning seven-league boots, we leap from point to point in history, bringing the theoretical into the presence of the practical, establishing thereby the living relationships which must obtain between idea and event in history; spiritually, we bring ourselves upon our "limit situation" through drawing out the dialectical implications of our cultural choices. The dialectical element in all human choosing is thus clarified, and by a series of abridgments out of history it is possible to bring about a prismatic breaking up of an original and hidden commitment.

The real objection to the critical retreat on the "being-nonbeing" relationship is that the modern mind has suffered such a succession of deceptions of spirit by metaphysical explanation that it will not now suffer another retreat into the abstract at the precise point where it has acknowledged its crisis and its need. For a crisis, by definition, the precise reversal of the procedure. It is the precipitation of a need out of the abstract, out of the precincts of reflection into the sphere of decision. For the crisis of the modern mind is not at bottom a crisis of the mind alone: it is a crisis of the spirit, and only secondarily a crisis of the mind—but, even here, of mind in relation to the spirit. Or, to put the same thing in another way, a crisis of history is never simply a matter for metaphysical speculation; it is a matter for personal *decision*. Reflection, in its infinite retreat on the idea, overreaches itself, qualifies its own processes elaborately, until it is seen to be a mere intellectual device substituting its processes for the present demand for action.

This is not to say that metaphysics has not its legitimate sphere of operation, or that it has no bearing upon the historical, or that a *belief* in Aristotelianism might not be preferable, for example, in our present situation, to a belief in Marxism. It is to say, rather, that the historical has to do with man as a creature in motion, *in actu,* with man in the practical context of a crisis situation. Theory of life, in such circumstances, is concerned with the *way of life* and with the means of attaining it.

To protect this interest, we must distinguish sharply between philosophy as a "science" and philosophy as world orientation, between "pure" philosophy and what used to be called *wisdom.* We must also distinguish between metaphysics, or ontology, as an inquiry into the nature of ultimate reality, and metaphysics as a sophistry of the spirit, as an interloper into the sphere of religious immediacy. The first of these distinctions can be made by examining more closely the Renaissance attitude with its paradoxical denouement in recent literature. The second we may consider thereafter when the inner nature of the problem has been clarified.

The Renaissance attitude can be clarified if we accept provisionally the popular viewpoint: Medievalism had reached a point of *stasis,* which brought about in the thirteenth to the sixteenth centuries a crisis of affirmation, in which the pristine principles of Christian and classical vitality broke through the formalism—intellectual and ecclesiastical—which sought to encircle it. The succeeding centuries confused the essence of this new vitality, and so the period suffered by degrees that fatal amputation of the spirit which left the period doubly vitiated from within by (1) a rejection of the faith and (2) an appeal to self-sufficiency. The Renaissance-modern mind, therefore, proposed to itself a twofold experiment—an experiment in thought and an experiment in culture—the one an attempt to find meaning by way of reason alone, the other an attempt to ground the self creatively upon its own limitless powers. The failure of these experiments brings us to the true crux of all human choosing and instructs us in our fundamental poverty apart from God.

Chapter III

THE EXPERIMENT IN THOUGHT

THE FIRST OF THESE EXPERIMENTS—THE EXPERIMENT IN THOUGHT—
presents an elaborate unfolding of the Renaissance attitude at the
point where self-sufficiency seeks to justify itself as the *autonomy of
reason.* This autonomy of thought is presupposed in all the
systematic efforts of the period to construe itself, whether in the
constructive rationalisms of deism and the Enlightenment; the
autonomy of moral reason in Sir Francis Bacon's thought; the
pantheistic monisms of Bruno, Spinoza, and Goethe; the rationalistic empiricism of Locke; the naturalistic empiricism of science;
the positivism of Comte; or the period's initial intellectual doubt,
which was itself an indication of the period's intention to submit
all to the judgment bar of Reason in its singular autonomy. All are
facets of a basic attitude. The experiment rests back upon that
initial insistence of the Renaissance man that he would at all costs
discover *himself* regardless of consequences.

That the consequences would be favorable, he did not doubt.
There followed, beyond question, a temporary sense of release and
emancipation such as had not been witnessed in the Western
world for centuries.

This is a fact of great significance, too often minimized in recent reactionary judgments. Creatively, it took the forms that are
familiar: the burst of creativity of all artistic kinds in Italy; the
work of the Humanists in England, Holland, and France; the
precipitation of the Protestant break with the Church in Germany. The Revival of Learning was as integral to this emancipation as the Age of Discovery: they were aspects of the same
awakening. The authoritarianism of the Church was thrown
off. The scholastic tyranny in thinking was thrust aside. As Ana-

tole France observed, "At last men dared to think! Believing that they were thinking through the ancients, they thought for themselves." The lamp which Ficino kept burning in his study before the bust of Plato is a fitting symbol of the inverse release which Renaissance man obtained through worshiping himself via the bust of antiquity.

Nevertheless, despite its initial soundness, this turning to the self—to man and to the world—carried its own fatality: it was delimited by its presuppositions, by the antecedent decision to establish a new starting point, a starting point not within the radius of Christian faith nor within the purview of the Aristotelian bequest of self-evident first principles but a starting point within the self-sufficiency of man.

In this decision, this willful suspension of belief, this determination to doubt all but the immediate, there was much that was salutary. It thrust the individual back upon his private responsibility under God—if there were a God. It gave rise to the principle of the free criticism of experience, a principle that is neither unchristian nor unphilosophical. It appealed to experience and to each man's freedom, thrusting aside the immense veil of authority in which all truth had come to be cloaked. This principle was abetted, also, by the inestimable apostleship of Luther, who, in restoring to men the sense of direct responsibility to God, a responsibility not mediated either by priesthood or institution, resumed the Christian primacy of faith verified by the free criticism of experience. "Just as no one can go to Hell or Heaven for me, so no one can believe for me and so no one can open or close Heaven or Hell for me and no one can drive me either to believe or disbelieve." [1]

What happened subsequently was the real tragedy of the Renaissance. For these two principles—that of the primacy of faith and that of the free criticism of experience—were severed. The insights of Luther were accommodated to a dogmatic authoritarianism not less stringent than that against which Luther had protested; and the free criticism of experience became the notion

[1] Quoted in Reinhold Niebuhr, *The Nature and Destiny of Man* (New York: Charles Scribner's Sons, 1941, 1943), I, 84, n.

of free inquiry operating in the interests of empirical investigation. Thus the spirit of man, which had experienced the momentary release into a life of faith and wisdom, was hurriedly closed off from both by the interception of a new dogmatism on the one hand and an empirical reduction of the criticism of experience upon the other. This left the self both naked and exposed, desperately introverted, and subject to a dialectic of gradual disillusionment and frustration. Secularity displaced the faith; freedom was debased into "emancipation"; humanistic good sense shriveled into "enlightenment"; the individual lost his newly found dignity in the humiliating "discoveries" of a naturalistic science. Meanwhile faith, uncriticized by life and experience, congealed into a Protestant scholasticism, or eddied into pietism and the several sects or cults of religious experience (feeling) ; and free inquiry followed the path of rationalism, empiricism, utilitarianism, evolutionism, experimentalism, down to this present hour.

That which happened to the Renaissance discovery of the self under these circumstances is the clue to the entire period. The contradictory dissolution of the self results from the initial assumption of self-sufficiency and from the attempt to justify the attitude by way of the autonomy of thought. The contradiction becomes apparent the moment we bring the thought experiments into some relation with the facts. In so doing we apply the test of the practical (which is the medium in which a culture works) to thought's autonomy. Thought is forced out of its hermetic isolation in such a way as to reveal its own concealed motives. The autonomy of thought, whether in its skeptical, rational, subjectivist, or absolutist patterns, presents a practical failure to justify the attitude—makes clear, in fact, the untenability of the attitude itself. We are provided thereby with a clue to our real condition. We perceive, in short, the dialectical paradox which is at the root of Renaissance experience, the silent sorites which operates from the beginning the unhappy irony whereby the man who discovers himself in the beginning of the Renaissance loses himself at the end of the Renaissance.

i

This dissolution of the self as self-sufficient accomplished itself quickly in the experiment of Montaigne, who, while remaining nominally faithful to the Church, turned to the rigorous perusal of his own self.

Montaigne aimed to "love life" and to "cultivate it," finding Nature a "gentle guide" and regulating his life "after the ordinary human pattern, without miracle, without extravagance." [2] Thus, as Sainte-Beuve said, he may have appeared a very good Catholic—except for his not having been a Christian! Perhaps the only divinity that he acknowledged was Socrates, the prototype of all such "Know thyself" disciplines; albeit the discipline of Socrates differs centrally from that of Montaigne in that Socrates' study of himself never delivered him into a preoccupied self-indulgence of willful introspection. Montaigne's overtures to "custom" as his guide in moral conduct were consistent with his "universal doubt." Nor did he concede to custom any more than a wise man's deference to its accumulated wisdom—particularly when its wisdom accorded with his own. For by his "universal doubt" he appraised all things, and on that shield he shattered every lance that bore upon him. He succeeded even in doubting his own doubt without at the same time contradicting his standpoint. For if he doubted he would at any rate *know* that he doubted, and so break the universality of his premise; but this Montaigne avoided by giving his skepticism the famous interrogative form: *"Que scais je?"*—"What do I know?" Thus, as Pascal, his shrewdest critic, describes it, "his uncertainty revolves upon itself in a perpetual and restless circle, alike opposed to those who affirm that everything is uncertain and to those who affirm that everything is not so, because he will affirm nothing." [3] Montaigne concludes to a "pure Pyrrhonism." But a pure Pyrrhonism, while theoretically possible, is a *practical* impossibility.[4]

[2] *Essais,* III, 13.
[3] Pascal, *Conversation with M. de Saci.*
[4] M. Maritain states the problem of doubt most efficiently: "When they say that they [the skeptics] do not know whether any proposition is true, either they know

It is true that Montaigne achieved a "noble, Stoical elevation of mind" (Sainte-Beuve) by way of resting all upon this initial universal doubt; but his tastes nevertheless relaxed into a hedonistic dalliance, a moral epicureanism. In the realm of moral conduct he was like a man floating or wavering in indecisiveness. Montaigne could not even mount a horse like a philosopher, objected Pascal; for he could not help considering whether the horse had as much right to use him as he had to use the horse.

Thus in Montaigne the experiment in self which begins in the declarative ends with the interrogative. But the interrogative is reflexive, having the effect, on the one hand, of canceling decision with doubt and, on the other, of making doubt itself a decision: philosophy became, for Montaigne, *a learning how to die*! This is the dialectical result of a turning of self with a deliberate "nonchalance" toward salvation. The self is delivered, in a single lifetime, to the Stoical conclusion. Three centuries only are required to reduce the congenial fortitude of this Renaissance skeptic to its lowest terms: "Stoicism: the religion with only one sacrament—suicide!" [5]

We have already noted, however, that this skepticism of universal doubt was a doubt based not on humility but on pride—which accounts for the latent rationalism that pervades it. "All inclination and submission is due to them [the ecclesiastical authorities]," said Montaigne, "except the mind's. My reason is not framed to bend or stoop; my knees are." [6] Here again Pascal saw clearly: "He [Montaigne] destroys imperceptibly all that which passes for the most certain among men, not indeed to establish the contrary with a certainty to which alone he is the enemy, but merely to show that, appearances being equal on both sides, one knows not where to fix his belief." [7] There is a con-

---

that this proposition at any rate is true, in which case they obviously contradict themselves, or they do not know whether it is true, in which case they are either saying nothing whatever, or do not know what they say." Thus the only philosophy open to the "pure Pyrrhonist" would be absolute silence, "even mental," which, as we have noted above, is a *practical* impossibility! (*Introduction to Philosophy* [tr. E. I. Watkin; New York: Sheed & Ward], p. 181.)

[5] Baudelaire.

[6] *Essais*, III, 8.

[7] *Loc. cit.*

72

cealed vanity in this resolute negation which constructs nothing, which Emerson was not slow to see: "The first dangerous symptom [in Montaigne] I report is, the levity of intellect, as if it were fatal to earnestness to know too much." [8] There is, indeed, a certain distinction which comes with demonstrating to the world that you can indulge its vanities without being taken in by them, or even with showing that the world's seriousness is nine parts vanity. But this is not the highest seriousness and easily becomes a vanity upon its own account.

Montaigne was a symptom and a symbol. His wisdom was derived from the ancients. His weakness was derived from the autonomous self-sufficiency of the Renaissance, the skeptical vanity of which he was shrewd enough to see through but vain enough to share.

The latent rationalism in Montaigne's universal doubt is brought into the open by the man who was born four years after Montaigne died—René Descartes.

ii

"The cell where Luther argued with the Devil, the stove against which Descartes had his famous dream, the corner of the Bois de Vincennes where Jean-Jacques soaked his waistcoat under an oak on discovering the goodness of the natural man,—those are the birthplaces of the modern world." [9] However the count may rest with Luther and Rousseau, Descartes has been accorded this pivotal significance in modern thought.

Beginning with the "discovery of his own ignorance"—Montaigne's universal doubt—Descartes aimed at finding a ground for knowledge that would be stable, unyielding, and incontrovertible. This he found by running the principle of doubt to the ground. He disclosed in doubt itself the reality of thought. To doubt is to think. Hence, if I doubt, it is certain that I think. But if I think, it is certain also that I exist. Hence, his famous *"Cogito, ergo sum"* —the clue to his system.

It is to be observed, however, that this is no syllogism: it is an

[8] Essay on "Montaigne, or the Sceptic."
[9] Maritain, *Three Reformers* (New York: Charles Scribner's Sons, 1936), p. 14.

axiom. The conclusion is identical with the premise. It is a self-evident proposition. It was a starting point, from which Descartes proceeded to "accept as true what we perceive clearly and distinctly, and nothing else." He thence discovered the self-evident, innate idea of God, produced Anselmic fashion out of the presence in the mind of the idea of the perfect. Then, having got God, he was able to trust his immediate perception of the physical world, since God, its primal cause, is not malicious nor capricious but perfect and therefore trustworthy. The world could not be trickery, or dream, or some phantasmagorical caprice of Divinity wherewith God fascinates our eyes, teasing us into eternity and out again with puckish sportiveness. Thus he knew, by way of the reason itself, three things: (1) that we exist, (2) that God exists, and (3) that the extended world exists. Henceforth doubt was impossible, was superseded, in fact, by the unshakable conviction that "no opposing reason can be brought against me which should make me ever call it in question; ... and thus I have a true and certain knowledge of it. And this same knowledge extends also to all other things which I recollect having formerly demonstrated, as the truths of geometry." [10] He would extend this method of the mathematical reason to all areas of knowledge. His system was a deduction everywhere from simple and clear ideas, overcoming probability by necessary knowledge; but since mathematical knowledge alone is necessary, bearing in itself the axiomatic inevitability of clear ideas, all knowledge must therefore be mathematical. Thus Descartes, as Étienne Gilson describes it, committed "mathematicism"; or, as Maritain says, he imported into the sphere of the human the prerogative of the angel: intuitive knowledge, innate in origin and independent of the world of things.[11]

That is one way to refute Descartes: to show that he moved from the "probability" of the skeptic into certainty by way of mathematicism and angelism. But there is an even simpler way, as Kierkegaard noted in his *Journals*. The real trap in

[10] *Meditations*, V, 8.

[11] Gilson, *The Unity of Philosophical Experience* (New York: Charles Scribner's Sons, 1937), pp. 140 ff.; Maritain, *Three Reformers*, pp. 57 ff.

which to catch all these thinkers who start with the skeptical doubt implicit in "probability" is ethics:

> Since Descartes they have all maintained that during the period in which they doubted they might not make any definite statement with regard to knowledge, but that they might act, because in that respect one could be satisfied with probability. What a tremendous contradiction! As though it were not far more terrible to do something about which one was doubtful (for one thereby assumes a responsibility) than make a statement. Or was it because ethics was in itself certain? Then there was something which doubt could not touch! [12]

It is quite certain that Descartes was a creature who must act; and because he must act, he must think! This, however, was not his view of the matter. For what has Descartes done, that he should become "the father of modern philosophy"? He has affirmed the complete autonomy of the human reason. "Give me extension and motion," exclaimed Descartes, "and I will construct the world." ("He needed God," said Pascal, "only to give the initial fillip to set the world in motion.") But he did more than this: he turned the mind inward upon itself, revealing thought to itself, as Hamelin said. Hereafter "the Philosophy of Illumination, lighting heaven with the candles of the Encyclopaedia, will . . . continue the philosophy of clear ideas." [13]

This turning of the mind inward upon itself is, in Maritain's opinion, "the original sin of modern philosophy." [14] The mind is henceforth closed upon its own processes. It is shut off from the objects of knowledge. It is delivered into its own interiority. And, like Montaigne's doubt, which it will come in time to resemble in its pathos, it will revolve interminably upon itself in a perpetual and restless circle, seeking egress into Truth. For there lurked in its *"Cogito, ergo sum"* not merely the facility of a mathematical world view but the facility of a concealed redundancy: what it really meant was "I think, therefore I am a thinker"! To be a thinker is to deliver oneself into a mere know-

[12] Kierkegaard, *The Journals* (tr. A. Dru; New York, Oxford University Press, 1938), p. 114.

[13] Maritain, *op. cit.,* p. 76.

[14] *Ibid.,* p. 77.

ing; yet the end of life is not knowing but living; and the end of living is to arrive at some relationship with truth, and not merely at "thought which conceives itself."[15] For Descartes's act of thinking grasps only its own thought, or representation of some outward likeness vouched for by the divine veracity. In short, thought is severed from reality, as the thinker is severed from life. "The defect of Descartes's *Discourse on Method*," writes Unamuno,

lies not in the antecedent methodical doubt; not in his beginning by resolving to doubt everything, a merely intellectual device; but in his resolution to begin by emptying himself of himself, of Descartes, of the real man, the man of flesh and bone, the man who does not want to die, in order that he might be a mere thinker—that is, an abstraction.[16]

This was the equivocation which his thought contained. For Descartes aspired greatly. The aim of his labor was to enable him "to walk securely"; he would "go forward so slowly, and . . . be so circumspect in all things, that though [he] made but very slight progress, at least [he would] keep [himself] from falling." He proposed in his early manuscript "the project of a universal science which can raise our nature to its highest degree of perfection."[17] His project was "the most important in all the world."[18] He would accept nothing as true which did not respond to the test of the clear idea: he would sweep away all prejudices. But, behold, the man Descartes, while all this process of supplanting Aristotle was going on, made a concession! "As it is not enough," said he, "before beginning to rebuild one's dwelling house, to pull it down and to furnish materials and architects, or to study architecture oneself . . . but it is also necessary to be provided with some other wherein to lodge while the work is in progress," so he would accept the customs of his own time—Montaigne also observed the customs!—and adhere to the religion in which he had been instructed as a youth.

[15] Descartes, *Oeuvres*, III, 71.
[16] *The Tragic Sense of Life in Men and in Peoples* (tr. J. E. C. Flitch; London: Macmillan & Co., 1931), p. 34.
[17] Title of a manuscript sent to Mersenne. (J. P. Mahaffy, *Descartes*, p. 65.)
[18] Quoted by Gilson, *op. cit.*, p. 152.

"Yes, exactly," comments Unamuno, "a provisional religion and even a provisional God! 'And he chose the most moderate opinions 'because these are always the most convenient for practice.'"[19] Kierkegaard also has noted the ease wherewith the philosopher builds with his mind a stately palace for his thoughts while he *lives* in the dog kennel outside!

Descartes remained in bed until noon, disliked controversy, was as dogmatic as the dogmatism he opposed, and died of an inflammation of the lungs at the age of fifty-four years—just before he had completed the application of his method to medicine, which, he little doubted, would easily have kept him alive for a hundred years! His doubt was comic, holds Unamuno, like a man who acts as if he doubted without really doubting. His reason also was comic, in that it reasoned into knowledge without attaining truth—which was pathetic also in that the thinker, in ceasing to be a man, had nevertheless a progeny of thinkers like himself who carried to completion his experiment in the interiorization of the self.

The Cartesian *cogito,* it is true, is compared frequently with Augustine's retreat upon the self for his starting point in faith. "Descend into thyself," said Augustine, "enter thy secret place, thy mind."[20] There are several passages in Augustine which duplicate this appeal to that inmost "secret place" which is the undeniable point of purchase which we hold upon truth.[21] But the passage which most nearly approximates the Cartesian formula is found in Augustine's *De civitate Dei:*

If I deceive myself, I am. For he who is not cannot, clearly, deceive himself, and so I exist if I deceive myself. Since then I exist if I deceive myself, how could I deceive myself about my existence, seeing that it is certain that if I deceive myself, I exist? It follows, therefore, that even if I deceive myself, I must needs exist in order to deceive myself, and it is beyond all doubt that I do not deceive myself when I know that I exist.[22]

[19] *Op. cit.,* p. 108.

[20] *In Joan. evang.* xxiii. 10.

[21] E.g. (*De vera religione* XXXIX. lxxiii), "Everyone . . . who doubts whether there be truth, has within himself truth whereby he should not doubt."

[22] XI. xxvi.

A fundamental difference, however, between Augustine and Descartes is thus made clear: Augustine does not argue from his doubting to himself as mere thought or thinker, but to himself as an existing being. He does not overleap his creaturehood in order to deliver himself to untrammeled thinking. In the parlance of these times, he recognizes the existential qualification which surrounds and conditions all abstract thought. Augustine's "interiority" is thus qualitatively different from that of Descartes: it has existential validity; it is not thought which conceives itself.

This is even more evident from another passage in which, by similar argument, Augustine extends his conclusion a little in order to include being, living, and thinking. Here the argument is set forth in dialogue form, with "Reason" questioning Augustine:

> You, who wish to know yourself, do you know at least that you are? —I know it.—How do you know it?—I don't know.—Are you a thing that is simple, or that is composed?—I don't know.—Do you know whether you are moving or not?—I don't know.—But do you know that you think?—Yes, I know that.—Consequently, that you think at least is true.—It is true.—You know therefore that you are, that you live, and that you think.[23]

Augustine's larger awareness separates him from Descartes and gives to his thought an orientation that is different in kind from that of Descartes. Two differences are to be noted: the first, that whereas the Cartesian doubt argues to thought which conceives itself, the Augustinian doubt argues to a "therefore I exist," to existence as inclusive of being, living, and thinking; and second, that whereas Descartes's doubt leads to a "thinking" in which the mind is closed in upon its own processes, surreptitiously identifying truth with its own idea, Augustine's doubt leads him to "apprehend" truth as a "somewhat" other than his thought about it, and upon which his thought depends. Or, to speak the piece simply (a possibility at the end of an analysis and not at the beginning, where, though equally evident, the obvious is

[23] *Soliloquies* II. i.

overborne by the supposition that where there has been so much earnest cerebration there is surely more than meets the eye)—to speak the piece simply, the Cartesian experiment with the self recoils into solipsism.[24]

iii

There is nothing contradictory in solipsism. Solipsism does not defy the law of contradiction, which is the test of abstract reasoning. Solipsism merely affirms whatever is identical with itself, in which there is no contradiction. But the realm in which solipsism refutes itself is the realm of the practical, where the test is not the test of contradiction but the test of absurdity. For we are considering the Cartesian experiment not primarily for its own sake, as an abstract rational system; we are considering it as a solution to the highly practical problem of the Renaissance *attitude,* stemming from a naïve *belief* in the capacity of the self to interpret life from within its own resources and to order it. Both the Renaissance doubt and the Renaissance-modern reason are expressions of belief in self-sufficiency. The test of such an experiment is practical, not theoretical: it is aesthetic, ethical, and religious. It is cultural and teleological. Thus when Unamuno accuses the Cartesian doubt of being comical, he is in reality transferring it to the realm of the practical and noting its reduction to the absurd. For no matter how logically self-consistent the system may or may not be within itself, it is obviously absurd that the propounder of the system, in propounding what was more important than anything else in the world, should, by a series of irrefutable propositions, delete himself from the system which was to mean life and death for him and which was to enable him "to walk securely"—as if it were possible for one to saw oneself off speculatively from a limb of the cosmos and so dangle indifferently in a speculative void.

It is this distinction—the distinction between the speculative and the practical interests of the person—that T. E. Hulme had in

[24] "Solipsism, although no more than an intellectual exercise in philosophy, is synonymous, in psychology, with the negation of the personality." (Berdyaev, *Solitude and Society* [tr. G. Reavey; New York: Charles Scribner's Sons, 1938], p. 167.)

mind when he urged a distinction between "pure philosophy" and *Weltanschauungphilosophie,* or the "critique of satisfaction." Numerous official philosophers of the Renaissance culture share in the general Renaissance view of what goes to make up a satisfying destiny for man. They are satisfied with certain conceptions of man's relation to the world, and these conclusions (which are, in reality, antecedent to their formal reasonings) are never called into question. They comprise an antecedent world view and project a culture. Descartes worked out a most formidable metaphysical apparatus, in the form of a method which would be applicable to all areas of truth, without stopping to consider whether the reduction of life to mathematical norms would be satisfying to men once the feat were accomplished—or whether they might starve to death, like the venerated ass of Cortes! Hulme remarks:

> I remember being completely overawed by the vocabulary and scientific method of the various philosophers of the Marburg School, and in particular by Hermann Cohen's "Logik der reinen Erkenntniss." But one day, hearing Cohen lecture on religion, where his views are, as is well known, entirely sectarian, I realised very easily that the overwhelming and elaborate method only served to express a perfectly simple and fallible human attitude.[25]

Thus a man might be clad in a suit of armor so elaborate and complicated, proposes Hulme, that to a visitor from another planet who had never before seen armor he might appear like some inhuman, mechanical power operating with impersonal irresistibility. "But if he saw the armour running after a lady or eating tarts in the pantry, he would realise at once, that it was not a godlike or mechanical force, but an ordinary human being extraordinarily armed. In the pantry, the essence of the phenomena is not *arms, but the man.*"[26]

Voltaire, who also had a hand in lighting "the candles of the Encyclopaedia," dramatized this speculative futility after his own fashion in his narrative of Micromegas' visit to the earth. Encountering a boatload of philosophers while wading through

[25] *Speculations,* p. 19.
[26] *Ibid.,* 19-20.

our oceans, this gigantic visitor from Sirius scooped them out of
the sea between his two fingers. In the boat were disciples of
Descartes, Malebranche, Leibnitz, and Locke, who essayed to
instruct the giant and his companion from Saturn on the nature
of the soul. So wild were some of these learned assertions that
the interplanetary visitors were convulsed with laughter, which
precipitated the boat into the Saturnian's pocket. By way of repa-
ration for this discourtesy, Micromegas presented to them a book
which promised to lay bare the very essence of things. It was
placed in the Academy of Sciences in Paris, where a curious old
secretary one day had the temerity to open it. He found the
pages blank!

A more distinguished and, at the same time, a more representative example of thought in conflict with the covert human
attitude, was Immanuel Kant. Santayana has noted "the pathetic separation which existed between his personal beliefs and
his official discoveries." Certainly his formal and official discoveries comprise a most formidable apparatus of closely
reasoned postulations, armed with antinomies and equipped
with distinctions. Joubert feared lest he had sprained his mind
in reading him! This was the Kant who, in pursuing the nth
recoil of the reason on itself, as propelled by Descartes and as
accelerated by Spinoza, Malebranche, and Leibnitz on the one
hand and Locke, Berkeley, and Hume on the other, performed
his *Critique* on the pure reason and reduced it to impotence.
Each mind was shut in to its own perceptions and withdrawn
from essences by its very nature, so that it could know repre-
sentations of things only and never things in themselves. The
mind was reduced to such initial subjectivity that a dogmatic
agnosticism was implied. But there followed then Kant's "somer-
sault" into the practical reason, where God, freedom, and immortality were restored by way of the moral law and the categorical
imperative. Thus we see

a wizened little old bachelor, a sedentary provincial scribe, scrupulous
and punctual, a courteous moralist who would have us treat humanity in
the person of another as an end and never merely as a means, a pacifist
and a humanitarian who so revered the moral sense . . . that, after having

abolished earth and heaven, [he] was entirely comforted by the sublime truth that nevertheless it remained wrong to tell a lie! [27]

Which, from the standpoint of the practical, is not without its comic element. The Renaissance-modern reasoner had recourse in his search for satisfaction to the God of Sinai. Yet here also he was satisfied too easily—was content, that is, to subscribe to the official Renaissance satisfactions. He envisioned a God whose relations with the world were scarcely other than those of eighteenth-century deism, and concluded all within the ethic of the moral law, subordinating thereby religion to ethics instead of making ethics depend upon religion.

Another consequence of the Kantian influence may be noted. While it constituted a reply to both branches of Cartesian influence—the rationalist branch, which would conclude all within the reason, and the empiricist branch, which would conclude all within sensation—it nevertheless precipitated the Renaissance self into one more impasse; for the subjectivity of the selfhood implied in our incapacity to know things in themselves had the effect of cutting the self off from reality, and the self was shut in upon its own isolation in the tower of its private finitude. The results were extensive. What it implied is excellently stated by Francis Herbert Bradley:

> My external sensations are no less private to myself than are my thoughts or my feelings. In either case my experience falls within my own circle, a circle closed on the outside; and, with all its elements alike, every sphere is opaque to the others which surround it. . . . In brief, regarded as an existence which appears in a soul, the whole world for each is peculiar and private to that soul.[28]

Students of modern poetry will recognize this passage as the one which Mr. T. S. Eliot subjoined adroitly to the passage which he borrowed from Dante's *Inferno*:

> I have heard the key
> Turn in the door once, and turn once only!

[27] Santayana, *Egotism in German Philosophy* (New York: Charles Scribner's Sons, 1940), p. 55.

[28] *Appearance and Reality* (New York: The Macmillan Co., 1893), p. 346.

—for this door is at once the door to the contemporary soul locked in its tower of subjectivity and to King Ugolino of Pisa locked in his tower to starve. The key to Ugolino's tower was thrown into the river below, and his family starved about him one by one. Ugolino suffered the hallucinations of the dying: he imagined that he heard the key turn in the lock—the key that would rescue him from death and release him into life. The contemporary mind, in the modern poet's verse, is like Ugolino—locked in a tower of hopeless subjectivity, from which there is no egress into truth, and in which the spiritual life starves to death from a surfeit of its own barrenness.[29] Or—to change the figure but retain the judgment—we are, as Paul Valéry somewhere says, like Robinson Crusoes, exiled on our little islands of flesh, surrounded by ignorance, and ruling over the apes and parakeets which chatter our own soul's insularity.

iv

One more step remained, however, in the rationalist experiment of the self—the Hegelian experiment, exploiting the possibility that Kant was wrong and that the rational was the real. Not that there was any eagerness on Hegel's part to change the Renaissance attitude, or to construe life's meaning according to some new schedule of satisfactions. On the contrary, his experiment was but one more turning on the old Cartesian axis—or, in his own system, the last term of the dialectic itself, which, beginning with Descartes, had shuttled back and forth from thesis to antithesis, each time mounting higher on the back of each preceding analysis. It was ready now to culminate in Hegel's system: the final synthesis of thought with being, the coalescence of both subject and object in the Absolute.

"In this new age," he said of the period opened by Descartes,

the leading principle is thought, and thought which originates from itself, that interiority which is a universal feature of Christianity and the distinctively Protestant principle. It is now the principle universally admitted, to hold fast to interiority as such, rejecting, and regarding as im-

---

[29] Cf. T. S. Eliot, *The Waste Land*, l. 411.

pertinent and lifeless, externality and authority. In accordance with this principle of interiority thought, thought for its own sake, is now the pure quintessence of inwardness, interiority which posits itself for its own sake.[30]

Unfortunately, Hegel shows a marked tendency to identify his own system with Protestantism and his own idea with that of the Absolute. But the fact of "interiority" as the clue to the entire rationalist experiment is one that we may ponder with some care.

The Hegelian interiority is founded on the immanence of the Idea, the Absolute, both within man and within the world. "The truth is the whole. The whole, however, is merely the essential nature reaching its completeness through the process of its own development." [31] The pattern of this development is that of Being, or Absolute Subject, positing its opposite, a pure negativity, by a dialectical self-diremption implicit in its actualization of itself; which actuality, being posited, establishes a dialectical becoming, working its way upward once more into Being. "Everything depends on grasping and expressing the ultimate truth not as Substance but as Subject as well." [32] This Absolute, which stands both at the beginning and the end of the process, as well as within it (being, in fact, the process itself) is, from our present perspective, which is one of becoming, to be viewed as a *result*. Only at the end can it be viewed as what it is in reality. Thus contradictions in thinking, as well as contradictions in history, are but the necessary pathway of dialectical return to complete Subjectivity, the Absolute, the Whole—the process of "restoration and return to simplicity." [33] "True reality is [thus] merely this process of reinstating self-identity;" it is the dialectical movement in which the Absolute witnesses "the process of its own becoming, the circle which presupposes its end . . . and has its end for its beginning"; it is the "mediating with its own self in transitions from one state or position to the opposite," ever tending into the Idea. It is the Idea "mediating" itself, in which "mediating is nothing but self-identity working itself out through an active self-directed proc-

---

[30] *Werke* (Stuttgart, 1928), XIX, 328.
[31] *Phenomenology of Mind,* Preface.
[32] *Ibid.*
[33] *Ibid.*

ess." [34] Thus God is not only the Absolute but the Subject, "reflectively mediating itself within itself."

This system—which is like that of Parmenides [35] in that it is a world suspended between the terms "being" and "nonbeing," and like that of Plotinus in that the One returns interminably upon itself, following the arc of its own circularity into its ultimate cipherhood—nevertheless aims, like the system of Descartes, to begin without presuppositions—to begin with the pure reason, discovering within the instrumentality of the reason itself the meaning of the whole. But this, as Kierkegaard pointed out so brilliantly, is an impossibility; for the reasoner must, in the course of his reasoning, either abstract from existence or else abstract without relation to existence. If he abstracts from existence, he obviously does not begin with the reason alone, with "immediacy." If he abstracts without relation to existence, then the pure beginning with which he begins is, like pure being, a pure chimera; and the problem is precisely that of accounting for existence. Hegel, of course, assumes that the whole system of things, including the things of concrete existence, is implicit in the notion of being or in the system of reason itself; but this does not follow. Any amount of reflection upon the notion of pure being can reveal nothing beyond the bare categories of quality and causation. But bare categories are barren of particular events. Pure motion supplies no bicycles; pure space contains no heliographs. "Reason as a system of principles is only a formal outline of possibility, and contains nothing specific and actual. The actual is found, not deduced; it is a fact of experience, not an implication of reason." [36] Thus, Hegel's problem is precisely the problem of existence, which, for him, was the derivation of his principle of becoming.

How, then, did Hegel derive his starting point? Not by the immediacy of abstraction, but by reflection backwards toward the beginning—in actuality. But this is an endless reflection, an infinite regress, *die schlechte Unendlichkeit*. This regress into the

[34] *Ibid.*
[35] Cf. Parmenides' saying that "thinking and being are one and the same," rejected by Plato in the *Sophist*.
[36] Borden P. Bowne, *The Theory of Thought and Knowledge* (New York: Harper & Bros., 1897), p. 307.

"bad infinite" can only be stopped arbitrarily, by deliberately *choosing* to stop it. But to effect the beginning by a resolution of the will is to violate the terms of the system, which were that we should begin without presuppositions. Thus Hegel, in order to arrive at truth by abstracting without relation to existence, is nevertheless forced arbitrarily to make terms with existence, but by a decision of the will to think without relation to existence: that is, he succeeds in erecting the system by ignoring the presupposition of fact, and his talent is thus left free to circumlocute in infinite reflection within the circumference of determined abstraction. By the same token the system fails, because it does not really begin with immediacy.

But this was precisely the whole aim of the Renaissance: to begin without presuppositions and to spin reality by way of the reason reflecting on its own processes. The foregoing experiment would lead us to conclude that such an undertaking is impossible. But that is incredible; for it is, as Hegel said, what all take for granted and have taken for granted for lo, these centuries. Let us, therefore, reconsider. Hegel claims to begin with the immediate, with the beginning. But in the beginning this beginning both is and is not. Hegel begins, that is, with pure being, indeterminate immediacy, and sets over against it, "nothing, pure nothing." But pure being and pure nothing are, as he has pointed out, identical. And now, at the point where nothing passes over into being, at the point of the dialectical movement, there becoming is born. Becoming is, so to speak, extracted like the magician's rabbit from a hat that isn't there: or, more exactly, becoming is like the smile on Alice's Cheshire Cat after the Cat has disappeared: it is an abstraction grinning at us dialectically, suspended between nothing and pure being, which are identical terms. Thus Hegel begins with nothing: or, rather, he does not begin at all but is delivered into an infinite regressive series in which reflection basks in the warmth of an uncriticized tautology. For the whole movement, so called, erects tautology as the highest principle of thought.

What resulted from this experiment? Contradiction (becoming) became the very nature of actuality. The "abyss of objectivity [which] intervenes between man and God" [37] was eliminated. The Absolute became Absolute Spirit, and man was merged with the Infinite after the manner of the Indian's absorption in the Atman. Nevertheless, he was absorbed "dialectically," and certain practical consequences followed. Man was subordinated to the state, for the state was the higher unity. Above the state was the Absolute. The state, said Hegel, "is the march of God through the world." "All that man is he owes to the state; in that alone he has his being. All value that man has, all spiritual reality, he has alone through the state." [38] War, for Hegel, is not an accident but the means "whereby the ideal character of the particular receives its right and reality." [39]

Thus, as his absolute idealism was spiritualized into pantheism, or a monism of the spirit; and as, for him, thought and being coalesced in the immanent identity of the Idea; and as his theory of history justified thereby the principle of permanent revolution culminating in the deification of the state, it was not long before Marx and Engels and Lenin appeared, who, discounting the abstract rhetoric of the spiritualized Absolute, adapted the principle of permanent revolution to their own interests and brought the system to a close in dialectical materialism and the dictatorship of the proletariat. By this means dialectical materialism could fulfill the reason's adventure in complete interiority by subordinating the Renaissance individual to the state and by "rationalizing" the whole of mankind, reducing him to an economic category in bondage to "the good of the whole." In the passage from Hegel to Marx, Renaissance individualism ironically inverts itself into hero worship of the proletariat.

v

Let us consider now, briefly, what these examples of the Renaissance experiment with thought reveal.

First, it becomes clear that, so far as this effort goes, man in

[37] Berdyaev.
[38] *Werke* (Lasson ed.), VIII, pp. 90 ff.
[39] *The Philosophy of Law,* in *Hegel Selections* (ed. J. Loewenberg; New York: Charles Scribner's Sons, 1929), p. 464.

the Renaissance, thinking he had found himself, succeeded only in losing himself. In his skeptical premise of doubt, he lost himself in a philosophy that was a learning how to die. In his rationalist premise of self-affirmation, he ended in solipsism— and an inflammation of the lungs! In his critique of pure reason he ended in a closed tower of subjectivity, isolated and alone. In his identification of thought with being he ended in tautology, and a loss of himself in the collectivist mass-idea.

It is not this alone, however, that concerns us; it is the total consequence of the attitude—the total consequence of the determi- nation of the Renaissance man to live from within himself, with- out presuppositions, and on his own power. It is this initial prem- ise, this antecedent conclusion, to which the brief centuries form but an elaborate footnote. For essentially it is a reduction to the comic or to the pathetic wherever this vast intellectual effort is brought into relation with the practical. It is not merely that mod- ern man, having thrust his hand into the dovecote of truth, of which Plato speaks in the *Theaetetus,* brings forth a mechanical cuckoo instead of a living dove: it is rather that, like "the famous physician of one of Holberg's plays, his medicine, while taking away the patient's fever, took away also the patient's life."

"For an abstract thinker," as Kierkegaard says, "who refuses to disclose and admit the relation that exists between his abstract thought and the fact that he is an existing being . . . produces a comic impression upon us, however accomplished and distin- guished he may be, for he runs the risk of ceasing to be a man!" [40] Similarly, our philosophers of the period have been men of great accomplishment, whose facility for infinite reflection has been great but who have absent-mindedly abridged the whole problem of existence.

Such a development would not have been possible with the early Greeks. They guarded against this reflective autonomy by remind- ing themselves from day to day that philosophers also were hu- man. They cherished healthfully the anecdotes enforcing man's mortality: Thales falling in the well while walking with his eyes

---

[40] Quoted in Miguel de Unamuno, *The Tragic Sense of Life in Men and in Peoples* (tr. J. E. C. Flitch; New York: The Macmillan Co., 1931), pp. 109-10.

upon the stars; Diogenes, the ironist, succumbing to a bilious attack from eating ox-foot raw; Zeno going out of his way to avoid a dog whose bite would have embarrassed his attempt to be an absolute idealist. They would have reminded us that Descartes died with inflammation of the lungs just when his method was to make us live a hundred years, and that Hegel, who set forth the universal System, was graduated from Tübingen with an "inadequate knowledge of philosophy"! [41]

As for Kant, he still remains the giant mind of all this reasoned turbulence. Joubert protested, none the less, that many of his ideas were like ostrich eggs which had to be broken on one's forehead, and which, more often than not, were found to be empty! But at least Immanuel Kant the man leaped over the pure autonomy of reason to affirm the practical reason. And this was very human. For these formidable apparatus of learning cover over, like the suit of armor, the naïve attitudes of modern man: only, T. E. Hulme's lone knight of the pantry should be exchanged for Tennyson's four knights about the Castle Perilous, four formidable champions, but the last the worst—until a kitchen-knight unseated him and sent his helmet rolling in the dust. Then appeared within the frightened face of a little boy. Unhelmet our pretense, and we are children who "repeat by rote the sentences of grandames and of tutors."

"Skeletons of animals and bones of the dead!" cried Goethe when confronted by these wondrous cerebrations; and his Faust went searching in the nether realms a compensation for this dupery of the intellect. *"Drum hab' ich mich der Magie ergeben"*—"Therefore have I given myself to magic"!

But this also is a fallacy. Reacting from the faithless mind, we project the faithless culture—the second, or alternate, experiment of the Renaissance.

[41] *Hegel Selections*, p. x.

Chapter IV

THE EXPERIMENT IN CULTURE

IT IS TRUE THAT THE "CELL WHERE LUTHER ARGUED WITH THE DEVIL" is one of the birthplaces of the modern world. It is true also that a case may be made out for saying that he was the "first great Romantic, an immanentist, and a prophet of egocentrism;" but one should hesitate before calling him "a spoilt Saint," [1] for this is to disesteem the prophetic function. Erasmus, who had no cause to love Luther, was wiser than the Churchmen; for he discerned beneath the contention of the age the possibility that in fighting Luther he might be fighting God's will in the world. Przywara, too, in his brilliant analysis of the Augustinian bequest,[2] ought not to rejoice too hastily in Hegel's judgment that "it is the Protestant principle that in Christianity interiority should universally become conscious of itself as thought" and specify this as the "formal principle of Luther and Hegel, immanence even to identity." Perhaps the analogy of being does not apply here. Berdyaev also is hasty in classifying the Reformation as the second moment in the dialectical *decline* of the Renaissance.[3] This is at best a half-truth and begs the whole question as to the prophetic significance of the Reformation. The truth is that Luther and the Reformation are still an issue, and there are one or two trifling points that must be cleared up in a preliminary sort of way if we are to understand the Renaissance experiment in culture and the reduction to interior pathos toward which it passed.

Kierkegaard comes nearer to the facts when he suggests that the same thing happened to Catholicism that happened to the

[1] Maritain, *Three Reformers*, pp. 197, 14, 15, 30, 48, *et al.*
[2] See his "St. Augustine and the Modern World" in *A Monument to Saint Augustine* (London: Sheed & Ward, 1930), p. 251.
[3] See p. 61.

rest of the world: there appeared a Copernicus in the person of Luther who observed that Rome was not the center about which all things turned but only a peripheral fact. Luther was one who did not stop to consider that a row of syllogisms filed like dominoes would all fall down if he shouldered his way through their major premises. He did not consider primarily how his utterance would stand with Aristotle or the *Summa* of St. Thomas: he was concerned with how it would stand before God. He was a prophet. And a prophet frequently is greater than himself.

The prophet's "Thus saith the Lord" may be sound; his attempt, or that of his disciples, to formulate the same in accordance with Augustine and the Councils may not be. It is possible even that his prophecy will adjourn the Councils by superseding them. Disciples, too, do not always see the prophet's prophecy, but see themselves in it and use the prophecy to climb by; or, in their haste to love the prophet (which is no part of the prophet's prophecy), they may make haste to fit his utterances in with all the encyclicals to show that the prophet meant no great offense in upsetting the pattern of syllogistic protection which the thinkers have erected betwixt ourselves and the infinite imperative of God's Word.

Doubtless Carlyle was right in saying that Luther let loose the individual in the world. There was need for it. Spiritual recovery always begins by precipitating individuals out of the anonymous collectivity. But Carlyle's individual before man and the world is not Luther's individual before God. For Carlyle, Luther was a *hero,* who gave to every man a Magna Charta of individual liberty which might be used to override authority and to assert oneself if one were strong enough! But that is blasphemy—if indeed the man in question is not a hero at all but a prophet. For prophecy brings authority. It is spoken by a man *called,* appointed by God. His authority supersedes authorities. As between the hero and the prophet there is a qualitative difference. A hero is such by his own powers; a prophet is such by God's powers. To say that Luther was a hero is to estimate him aesthetically, on our own terms; not prophetically, on God's terms. And in the sense that the world saw in Luther a hero, releasing it into individuality and irresponsible liberty, it is right to say that Luther was at the source of the modern period. If to be modern is to place the focal point of human dignity in each man's responsibility as he stands alone before God, then Luther was a source of the modern experiment. Carlyle rejoices, however, in the wrong freedom, in Luther's Teutonic robustness, in the fact that he "did shake the forest in his magnificent ire" and so released the "individual," whose dialectical decline we have been tracing. The hero, as Kierkegaard would say, has only "an immanent teleology," whereas the prophet is "absolutely, paradoxically, teleologically placed." [4] The sense of Luther's being teleologically placed with reference to the whole disintegration of scholastic "logicism" (Gilson) is the real question at issue, and it cannot be lightly passed over by anyone whose critical perspective centers in the Cross and is not curtailed by its historical accommodations. Wherever this possibility is acknowledged, Luther becomes a true Copernicus of the spirit, making God, not man, the center of the universe. Wherever it is not acknowledged, he becomes the first Romantic, an immanentist, and a prophet of egocentrism.

Three things, then, we must note in Luther's prophecy: first, his recovery of the prophetic dimension in Christian awareness; second, his renewal of the dialectical understanding of man as sinner; third, his proclamation of the theocentric idea of love as over against the egocentric attitude of medievalism. These reorientations of man in the world both stand over against and help to explain the Renaissance culture in its Faustian, romantic, and mystical experiments.

i

First, then, Luther resumed the prophetic imperative of Christianity by placing man once more directly before God. "God and my soul" was not more Augustinian than it was Lutheran. "When you lie upon your deathbed you cannot console yourself by saying 'The pope said thus and so.' The devil can drill a

[4] "Of the Difference Between a Genius and an Apostle," pub. with *The Present Age* (London: Oxford University Press, 1940), p. 160.

hole through that assurance. Suppose the pope were wrong? Then you will be defeated. Therefore you must be able to say at all times: 'This is the word of God.'" [5] Which is what Erasmus had in mind when he proposed the little conundrum as to the future of the poor man who died when the priest had got him prayed only half way into heaven! "No one can go to Hell or Heaven for me," Luther says. Or, as Erasmus put it: "God Almighty knows a knave as well in a Franciscan's habit, as in a buff-coat!" [6] Before God we stand alone; and our responsibility is to him; and we are responsible.

Luther's understanding of sin stems from this. He considers sin personalistically, not rationalistically. It is not so much a matter of the corruption of our nature as it is the complete turning from God of the whole person, and hence a perversion and a defiance. Sin is "what one lives and does *outside faith* in Christ." [7] Unbelief is of the very essence of sin. "Unbelief is in all men the chief sin, even in Paradise it was the beginning and the first of sins, and it probably remains the last of all sins." [8] This was the overt and covert defection of the Renaissance attitude, as we have seen: the willful suspension of belief, the *"Que scais je?"* of Montaigne, the discovery of truth without presuppositions—itself a presupposition, grounded in unbelief. The results of such unbelief are, as Luther saw, twofold: (1) the heart is curved inward upon itself—*"Cor incurvatum in se"* [9]—so that it suffers that vicious egocentrism in which we "revolve around ourselves" instead of relating ourselves to God; and (2) this turning inward of the self upon itself becomes a self-propagating fatality which the self cannot throw off since it feeds upon it daily by its own determination in unbelief. This also foreshadows the Renaissance experiment in culture. For the dialectical implications of this fatality are traceable everywhere in that culture.

The third point—Luther's theocentric idea of love—is not less revealing, for it helps to distinguish between Reformation in-

[5] Quoted in Niebuhr, *The Nature and Destiny of Man*, I, 60.
[6] "The Rich Beggars, *Colloquies* (tr. Sir Roger L' Estrange; London: 1680).
[7] EA, vol. 12, p. 111.
[8] WA, vol. 46, p. 41.
[9] *Römerbrief* (Ficher), II, 184.

fluence and medieval influence on the Renaissance passion for individuality. Luther's objection to Catholic piety rested precisely in its egocentrism, its tendency to put man in God's place. For him the Catholic doctrine of love was "an egocentric perversion"—a moralism, a eudaemonism, placing the center of gravity within ourselves. It centered in our love for God *(eros)* rather than in God's love for us *(agape)*. Catholic piety was saturated everywhere with Neo-Platonism, which from Plotinus on was acquisitive and self-possessive. This is the erotic motif. Medieval thought was characterized by "the upward tendency," by "heavenly ladders," by the *via unitiva,* by a way of ascent to God through our own powers. This motion was latent, also, in the rational theology of Scholasticism, in the analogy of being itself, whereby we reason upwards through the several degrees of being (knowledge) to beatitude, which is itself a eudaemonistic consummation. In medieval mysticism this consummation took the form of mystic union, ecstasy, absorption; or, in the words of Sir Thomas Browne, it aimed at "Christian annihilation, extasis, exolution, liquefaction, transformation, the kisse of the Spouse, gustation of God, and ingression into the divine shadow!" [10] It also took the milder form of moralism and the imitation of Christ. This is Christian; but, as Luther said: "We ought to do this! Good! And then you will be saved! No! I grant that Christ is to be imitated, and the shedding of His blood; but by this I am not saved." [11] Thus, one might decide to imitate Christ via celibacy (a self-stultifying doctrine if universalized) because Christ never married; but one is not saved thereby. Or one might choose to be a pacifist because Christ was no warrior; but one is not saved thereby. Luther does not deny good works, which are of the law; but he rejects the notion that we are saved thereby.

Or, to put it in the milder terms of Erasmus: "No man can be said to keep the Law but he that observes the Will in it of the Law-Maker." [12] There is a difference between observing the

[10] *Hydriotaphia.*
[11] WA, vol. 7, pp. 33, 29 ff.
[12] "The Religious Treat," *Colloquies.*

Law as one might observe a code, or custom, or the rule of the Church, and obeying it as a response to God's will. For the latter presupposes the relationship of faith, whereas the former substitutes a moralism for it.

The attitude of Erasmus may be understood from this. "The first place must be granted to the Authority of the Holy Scriptures," he said; "but, after that, I find among the Ancients . . . certain precepts . . . so clean, so sincere, so divine, that I cannot perswade my self but they wrote them by Holy Inspiration." That is to say, granted the primary premise of faith centering in Jesus Christ, much moral wisdom of the ancients, which consummates otherwise in rationalism of various hues, is given its true center; for the wisdom of the ancients at any rate adhered to the vital union of thought with life, pursuing a right relation with the True, the Good, and the Beautiful. Their wisdom, therefore, is "human"; and it does not, as Gilson would say, betray the mind or heart into "logicism" or "theologism." [13] Erasmus would prefer, therefore, to "lose all Scotus, and twenty more such as he, than one Cicero, or Plutarch." It was not that he was "wholly against them neither"; but he saw clearly how medieval piety and practice had so narrowed the vital union of faith with criticized experience that he saw more "pious inclinations," more "absolute resignation of himself to the Divine Will," in Socrates than in much official Christendom. Hence his rhetorical cry, *Sancte Socrates, ora pro nobis!"*—"Holy Socrates, pray for us!"

It is quite true, on the other hand, that Erasmus could not go the whole way with Luther either, for the obvious reason that Luther so tended to absorb God's love (ἀγάπη) into God's grace that he came nigh to asserting in relation to man a determinism of God's will.

This, however, is not our present argument. We wish merely to stress the fact that Luther opposed the anthropocentrism of medieval mysticism, piety, and good works and set over against

[13] Cf. Gilson, *The Unity of Philosophical Experience,* chaps. i-ii.

it a theocentric conception of God's love, as that which is above all necessary to salvation:

"To pluck up, and to destroy, and to overthrow," namely, everything that is in us (i.e., all that of ourselves and in ourselves pleases us), "and to build and to plant," namely, everything that is outside us and in Christ. . . . For God wills to save us not by domestic, but by extraneous righteousness and wisdom, not that which comes and springs from us, but that which comes from elsewhere into us, not that which originates in our earth, but that which comes down from heaven. Therefore, it behoves us to be instructed in a righteousness altogether external and alien. Wherefore it is first necessary that our own and domestic righteousness should be rooted out.[14]

In short, Luther's protest was primarily theocentric and not egocentric, and the charge of anthropocentrism laid against him must be qualified on behalf of his prophetic aim. Niebuhr is much nearer to the truth when he suggests that Renaissance individualism is something new under the sun—that it is a compound of Christianity transplanted into the soil of classic rationalism, producing the new concept of individual autonomy. The subsequent development of this autonomy, however, is related not to the Protestant idea of the individual's sole responsibility to God but to the medieval mystical idea of the infinite potentialities of the human spirit. "A straight line," argues Niebuhr, "leads from Meister Eckhardt to Nicholas of Cusa." [15] It leads farther than that: it leads from Plotinus via Dionysius the Areopagite through Eckhardt and Nicholas of Cusa on to Victor Hugo and the French and German Romantics.

In all these ways prophetic Christianity, recovered momentarily in Luther, stands against both medievalism and the autonomous individual of the Renaissance; but its affinities with Renaissance culture *seem* clearer because the Renaissance used the prophecy to gain its autonomy apart from the all-important responsibility to God. It sought to retain the proph-

[14] *Römerbrief*, ii, p. 3, 3f.; 2, 4ff. Quoted in Nygren, *Agape and Eros*, Pt. II, Vol. II, p. 464. This work may be consulted for a thorough documentation of this far-reaching distinction.

[15] *Op. cit.*, I, 61.

ecy rationalistically and independently without its presupposition in faith.

ii

This however, was not possible. The antecedent doubt deprived the prophecy, so truncated, of power. The individual, apart from God, turned inward on himself—*Cor incurvatum in se*—and the Christian fatality set in. "Man has either God or an idol." Or, to postulate the dialectic from Pascal, who put his finger on the weak spot of the age:

God alone is man's true good; and since man has left God it is a strange thing, that there is nothing in nature that has been able to fill his place: stars, heaven, earth, elements, plants, cabbages, pears, animals, insects, calves, serpents, fevers, plagues, war, famine, vices, adultery, incest. And since he has lost the true good, everything may equally appear to him such, even his own destruction, although so contrary to God, reason, and nature combined. Some seek it in authority, others in curiosities and science, others in voluptuous pleasures. . . . Philosophers have said: Return into yourselves, you will find there your good; men do not believe them, and those who do believe them are the most empty and the greatest fools.[16]

That Pascal knew whereof he spoke and understood it, and that the age did not, may be seen by placing side by side two passages, the first from *Hamlet*, the second from Pascal:

What a piece of work is a man! how noble in reason! how infinite in faculties! in form and moving how express and admirable! in action how like an angel! in apprehension how like a god! the beauty of the world! the paragon of animals!

So speaks the doubtful Dane, whose vacillation, whose "psychopathic doubt," whose *défaillance,* has been the wonder and despair of critics down to this present hour. Shakespeare "is a medieval overtaken by the immense perturbation of the Renaissance." [17] Shakespeare, who has read Montaigne, and who borrows like a genius, writes a play which borders on the metaphysical—"to be, or not to be"—and in which the hero's

[16] *Pensées,* 248.
[17] P. H. Frye, *Romance and Tragedy* (Boston: Marshall Jones Co., 1922), p. 290.

> . . . native hue of resolution
> Is sicklied o'er with the pale cast of *thought!*

Pascal, a man of faith, who understands this doubt, knows no such hesitation:

> What a chimera, then, is man! what a novelty, what a monster, what a chaos, what a subject of contradiction, what a prodigy! A judge of all things, feeble worm of the earth, depositary of the truth, *cloaca* of uncertainty and error, the glory and the shame of the universe!

Here we see a difference—a qualitative difference—between man the paragon of animals, and man the glory and the shame of the universe. Man's resplendent powers, newly released in the Renaissance individuality, do not emerge as triumphantly as they ought in that "paragon of animals"! True, in Pascal there is no great triumph either, save that of candor. There is a shadow from above. But in Hamlet there is shadow from within.

The paradox of the Renaissance was that it called upon a pagan God against the background of a Christian doubt. T. S. Eliot suggests that in Elizabethan individualism the Senecan attitude of pride, the Montaigne attitude of skepticism, and the Machiavellian attitude of cyncism combine.[18] Shakespeare's skepticism is notorious; but this does not account for Hamlet altogether. Hamlet is debilitated from within. His behavior is, in the last analysis, not determined by effective choice but by inertia of the action, a fate that ironically disposes of the issue by way of a coincidence of circumstance that could not endure deferment of these wills—a kind of Christian nemesis, to speak paradoxically, at once impersonal and fortuitous. This is a profound irony, and accounts for the blasphemous tincture in the Shakespearian doubt. To be a pagan is no longer possible, for the Cross has intervened betwixt antiquity and the Renaissance. Naïveté has been lost.[19] Therefore, Shakespeare "is at his great-

---

[18] *Selected Essays* (New York: Harcourt Brace & Co., 1932), p. 112.

[19] A comparison of Hamlet with Orestes marks the contrast, not only between naïveté and complexity, but between character and act, and between fate as circumstance and fate as sustainer of the moral order. Prosser Hall Frye's excellent com-

est when describing great spirits in chains!" [20]—Hamlet, Lear,
Macbeth. For Shakespeare's drama is religious drama: it is
interiority that matters in it. The hero falls a victim to the
antecedent doubt, which empties into indeterminate reflection,
until ironic circumstance overtakes the man who cannot choose
to be. Shakespeare poses everywhere a question for which he
has no moral solution: and he is great depicting doubt converg-
ing dialectically upon despair. This profound skepticism has
been often summarized:

> Yea, all which it inherit, shall dissolve
> And, like this insubstantial pageant faded,
> Leave not a rack behind. We are such stuff
> As dreams are made on, and our little life
> Is rounded with a sleep.

Or, again:

> Tomorrow, and tomorrow, and tomorrow
> Creeps in this petty pace from day to day
> To the last syllable of recorded time,
> And all our yesterdays have lighted fools
> The way to dusty death. Out, out, brief candle!
> Life's but a walking shadow, a poor player
> That struts and frets his hour upon the stage
> And then is heard no more; it is a tale
> Told by an idiot, full of sound and fury,
> Signifying nothing.

These and countless other passages lay bare the human plight
as it presents itself in all the varied ironies of guilt, indignities,
and shame, and in which the whips and scorns of time that
Hamlet knew seem but ampler adumbrations of Shakespeare's
own lament from the *Sonnets:* "Tir'd with all these, for restful
death I cry." Here again the self is "bent back upon itself."
Even its doubt is ironic because it fears there is a God; yet its
sense of guilt will never reach repentance, since its fear of God

---

parison of Shakespeare with Sophocles in his *Romance and Tragedy* is an admirable
study of this kind.
[20] G. K. Chesterton, *Chaucer* (London: Faber & Faber, 1932), p. 240.

is itself ironically curtailed by the antecedent doubt. "The knot of our condition," says Pascal, "takes its twists and turns in this abyss."

iii

If *Hamlet* is the symbol of Renaissance individuality enervated by doubt and overborne by circumstance in a negative determination, a likelier symbol of the Renaissance culture will be found in *Faust;* for in *Faust* doubt is positively determined toward despair.

A transition from the one to the other might be devised by way of *Lear;* but Lear is still a victim, not a positive protagonist. There is much truth in Spengler's remark (for whom *Faust* is the symbol for an entire culture) that "Lear is at the last a mere name, the axis of something unbounded"[21]—though one must add that its rotation is intensive, not expansive, as with the later Romantics. Faust, on the other hand, is an anode, not a cathode, to this doubting. He *chooses* evil: "Therefore have I given myself to magic!" Against the background of his doubt, he chooses. He effects a decision. What he cannot have by faith, he will have by magic. Which also is a willfulness, a disguised ambition to "bind the world" (Berdyaev). Being a creature of the Renaissance—an autonomous individual, one whose knees will bend but whose mind will not—he will take the Kingdom by force, since he is incapable of surrender in faith. But he will have all this at the cost of his soul. That is the price which Renaissance culture exacted for its benefits. Man becomes infinitely clever, like Faust: he has knowledge without wisdom; he conquers the world without conquering himself; he is given Helen, herself the renascent Culture, without recovering his soul thereby.

> Her lips suck forth my soul; see where it flies!
> Come, Helen, come, give me my soul again.
> Here will I dwell, for Helen is in these lips,
> And all is dross that is not Helena.

Poor Faust! These kisses of the gentle Culture take our souls

[21] *The Decline of the West* (tr. C. F. Atkinson; New York: Alfred A. Knopf, 1926), I, 129.

Faust

away. And "where we are is hell, and where hell is there must we ever be"—as Mephistopheles explains. The dialectic doubt, prosecuted with ambitious energy, pursues the phantom hope until itself precipitates despair. Then, too late, Marlowe's Faustus cries: "See, see, where Christ's blood streams in the firmament!" —one drop of which, he knows, would suffice to save him.

The tenacity of this legend, which arose in medieval times and persists through Marlowe into Goethe, indicates how deeply it has entered into human consciousness as a parable of our defection. In medievalism, Doctor Faustus sold himself to the devil to quench his thirst for knowledge. It was "a parable of the impotent yearnings of the spirit of the Middle Ages—the belief that they could only recover the lost treasure [of pagan learning] by the suicide of their soul."[22] Of Marlowe's *Faustus* a recent critic writes: "He penetrates more deeply into the experience of a mind isolated from the past, absorbed in the realization of its own destruction."[23] It is the modern mind's absorption in the processes of self-destruction that betrays in it the Faustian dilemma and the Faustian despair. For doubt, when positively determined—that is, when we pursue its implications to the end—issues in despair. But this despair is paradoxical. It is the last extremity of willfulness wherein the premises we chose betray themselves for what they are and aggravate their own denial. Yet this is to deny ourselves as doubters. So we come full circle and are thrust upon the crux of all initial choosing, the crux of faith or unbelief once more— which choice we will not choose, for there is always one more idol that our magic can construe.

This paradox of doubt with its evasions is at the very heart of Goethe's more complex attempt to satisfy the soul apart from faith—more complex because two hundred years have passed, and pantheism, rationalism, and romanticism have intervened. Marlowe's drama is more simple and more penetrating because the faith itself is clearer as the background of the doubt and so supports it. Two hundred years of compromise and immanence have blurred all this. God himself has been interred within the All.

---

[22] Symonds, *The Renaissance in Italy*, I, 354.
[23] Miss Ellis-Fermor, quoted in T. S. Eliot, *Selected Essays*, p. 113.

When Faust seduces Margaret he preaches pantheism, a godly sophistry:

> Sweet one! My meaning do not misconceive!
> Him who dare name
> And yet proclaim,
> Yes, I believe?
> Who that can feel,
> His heart can steel,
> To say: I disbelieve?
> The All-embracer,
> All-sustainer,
> Does He not embrace, sustain,
> Thee, me, himself?
> Lifts not the Heaven its dome above?
> Doth not the firm-set earth beneath us lie?
> And beaming tenderly with looks of love,
> Climb not the everlasting stars on high?
> Are we not gazing in each other's eyes?
> Nature's impenetrable agencies,
> Are they not thronging on thy heart and brain,
> Viewless, or visible to mortal ken,
> Around thee weaving their mysterious reign?
> Fill thence thy heart, how large soe'er it may be,
> And in the feeling when thou'rt wholly blest,
> Then call it what thou wilt—Bliss! Heart! Love! God!
> I have no name for it—Feeling is all in all.
> Name is but sound and smoke
> Obscuring Heaven's glow.

This is the apotheosis of feeling, a Romantic reaction to the Stoic barrenness of the rationalist enlightenment. Nature has been deified. Man is nature's angel. God is present in him, and man feels his presence. Gretchen's comment feebly falls, like our inconstancy:

> There's something wrong about it; much I fear
> That thou art not a Christian.

Aye, there's the nub of the matter. Faust was not a Christian. He had studied philosophy, jurisprudence, medicine, and theology, only to discover that we *can know nothing;* and so he had given himself to the devil for the sake of enlightenment!

Goethe was, however, too shrewd a man to be long deceived by this reactionary movement which, in turning from the reason, turned once more to self—but to the self of temperament, of feeling, and of infinite longing. *"Das Ich soll sein!"* Goethe came to see that all this profligacy of feeling was rooted in sentimentality and was at bottom psychopathic. Authors who were betrayed by it, together with his own Wertherian disciples, he came to look upon as "hospital poets." The romantic, he said, "is sickly." All the same, Goethe remained a pantheist, an immanentist, and a Spinozist.

> God dwells within, and moves the world and moulds;
> Himself and nature in one form enfolds:
> Thus all that lives in Him and breathes and is,
> Shall ne'er His presence, ne'er his Spirit miss.

Or, more precisely: "Nature works after such eternal, necessary divine laws that Deity himself could alter nothing in them"! Goethe's *Faust* suffers from this involution. It is founded on a pantheistic monism yet parades a dualism of the spirit—man and the medieval devil. But closer scrutiny reveals that Mephistopheles is not a Christian devil! He is a mask. He is the pantheist's roundabout way of producing good. He is a foil for doubt.

This Faustian doubt, together with its implications, is clarified by two of its symbolic episodes.

The first is Faust's union with Helen, symbolizing the marriage of the Teutonic with the classical spirit. The product of this union is the child Euphorion. Euphorion is wild and irrepressible. He leaps upon the rocks and climbs up higher to the cliff's edge, where he fain would fly:

> Ever higher must I clamber
> Ever farther must I see.

And he leaps, only to fall like Icarus before the feet of Helen and Faust. Therein we see the tragic consummation of Romantic culture, the unnatural product of the classic culture and the Teutonic spirit severed from the Faith.

It is often pointed out that the sorrowful flight of Euphorion in Goethe's *Faust* was inspired by the character and career of Lord Byron, whom Goethe admired excessively. It also reflects, however, the tragic situation of the Faustian soul, which is caught, like Goethe himself, in a recoil from the immediate, the momentary, the fleeting, which it nevertheless endlessly pursues.

This paradox is further dramatized in the death of the aged Faust. For Faust, having sought in vain to satisfy his longing by every divertisement which Mephistopheles could conjure, turns at last, like a good Stoic and a good humanitarian, to his fellow men. He aspires to dig canals for them, and to build a kingdom. In this turning, says Spengler, "Goethe presaged psychologically, the whole future of Western Europe." The eighteenth and nineteenth centuries, having plumbed both the rationalist enlightenment and the romantic agony to their depths, and finding there, like Lucretius' plumb line in the universe, "no bottom," thrust their longing outward to absorb it and abstract it into "modern Europe's state-provision, humanity-ideals, world-peace, 'greatest happiness of the greatest number' "—the "purely practical, far-seeing, outward-directed activity." [24] This turning is the last evasion. It is the "learning how to die"; it is what Baudelaire calls the "necessity to work, if not by taste, at least by despair: since to work, is less boresome than to amuse oneself." [25] It is a failure of spirit and a loss of creativeness. It is a pragmatic acquiesence in the objective order of the finite world, a submission of the human to the nonhuman, and of the personal to the general. It is an ironic denouement of the Faustian complicity. The aged Faust, at the end of his hundred years, blind and ambitious for his earthly city, directs the workmen in what he takes to be the digging of the canal—but which is, in reality, the digging of his own grave!

This is not inconsistent with the plot of the whole. Having turned from Christian faith, Faust first aspired to conclude all within the immediacy of feeling. This palled, and Goethe's second dogma offered a new foothold: *"Am Anfang war die*

---

[24] Spengler, *op. cit.*, I, 355, 354.

[25] "Faust founds his kingdom because he must do something." (Santayana, *Three Philosophical Poets* [Harvard University Press, 1910], p. 181.)

Tät"—"In the beginning was the deed." But against the background of doubt this merely led to a Stoical doctrine of works, wherewith Goethe aimed to redeem himself.

> Who ceaselessly doth strive will merit
> That we should save and make him ours.

So speak the angels at the close of *Faust,* in the passage which Goethe himself has indicated as the key to the drama. Romantic longing passes over into striving, though the striving should be infinite. An immanental subterfuge masked by Stoic pride, but always crying in the final dark, *"Mehr Licht! Mehr Licht!"*

iv

The term put forward in the German Romantic period to describe this aggravated perplexity of spirit was *Weltschmerz,* to which our English equivalent "world pain" does scant justice. It is "the Romanticist's agonistic manner of re-discovering Hell!"[26] But to return to T. E. Hulme's appraisal, referred to above, Romanticism is a prime example of the pursuing of perfection on the plane of the human. This implies a transposition of the problem of moral evil. The dogma of original sin is exchanged for a naïve belief in the natural goodness of man.

Here again we see how the Renaissance attitude differs from the medieval attitude in that perfection is located within man and not above him, and that man is no longer regarded as exhibiting in himself—or within nature—any radical defect such as the medieval consciousness recognized.

Suppose now, says Hulme, that we imagine a man situated at some point on a plane. And then we locate perfection where it ought not to be, that is, somewhere on this human plane. From the point where the man stands roads radiate in several directions. The Romanticist supposes that perfection is to be sought along some one of these roads. Since nothing actual apart from God can

[26] S. R. Hopper, "Goethe in Our Time," *Congregational Quarterly,* London, XVII. (April, 1939), 2.

be perfect, this is an imposture; none the less we persist in it and follow out these several horizonal possibilities, only to discover that perfection is not to be found on any one of them. Thus time after time the soul is thrust back upon itself. This makes for *Weltschmerz* and romantic agony.

This description is accurate enough as far as it goes, and to illustrate it exhaustively from the infinite strivings of Romantic ingenuity and longing would be an almost interminable enterprise.[27] There are, however, one or two aspects of the Romantic experiment which we may not pass over; for Romanticism, as the leap from reason into feeling while the antecedent doubt remains constant, is that extreme aggravation of the soul which is the mark of Renaissance culture in the eighteenth and nineteenth centuries.

Rousseau, for example—"Descartes's angel acting like a beast" [28] —has become the recognized example of the Romanticist who finds perfection in the self and locates evil in our institutions. He also prosecuted his beliefs with religious fervor. "Only Rousseau can seduce you from the Christian faith; and only the Christian faith can save you from Rousseau," said Joubert. For by placing perfection in the self Rousseau discovered the natural goodness of man. Thus man, being naturally good, so long as he acted wholly from his natural impulses, would find perfection in himself. In this dislocation of the religious dogmas all the Christian doctrines were paraphrased. Grace, which is a power from on high, was paraphrased in Rousseauistic feeling. Christian sanctity was parodied in Rousseau's doctrine of the "beautiful soul"—*"la belle âme"*—wherein simplicity and sympathy became the prime characteristics. Rousseau's Julie could have "no surer guide than her heart"; she could "give herself up to it without scruple, and to do right [had] but to follow it." A religion of Humanity was projected.

It has been acutely remarked of Rousseau that "he loved man-

---

[27] Cf. Irving Babbitt, *Rousseau and Romanticism;* Paul Elmer More, *The Drift of Romanticism (Shelburne Essays, Eighth Series);* Ernest de Seillière, *Romanticism and Religion;* Mario Praz, *The Romantic Agony; et al.*

[28] Maritain.

kind in general and hated men in particular." Precisely. What is wanting here is love for *men*. The love of man in the abstract is a subterfuge; it is a self-indulgence. It is a new religion in which the self is lost. Said Schleiermacher:

> All exists in vain for him who sets himself alone. In order to take up into himself the life of the World-Spirit [*Weltgeist*] and have religion, man must first have found humanity, and he finds it only in love and through love. For this reason these two things are so closely and indissolubly united; a longing for love, ever fulfilled and ever renewed, forthwith becomes religion. . . . Humanity itself is for you the true universe.

This Universal Spirit is at bottom pantheistic. It is Nature with a capital *N*. It is a projection of the "longing for the infinite"— *das Unendliche*—on the one hand, and an immanental interiorizing of the Universal Spirit on the other. Thus, while it projected on the plane of the human a humanitarian parody of Christianity, such as we find in Tolstoi, whose derivation from Rousseau is notorious [29]—a religion of service, brotherhood, and concern for "humanity"—its more characteristic expression was a mysticism which turned the spirit inward upon its impotence. The turning to oneself in one's uniqueness is, on the one hand, an affirmation of Renaissance individuality; but it is, on the other, a confession of solitude and a self-deification. *Mich führt alles in mich selbst zurück,*" said Novalis—"Everything leads me back into myself!" (*Cor incurvatum in se!*) Rousseau (like Montaigne) would give to the world the full benefit of his study of himself. "I want to show my fellows a man in all truth of nature," he wrote in his *Confessions.* "Happiness on earth depends on the degree in which we withdraw from things and draw closer to ourselves." For "we are sustained by our own substance, but it is never exhausted." [30] His beatitude, his aspiration, was to be like God, who enjoys "nothing save himself and his own existence"; thereby he wished to be "self-sufficient, like God." [31]

---

[29] See Milan I. Markovitch, *Rousseau et Tolstoi, passim.* See also his second volume, *Tolstoi et Gandhi,* for an elaborate documentation of the manner in which these religious accommodations have been carried over into these present times.

[30] Letter to Henriette, Nov. 4, 1764.

[31] *Rêveries,* promenade v.

This self-deification results from the withdrawal of the self from the objective world order, or from the pantheistic reduction of God, man, and nature to an undifferentiated monism, in which man, perforce, must rely on his self-sufficiency. This self-sufficiency affirms itself in one of four ways: by way of humanitarian deification of man in the lump—the aggregate Humanity —a philanthropic, ameliorating self-worship which passes quickly into Marx and loses the self in collectivity and the state, Hegel conspiring; or by way of projecting itself above itself, Nietzsche-wise, to erect the superman, in which the self is lost through the willful deification of its own powers in infinite possibility, yet avenging this abstraction through a will to power and worshiping the master individual or the master race; or, after the manner of Freud, by way of holding the ego as its own object of worship, culminating in narcissism; or by turning to the mystical, as in Hugo and Novalis, and losing the self in endless longing for the infinite.

Berdyaev believes that this dissolution of the self in modern Romanticism results from the coming together of three things: new philosophical interpretations of the ego's function in the discovery of truth, a new scientific outlook, and the idea of the freedom of conscience.[32] This is true, but in the sense already noted—in the sense, that is, of a perversion of Luther's prophecy and not in the sense of its fulfillment.

For the Romantic appeal was not to Luther but to the medievals. The Romantic nostalgia for the Middle Ages was not peripheral; it was central to one entire phase of Romanticism. A line of descent must be traced backward at least as far as Plotinus for the Romantic "longing for the infinite." Schelling, too—who turned poetry into philosophy as Novalis turned religion into poetry—is prefigured in Plotinus: "This is the spirit that Beauty must ever induce,—wonderment and a delicious trouble, longing and love and a trembling that is all delight." [33] Novalis' "mystic yearning" is like Plotinus' declaration that "our concern is not

[32] *Solitude and Society*, p. 99.
[33] *Enneads* I. vi. 4.

merely to be sinless but to be God." [34] This illuminates the remark of Sister Catrei, Meister Eckhart's pupil, who, when coming out of an ecstatic trance, exclaimed: "Rejoice, O Master, for
I have become God!" or the remark of the woman in Victor
Hugo's salon when the great Romanticist was himself mystically absorbed: *"Chose sublime!"* cried she, *"un Dieu qui croit en
Dieu!"* [35] Mme de Staël was not far wrong when she remarked
of Schelling's description of immortality as a return of the soul
to the All Soul: "This immortality bears a terrible resemblance
to death!" [36] The accents of Plotinian mysticism may be found in
the Pseudo-Dionysius, St. John of the Cross, St. Theresa, Ruys-
broeck, and elsewhere throughout medieval mysticism. Between
the medieval mystic and the later Romantics, Giordano Bruno
has intervened to pantheize the idea of the infinite. But the underlying monism, spiritual or pantheistic, remains unchanged, as
does the erotic ascent by our own powers.

Paul Elmer More, indeed, would push the origin of these
longings back to Greece itself, where Western philosophy was
affected by Eastern religion, and where the notion of *apeiron,*
mere boundlessness, was introduced. To this the Greeks opposed a controlling *autarkeia,* an ideal of self-sufficiency which
sought "to convey the sense of pure infinity, not by the sug-
gestion of vague unlimited forces forever striving for expansion,
but by absolute control at the center." [37] But self-sufficiency
makes for the recoil into the several rationalist experiments,
whether Stoical, Epicurean, or skeptical. If relieved by mysticism, it concludes to a dissolution of the self in infinite longing or to an intensification of the self in terms of feeling. If
protected by a willful self-sufficiency, it returns to the rationalist discipline of learning how to die. In either instance what is
lacking is religious humility, such as Erasmus saw in Socrates

---

[34] *Ibid.* I. ii. 6.

[35] Henry Adams, *The Education of Henry Adams* (Boston: Houghton Mifflin Co.,
1918), p. 143.

[36] *De l'Allemagne,* III, vii.

[37] *The Drift of Romanticism, Shelburne Essays, Eighth Series* (Boston: Houghton
Mifflin Co., 1913), p. 22. Cf. Irving Babbitt, *Rousseau and Romanticism* (Boston:
Houghton Mifflin Co., 1919), p. 253.

—"absolute resignation of himself to the Divine Will." The Socratic daemon, acting upon Socrates as a negative check upon expansive action, stands dramatically opposed to the medieval ladders of mystical ascent [38] upon the one hand, and to the rationalist self-sufficiency upon the other.

It obviously has nothing in common with Romanticism, understood either as a pantheistic longing for the infinite or as a reaction from rationalistic self-sufficiency into the alternate self-sufficiency of the apotheosis of feeling in the natural man.

The autonomy of self is lost in either case, and Romanticism remains at best another modification of the Renaissance experiment in self-sufficiency apart from faith.

One more possibility remained, however. What could not be done by reason or by nature might be done by culture, which projects a moral order based upon the accumulated wisdom of the past.

V

To rehearse the foregoing in another turn would make for weariness—such weariness, or ennui, as our age itself now suffers, fatigue of its own recoil. The comparative health of Matthew Arnold's "culture," brings, however, some relief. As an apostle of sweetness and light, and as a proponent of the best that has been

---

[38] "Unto this Darkness which is beyond Light we pray that we may come, and may attain unto vision through the loss of sight and knowledge, and that in ceasing thus to see or to know we may learn to know that which is beyond all perception and understanding (for this emptying of our faculties is true sight and knowledge), and that we may offer Him that transcends all things the praises of a transcendent hymnody, which we shall do by denying or removing all things that are. . . .

"It is not soul, or mind, or endowed with the faculty of imagination, conjecture, reason, or understanding. . . . It is not number, or order, or greatness, or littleness, or equality, or inequality. . . . It is not immovable nor in motion, or at rest, and has no power, and is not power or light, and does not live, and is not life; nor is It personal essence, or eternity, or time; . . . nor is It one, nor is It Unity, nor is It Godhead or Goodness; nor is It a Spirit, as we understand the term, since it is not Sonship nor Fatherhood; nor is It any other thing such as we or any other being can have knowledge of; nor does It belong to the category of nonexistence or to that of existence. . . . It transcends all affirmation by being the perfect and unique Cause of all things, and transcends all negation by the pre-eminence of Its simple and absolute nature—free from every limitation and beyond them all." (*Dionysius, the Areopagite, on the Divine Names and the Mystical Theology*, tr. C. E. Rolt [New York: The Macmillan Co., 1920], ii, iv.)

thought and said in the world, Arnold at least held out to us one more resort, the resort of eclectic sanity. The rule of measure and of sense and of high seriousness was at the least a helpful relief from the overwrought anxieties of the Romantics and from the arid reason of the Enlightenment. The Greek sense of proportion, the Olympian wisdom of Goethe, the Aristotelian poetry more real than history—all this recalled man to himself and recovered what was sound in the Renaissance appeal to the classical idea of man.

Arnold was, however, too keen a critic not to sense the tension. His early "wandering between two worlds," the melancholy, long-withdrawing roar of faith by Dover Beach, suggested that the world

> Hath really neither joy, nor love, nor light,
> Nor certitude, nor peace, nor help for pain;

while his

> Poor fragments of a broken world,
> Whereon men pitch their tent!

all testify to his awareness of the breach. In his "Empedocles on Etna" he feels, like so many of his contemporaries,

> . . . the agony of thirst,
> The ineffable longing for the life of life
> Baffled forever,

which, nevertheless, men ceaselessly pursue with thought and mind, until they are forced back into

> . . . this meadow of calamity,
> This uncongenial place, this human life:
> And in our individual human state
> Go through the sad probation all again,
> To see if we will poise our life at last,
> To see if we will now at last be true
> *To our own only true, deep-buried selves,*

Being one with which, we are one with the whole world;
Or whether we will once more fall away
Into the bondage of the flesh or mind,
Some slough of sense, or some fantastic maze
Forged by *the imperious lonely thinking-power.*

Empedocles leaped into Etna, so that it might be thought he had arisen into heaven—so that he might be worshiped as a god!—but lost one slipper when he leaped. How like mortality! How like the Renaissance!

Arnold turned to discipline and morals, to Goethe, to Spinoza, and to Marcus Aurelius. He turned to God and the Bible—found "morality touched with emotion" and "something not ourselves which makes for righteousness." This was much, but not enough. It rises not to faith. It rests in resignation.[39] Arnold's appeal is at best a moralism which subserves the law. It is appraised, indeed, by Arnold himself when, at the close of his essay on Marcus Aurelius, he writes: "We see him wise, just, self-governed, tender, thankful, blameless; yet, with all this, agitated, stretching out his arms for something beyond,—*tendentemque manus ripae ulterioris amore."*

So ends the Renaissance—multiform, kaleidoscopic, skeptical, rational, mystical, romantic, self-sufficient, proud; yet, for all this, agitated, stretching out its arms for something beyond. Or, to summarize its cultural experiment after the contemporary fashion—

Shakespearean fish swam the sea, far away from land;
Romantic fish swam in nets coming to the hand;
What are all those fish that lie gasping on the strand? [40]

[39] Arnold, on the occasion of the death of his son, turned to the *Meditations* of Marcus Aurelius for consolation.
[40] "Three Movements." From *The Collected Poems of W. B. Yeats.* By permission of The Macmillan Company, publishers.

Chapter V

THE FOCAL POINT OF CRISIS

THERE IS A POINT AT WHICH IDEA AND EVENT ESTABLISH PROPHETIC relationships and project a destiny. There is at the surface, as Emerson says, "infinite variety of things; at the center there is simplicity of cause." What we aim at is to pare away the surfaces in order to lay bare these causal simplicities. What we have presented, therefore, is a series of critical abridgments.

Such abridgments vary in degree; they may also vary in kind. "A high-flown journalist named Rousseau," says Mr. Friedell, "writes a couple of bizarre pamphlets, and for six years a highly gifted people tears itself to pieces. A stay-at-home scholar named Marx, indifferent to and ignored by society, writes a few fat volumes of unintelligible philosophy, and a gigantic empire alters its whole conditions of life from the base upward." [1] These are obvious abridgments. They are the same in kind as that of M. Maritain cited above: "The cell where Luther argued with the Devil, the stove against which Descartes had his famous dream, the corner of the Bois de Vincennes where Jean-Jacques soaked his waistcoat under an oak on discovering the goodness of natural man,—those are the birthplaces of the modern world." The two abridgments vary quantitatively; but they make the same appeal—the appeal from results and practical effects to the centripetal cause. They seek the axis of control to which the idea projects may be tied, and which obscure the center by their whirlings. They run the risk of fatal partiality, of distorting the truth by an incomplete preclusiveness. There were, besides Luther, Descartes, and Rousseau, other sources of the modern

[1] Egon Friedell, *A Cultural History of the Modern Age* (New York: Alfred A Knopf, 1930), I, 27.

world: the decay of Scholasticism, the recovery of Greek human-ism, the renewal of biblical faith. An abridgment, in order to justify itself, does not require that all the elements in a movement be recounted; it requires that all that is essential to the movement be recounted. What is essential is the clarification of the central principle.

In the foregoing abridgments we have specified the Renais-sance-modern world view as stemming from a shift in attitude toward man and his place in the cosmos. This turning "to man and to the world" was founded, as we have seen, upon an ante-cedent doubt and buttressed by naïve faith in self-sufficiency. The experiments in thought revealed the paradoxical nature of this blend of doubt and self-assertion. The turning to the autonomous reason resulted in skeptical impotence (Montaigne), in solipsism (Descartes), in subjectivity (Kant), and in tautology (Hegel). In all of which there is discernible a pattern of introversion where-by the self turns in upon itself and yearns for egress into truth. Similarly in the experiments in culture, the prophetic utterance of Luther, which brought the individual to his place of dignity *before God,* was lost by those successive thinkers who wished to preserve the dignity—but immanently and rationalistically, independently or magically, romantically or eclectically. Thus in *Hamlet* we be-held the Renaissance individual enervated by doubt and overborne by circumstance in a negative determination; in *Faust* this doubt was positively determined toward despair; in its longing for the infinite the soul returned by disillusionment back in upon itself in what has since been called romantic agony; and in the sanity of Matthew Arnold we saw eclectic wisdom compound-ed with a Stoic pride whereby a reasoned self-sufficiency main-tained itself by morals and by resignation. Matthew Arnold (morals and resignation) is the Stoic counterpart at the end of this development of Montaigne's Epicureanism (morals and hedon-ism) at the beginning. The pattern of the Renaissance turns in upon the self and thus expounds by dialectical unfolding what Luther knew as sin: *cor incurvatum in se*—the self's refusal to acknowledge its relationship to God.

Culture is the construct in fact of human wishing and desiring. It is the soul of man writ large in any epoch. It is the conversion into artifacts, through music, art, architecture, letters, sculpture, and other means, of the ideas and aims which accompany a basic attitude. Through such selected means it expresses its true spirit, and all its works are significant by virtue of the spirit which informs them.

This view of culture does not contravene the opinion of those philosophers of history who draw a sharp distinction between culture and civilization. The views of men like Spengler and Berdyaev merely serve to intensify the conclusions to which we have already been driven. According to this German way of thinking, "Culture, having lost its soul, becomes civilization." [2] As our spiritual capacity for the creation of values declines, or lags, or atrophies, civilization supplants it. The will to power supplants the will to value. The "enlightened" reason moves toward the rationalization of mankind. Economic materialism "is the typical philosophy of an age of civilization." This triumph of the enlightened reason produces civilization which depersonalizes, reduces man to the abstract, dominates him by economics, and concludes to the pragmatical and mechanical. "The relation between ends and means is reversed and perverted." We live for "life" which is no longer life; and this "life" is the death of culture, as it is the death of transcendent values. It is what Spengler describes as the "decline" of the West. These conclusions correspond closely with what we have set forth above in our series of experiments: that if any culture commits itself to premises which deny the primacy of the God-relation, or suspends the question as to the nature of the spiritual, or attempts to be spiritual while declining the responsibilities of the spiritual, that culture has committed itself beforehand to an internal process of decline. It will pass into civilization as defined.

When, however, philosophers of history such as Berdyaev and Spengler go a step further and say that culture *must* pass over into civilization, of the kind described, we must demur. It is true that our culture has done so; it is true that other cultures have

[2] Berdyaev, *The Meaning of History* (tr. G. Reavey; New York: Charles Scribner's Sons, 1936), p. 216.

arisen and have declined, and that in declining they have passed through some such proximate stages. The mortality of cultures cannot be denied. But that a culture must decline implies a metaphysical fatality of such rigor as to empty the historical entirely of the personal categories. This is a profound misunderstanding. Yet the foregoing experiments resemble precisely this view. They resemble it despite the fact that their argument is exactly the reverse of this causal strait-jacketing of human experience.

The resemblance is due to the fact that there is a causal factor in every dialectical unfolding, but even more to the fact that our authors of world histories also employ the device of abridgment. Their abridgments are more elaborate and will frequently pass, as in the late voluminous interpretations of Professor Arnold Toynbee, into six or seven volumes of five hundred pages each. They are approximations for all of that. If we were obliged to wait until some philosopher of history had contrived to get all the facts of all the cultures into his volumes (thus guaranteeing empirically the authority of his statement), we should, in fact, have to wait interminably; for the approximation is at best relative, and the possibilities for an inclusive compendium of all the facts are infinite.

This is true equally of Spengler's interpretation of the rise and fall of civilizations after the pattern of the seasons—spring, summer, autumn, and winter. This is an aesthetic abridgment of the problem. Mr. Christopher Dawson employs the same kind of metaphysical-aesthetic abridgment in his use of the mother-daughter analogy. Mr. Yeats uses the phases of the moon. Berdyaev falls back upon the being-nonbeing stratification. Goethe's preference for the spiral view, as against Eckermann's acceptance of the cycle, is a judgment of the same order. There is a sense, even, in which Plato's notion of time as a "moving image of eternity" is a metaphysical-aesthetic abridgment. Hegel's systematic exploitation of the historical in his all-inclusive shuttle work of becoming, dialectically teetering in a one-two-three progression like a three-legged robot, is also an abridgment which reduces the historical to a universal metaphysical compulsiveness. The unconscious philos-

116

ophy of history held almost universally today—the Darwinian view—is a causal evolutionism, designed after the analogy of the geological process, unfolding indefinitely like the two sides of a gully, or ascending mystically by way of some discursive protoplasmic *analogia vitae.*

The interest of our own abridgments has been altogether different *in kind.* The milieu of history exhibits, we have held, a dialectical unfolding which brings our hopes and sophistries out into the open by transferring them from the sphere of reflection to the sphere of decision, enforcing on us, by the terms of our own choosing, the true nature of the human situation. In the moment of crisis men are thrust *out* of the sphere of reflection and into the sphere of decision, which is the sphere of history. History has, therefore, a positive significance. It becomes the medium for a fresh transfiguration of the world.

One thing is clear, however. There can be no transfiguration of the world by flying from our aeon's perplexity, for that would be like trying to leap over our own shadows. We must enter deeply into the aeon's despair, and at the same time use the aeon to enter deeply into ourselves in order to reach the point of inmost determination for the newer understanding of ourselves. This is itself a crisis. A crisis is the point at which the inner contradiction of a period's assumptions reaches its maximum of tension and bursts asunder for want of an inner principle of control. This crisis is felt by all who are a part of it as a loss of confidence and unity. The peripheral centers about which the common lives of men are built lose their cohesiveness because the larger center has been destroyed.

> Now all things melt and shift in the moon's light.
>
> . . . .
>
> The knowledge you had at morning by the night
> Will cope with nothing . . .
>
> . . . .
>
> It is the moment of the whirlpool, moment
> Of the abyss where all things stream.[3]

[3] Archibald Fleming, Sentry's speech from "The Destroyers," *The New Republic,* July 13, 1938, p. 273.

In such a moment we experience that singular isolation which comes from having no foundation either for faith *or* for doubt. In such a moment one of two things happens: either the soul turns inward to exploit the irony of its uncertainty, or the soul reacts into some former synthesis of knowledge. The first turns inward. The second is an outward movement though it turns back into the past. The first is the more profound turning, since it must issue in despair or faith. The second is the more deceptive, since it quotes hope at precrisis figures. But both imply that we have changed our attitude; and since we experience both turnings in our world today, it is clear that we have abandoned or qualified the Renaissance way of looking at the world.

To examine these two turnings, therefore, is to clarify the focal point of crisis. For the turnings are, when taken together, the outward and the inner aspects of the soul's dilemma. We shall examine each, therefore, in turn and show how they renew the basic issue of the Renaissance, but in a form which requires a recovery of the original grounds of Western civilization.

i

The pattern of·introversion already apparent in the Renaissance experiment in the autonomy of reason, and even more apparent in the great works of the creative imagination throughout the period, is brought to its sharpest focus in the time of crisis.

This is revealed in the dilemma of poets and artists, of those who would creatively translate the epoch's attitude into works of culture. On the one hand, the creative possibilities of doubt have been exhausted; for doubt is negative and offers possibilities to the thinker or the creator only so long as it has something positive to work against. The modern poet, to make the example concrete, must either produce "images" (roses, fogs, and urns—of which there is no doubt), or he must find a foothold in the principle of enervation itself—the primary doubt. He finds himself shut in upon this annihilating ambiguity:

> We need a theme? then let that be our theme:
> that we, poor grovellers between faith and doubt,

the sun and north star lost, and compass out,
the heart's weak engine all but stopped, the time
timeless in this chaos of our wills—
that we must ask a theme, something to think,
something to say, between dawn and dark,
something to hold to, something to love.[4]

Such is the foothold of poetry today: it takes its foothold in the fact that we have no foothold.

On the other hand, the self-sufficiency of man experiences today its own reduction to the absurd. To be consistent with his principle, man must continue to assert himself. But the principle itself has led him to absurdity. To assert his self-sufficiency at the price of self-absurdity is a contradiction of the principle. Its precipitate is irony. It feeds upon itself:

> In the desert
> I saw a creature, naked, bestial,
> Who, squatting upon the ground,
> Held his heart in his hands,
> And ate of it.
> I said, "Is it good, friend?"
> "It is bitter—bitter," he answered;
> "But I like it
> Because it is bitter,
> And because it is my heart." [5]

This is the alternate foothold of modern poetry—in the bitterness of disillusionment, which, because it is our own, gives us something to feed upon. Such a choice of ourselves moves, however, either toward the knowledge of ourselves as sinners, which would be to abandon the Renaissance religious doubt, or toward the knowledge of despair, which would be to abandon the Renaissance self-sufficiency. The dilemma of the modern soul reveals that it *has* abandoned the Renaissance attitude in so far as this was founded on the antecedent doubt and on the principle of self-sufficiency. The irony arises from the soul's attempt to live creatively out of an attitude already abandoned.

[4] Aiken, *Time in the Rock* (New York: Charles Scribner's Sons, 1936), p. 2.
[5] Stephen Crane, *The Black Riders,* in *The Work of Stephen Crane* (ed. Wilson Follett; New York: Alfred A. Knopf, 1926), Vol. VI.

Theologians and critics of culture, up until very recent times, have naïvely ignored the growing consciousness of this inner dilemma; yet it is one of the most significant and, in an inverted sense, most prophetic signs of these times.

The consciousness of this dilemma goes back at least as far as Baudelaire, whose irony, whose narcissism, whose virile rejection of the prevalent mood, combined to make him a point of departure for a new development in poetry.[6]

Baudelaire was keenly aware of the coming crisis:

> The world is coming to an end. . . . I do not say that the world will be reduced to the foolish disorder of the South American republics,—that perhaps we shall even return to the savage estate, and that we shall go, across the grassy ruins of civilization, to look for pasture, tinder-box in hand. No. . . . We shall perish precisely by what we expected to live by. The mechanic will so far have Americanized us, progress will so far have atrophied the spiritual part in us that nothing amongst the sanguinary, sacrilegious, or antinatural dreams of the utopists could possibly be compared to its positive results. . . . It is not by any particular political institutions that the universal ruin (or universal progress; the name matters little) will manifest itself. It will be by the acquiescence of our hearts.

This foreboding was not peculiar to Baudelaire. It is found in Goethe before him, as in Flaubert after him. The terms are only slightly different. Goethe said:

> Mankind will become cleverer and more perspicacious, but not better nor happier nor more energetic. I foresee the day when God will no longer take delight in his creatures, and will once again have to annihilate the world and make a fresh start.

And here is Flaubert's prediction:

---

[6] To trace this development is not our present concern; but, to signify the change in attitude which it entailed, one has only to call attention to the titles of certain much-discussed works of art which follow in the line of this development—Baudelaire's *The Flowers of Evil*, Rimbaud's *Une saison en enfer*, Laforgue's and MacLeish's *Hamlet*'s, Vondel's *Lucifer*, Ezra Pound's *Draft of XXX Cantos* (his abstract for a contemporary hell), T. S. Eliot's *The Waste Land*, and others. All retain a starting point within the Faustian dilemma but add the new dimension, the *double-entendre* of irony, which thrusts the motion forward and inward into good and evil in an absolute reference.

If society continues on its present path I believe we shall see the return of such mystics as have existed in all the dark ages of the world. The soul, unable to overflow, will be concentrated in itself. We shall see a return of world-sickness—beliefs in the Last Day, expectation of a Messiah, etc. But all this enthusiasm will be ignorant of its own nature, and, the age being what it is, can have no theological foundation: what *will* be its basis? Some will seek it in the flesh, others in ancient religions, others in art; humanity, like the Jewish tribes in the desert, will adore all kinds of idols.

Flaubert goes on to point out that the age will be ripe for satires comparable to the *Satyricon* and the *Golden Ass* but conducted on the psychical rather than the sensual plane.

Neither Goethe nor Flaubert penetrates so deeply as did Baudelaire. Goethe, as we have seen, was not alarmed at his own prophecy. Like other prophecies in an expansive age, it was rhetorical. He did not seek a radical cure. He accommodated himself easily within a slightly idealized and Hellenized Spinozistic Stoicism. Flaubert also, like Rainer Rilke in recent times, took refuge in "a kind of aesthetic mysticism." "When there is no encouragement to be derived from one's fellows, when the exterior world is disgusting, enervating, corrupting, and brutalizing, honest and sensitive people are forced to seek somewhere within themselves a more suitable place to live." "I am a mystic at bottom, and I believe in nothing!" (*Cor incurvatum in se!*)

Nietzsche saw it also, as "the rise of Nihilism," which he prophesied in the Foreword to his *Will to Power*:

The future speaks in a hundred signs. This destiny announces its coming everywhere. . . . The whole of European culture has felt the torment of suspense, growing from decade to decade, like an impending catastrophe. . . . Nihilism stands before the door.

The "decline of Christianity" (*Der Untergang des Christentums*) implies the loss of sanctions and the passage into nihilism. The will to value will be replaced by the will to power. Nietzsche welcomed this. He became a prophet of that dark melancholy which now lies heavy on the world.

Baudelaire was no nihilist. His irony is too profound. His narcissism is too hard. He knows that he is caught within the fatal dialectic of his time. But he knows it fundamentally, in terms of man's condition and his willfulness:

> When an exquisite poem brings tears to the eyelids [*au bord des yeux*], these tears do not witness to excess of enjoyment; they are the witness rather of an irritated melancholy, of a postulation of nerves, of a nature exiled in the imperfect, and which would like to take immediate possession, even on this earth, of a revealed paradise.[7]

As for civilization, it is to be found not in gas or steam but "in the diminution of the traces of original sin." [8]

We need not overlook Baudelaire's dandyism, his Satanism, his boredom, his grossness, his psychopathic exploitation of his own neuroses, his dramatization of his own psychoses, or the fact that his poetry was "the apology of despair." We merely note the new dimension in it. "The wearisome spectacle of the immortal sin" is not the same thing as the ennui of André Gide: "Between desire and boredom our restlessness balances. The whole of humanity looks to me like an insomnia victim who tosses to and fro upon his bed without being able to sleep." [9] Gide's victim of insomnia is a case for psychotherapy; Baudelaire's "wearisome spectacle of the immortal sin" is a subject for redemption.

Baudelaire recognized that the Renaissance-modern man would take the Kingdom by force, and on this earth even, but without repentance; that he would create a revealed paradise by his own efforts, and by ignoring the revelation; that he would discover perfection within himself and within his world, refusing to know himself as a creature exiled in the imperfect. Baudelaire knew the solitude of saints, but he was no saint. So he produced his flowers of evil and composed "litanies of Satan." His ironies enforced his isolation. His great achievement was that, in a world where men were nothing, he became—a sinner. He *wished* to be self-sufficient like the others and to found himself on doubt; but he *knew* that he could not.

This is the dilemma which confronts the modern poet and

---

[7] *L'Art romantique*, VIII.
[8] *Journaux intimes*, "Mon coeur mis à nu," 58.
[9] *Les nourritures terrestres* (Paris: Gallimard, 1897), p. 104.

which he everywhere exploits—whether it be the French poet Rimbaud praying Satan for "a fork-thrust," a "drop of fire" to reassure himself that his spirit is alive; or the German poet Rainer Rilke discovering that "we live our lives forever taking leave"; or the Anglo-American poet T. S. Eliot discovering "the hollow men" of the present world. The turn is inward into the irony of the human condition apart from God.

Now irony is itself a profound turning and is an indication that the Renaissance attitude of optimism and unlimited hope has been abandoned. Irony is not merely double edged. It also brings together two dimensions: the temporal and the eternal. And it juxtaposes them by its ironic contradiction in such a way as to make it clear that the one is not the other. It also brings the soul to bay when its terms are thoroughgoing, not in such a way as to focus on the temporal, but in such a way as will expose the temporal to the eternal. This signifies, when applied to man in history, that we have explored all the horizontal possibilities. We have sought perfection at the end of all the horizontal roads, only to find each a dead end thrusting back upon the mid-point, turning the mind backward upon itself and forcing the soul inward upon its central isolation. Like the snake swallowing its own tail, it ends in "an *infinite* straight line *perpendicular* to the plane." [10] The human spirit suffers a recoil into the religious attitude. Perfection is no longer posited upon the human plane but must be sought above the human, and the tragic significance of life apart from the divine is ironically disclosed.

To disclose in such wise the radical imperfection of the soul on its human level is to disclose its inner contradiction together with its dialectical motion to and fro upon the plane of doubt. This is the plane of fatal ambiguity apart from God, which intercepts all hope and breeds despair, and which repeats itself in all our utterance.

Irony takes its standpoint in the living thought, in the relation between the individual and the idea or event. Mr. T. S. Eliot's *The Waste Land*—referred to above—derives its power from its

[10] Hulme, *Speculations*, p. 34.

123

ironic juxtaposition of our disintegrated culture with the unity of ancient culture, all in an abstract manner; yet the contradiction thus established forces the consciousness inward infinitely upon its sense of moral impotence and ethical responsibility. The abstract aridity of the poem's accidents is transferred to the soul, where it festers into the religious question: life or death, hope or despair. Thus, in the profoundest sense, irony may assist in bringing the rebellious soul, the soul curved in upon itself, to the point of moral choice, disclosing the contradiction between our supposed self-sufficiency and the soul's need for an absolute object of faith. Irony never beholds this object in itself. It nevertheless leads the individual up to it and there abandons him. Irony presents dialectically the discrepancy between our finite horizontal hopes and the infinite religious demand.

Irony in this form has one advantage over prophecy. As Kierkegaard would say, its dialectic "wounds from behind." It takes the subject, the rebellious soul where it is, in the curvature of its own doubt, the soul concurring. It complies with the soul's orbit of recoil upon itself but abstracts outwardly from the motion, so that the soul is left stranded by its own recoil before the contradiction of the religious demand. Which is ridiculous—the soul concurring! To quote once more from Stephen Crane:

> I saw a man pursuing the horizon;
> Round and round they sped.
> I was disturbed at this;
> I accosted the man.
> "It is futile," I said,
> "You can never ——"
>
> "You lie," he cried,
> And ran on.[11]

The infinite responsibility and our finite impotence are here juxtaposed as the ideal and the actual. The ethical question is posed by exploiting the soul's willingness to follow its own folly aesthetically. Its truth assaults us from behind. From behind what? Our

[11] *Op. cit.*

124

pride! Human pride and human folly are juxtaposed. Laughter hears its echo in the empty cavern of its pride.

Irony may have, therefore, prophetic significance; or it may be a medium of covert repentance, an adroit confessional. But it confronts the issue without responsibility. It retreats into the aesthetic and shuns decision through its art. It refuses its apostleship by escaping into its medium. The decision is what it cannot come to; it can only present aesthetically the *need* for the decision. Decision steps beyond the bound of irony. It is for this reason that irony is the last evasion, the sole remaining "hide-out" of the modern soul. For in irony the poet can abstract ironically from his condition: he can prove his intellectual superiority to this dilemma, can confess the guilt of all—his own included—*without responsibility*. The poet can, by virtue of the double motion of his irony, abstract from his condition and at the same time confront it, both acknowledge it and remain detached from it, and so preserve his life in it.

But to preserve one's life between abstraction and confession is itself an irony. It is the irony of irony. Like Victor Hugo's *The Man Who Laughs,* such a soul would be pathetically contorted into a perpetual misrepresentation of itself just as the child's features were distorted into a changeless grin which it bore through life, enduring hardship, pathos, and deep tragedy beneath a living mask of laughter. Life could endure this; but the spirit cannot. It will end in apathy, despair, or transformation by an act of faith.

Even Heine, master of irony as he was, reached the point where his own irony doubled back on him. "Alas," said he, "the irony of God weighs heavily upon me! The great Author of the universe, the Aristophanes of Heaven, wished to show the petty, earthly, so-called German Aristophanes that his mightiest sarcasms are but feeble banter compared with His." [12] He was compelled to abdicate. "I come back into the humble fold of God's creatures."

By irony we pass through irony. We apprehend the basic contradiction in the heart of man. This is the contradiction of sin, of

---

[12] *Confessions.*

the fact that God's creatures presume to deny him. Today our poets and culture spokesmen pass into the inverse prophecy and covert confessional of irony in all its forms. It culminates in despair, where poets commit suicide, or are jailed, or are converted to religious faith. In this sense it is true, as Ezra Pound has said, that the poets "are the antennae of the human race." They are so, not because they see ahead, but because they see within. The childlike wonder which the poet has in times of faith becomes a childlike cry of pain in times when faith is gone. And this is true even when the childlike need is "intellectualist," as in modern times—that is, when it is surrounded by a barbed-wire hedge of conceits and sophistication. Irony in the twentieth century has swallowed itself and projected the infinite straight line of faith perpendicular to the plane of horizontal doubt. Herein we see how man "upon the road of natural perfection encounters sin"; we see that he is a creature "inevitably stigmatized, who carries either the wounds of the old Adam, or those of the Crucified." [13]

Irony precipitates the religious question. By poesy, and by traversing poesy, both thought and culture are brought to bear upon the question of the soul's eternal destiny. Such ironies comprise a living record of the *unfolded* dialectic of a willful attitude. This is prophetic of a new decision. Poetry will not save the world. But poetry can force the soul into the precincts of its last evasion. It can strip away the final vestiges of pride. It can expose the soul to its imperfection and its situation in a world of sin and tragic circumstances. It can, in brief, deprive our Protean souls of their evasive powers, until

> Changed to ourselves by this enforcing hand
> We lay like silver naked Proteus on the sand:
>
> The pelt fell from us and the sea-cow's shape
> The fish's scarlet the shark's wrinkled skin
> The seal's eyes and the brine encircled nape
> The foam's evasion the down-diving fin—
> All cheats and falsehoods of our vain escape:

[13] Jacques Maritain, *Réponse à Jean Cocteau* (6th ed.; Paris: Librarie Stock, 1926), p. 31.

Changed to ourselves, sea-sleeked and dripping yet
Our limbs lay caught and naked in the taking net.[14]

ii

The crisis of culture makes clear not only that the soul is brought to bay but that a reorientation of our culture must be brought about. There is required, therefore, an outward as well as an inward turning. In its first phase the outward turning is necessarily a turning backward along the way that we have come. In the anxiety of crisis the mind seeks the sources of historic error. It seeks to correct its error by appeal to previous epochs. In order to see forward into the future, there must be a reflection of the prophetic vision against the past. It is necessary, as Jaspers says, to pass through the lost domain of truth in order to revise it possessively.

This is the moment of "reaction," in which the isolated soul seeks shelter in some previous synthesis of life and knowledge. In the moment of reaction we have the appearance of going backward. We seem to defy the principle of "progress," to which the modern mind has attached itself so firmly.

A crisis, however, may become so thoroughgoing as to call in question all hypotheses. It may thrust us absolutely upon our "limit situation." "Progress," as a measure for value and meaning, is of no significance until its goals and standards are defined. It is therefore quite possible that a person appearing to "go backward" may in reality be going forward. As Pascal said, "When everything moves equally, nothing moves apparently: as on a ship. When all things go towards disorder, nothing seems to go thither. He who steps, causes, like a fixed point, the recession of others to be remarked." T. S. Eliot puts it even more crisply:

> In a world of fugitives
> The person taking the opposite direction
> Will appear to run away.[15]

[14] Archibald MacLeish, "Men of My Century Loved Mozart," from *Collected Poems, 1924-1933* (Boston: Houghton Mifflin Co., 1933), p. 89.

[15] *The Family Reunion* (New York: Harcourt, Brace & Co., 1939), Pt. II, scene 2.

In the time of crisis we must consider these "reactions" careful-ly. When it is clear that we have gone wrong on first principles, we must either recover the principles or experience a moral purga-tion or do both.

One danger, nevertheless, is evident. If we are to pass through the lost domain of truth, we must do so in order expressly to re-vise it possessively. This is a critical task, for it implies selection and rejection in the light of some principle of eternal significance. Therein, however, lies the difficulty. The crisis, we have said, be-trays the lack of such a principle. The crisis is a negative dis-closure. It discloses to us not a standpoint but the absence of a standpoint. It ends not in affirmation but in the need for affirma-tion. In proportion, therefore, to the desperation of the crisis, the heart will clutch eagerly at former patterns and try to rest in them.

Any reaction which makes of any past epoch an object of wor-ship, or which chooses such an epoch as a means of avoiding the possessive revision of its principles, or which uncritically projects such an epoch as an objective idealization by means of which it escapes the responsibility of a new compendious decision in faith, is a betrayal. It is an escape from the issue. It is a retreat from freedom. It is an attempt to avoid the pain of reorienting the mind, on the one hand, and the venture of faith upon the other. It hopes to avoid the new decision by resting in the previous de-cision. As over against the risks of faith, the soul seeks some cer-tainty or some authority which will certify for it the nature of truth and the patterns for action.

The reactions of our day take this form. The totalitarian states are absolutist. They make a total claim upon the individual. They resolve his destiny by subordinating it to the state. The regi-mentation which they impose supplies the order and the authority which men in the period of uncertainty require. These totalitarian philosophies are reactionary. Freedom has failed, it is held; it has made for weakness, for exploitation of the weak by the strong, for a false emphasis on the equality of all men. The individualism of so-called democratic states is but a smothered tyranny exercised by capitalists over the workingmen. If it is asked why educated men could acquiesce in the rise of totalitarian ideologies, the an-

128

swer is not difficult to find. The best minds, as well as the humblest, have been enervated by the antecedent doubt on which the Renaissance experiment was based. This doubt, moreover, was a religious doubt. The Renaissance man no longer believed in Christianity as he received it from the medieval world. Copernicus had shattered that world view cosmologically as Luther had shattered it religiously. Science and reason became the certainties for modern man. But the ideal of science accords quite well, from one point of view, with the notion of the rationalization of all mankind. The rationalization of all mankind becomes the rationalization of society, which leads by easy steps to regimentation on behalf of the state.

Totalitarian ideologists are also anti-Christian. They are right in seeing in Christianity their greatest foe. For whether the Renaissance recognized the fact or not, the true origin of its notions of freedom and the inherent dignity of the individual was Christian. Christianity also makes a total claim upon the individual. It makes it in the name of God and not in the name of race or state. Totalitarianism renews today the opposition between God and Caesar. Totalitarianism is a reaction into paganism. In other words, it is a reaction not only against the Renaissance-modern postulates but against the whole of Christendom. It is a great rejection. Its success would be the end of the West as we have known it since the beginning of the Christian era.

As over against this, we see in the world today prophetic voices recalling us to the basic faith on which the West was founded. Democracy itself, as it seeks to justify its opposition to the totalitarian claims, must discover increasingly the Christian origin of its fundamental beliefs about man. This, however, is not reaction. It is an appeal to faith. Reaction takes the form of an appeal to authority.

The more obvious forms of religious reaction are those which would hurry us back into Reformation theology or into the medieval synthesis. The one appeals from the risks of faith to the external certainties of the Word; the other appeals to the external certainties of the institution and the system. The former appears most notably in the "crisis theology" of Karl Barth, the latter in the work of the Neo-Thomists.

Concerning the former we shall remark little here. It appears that Barth's appeal was courageous and prophetic, but there was in it something desperate and willful. It is founded in a despair of God which is authentic, but it seeks a way to God by desperation and the will to believe. Just as G. K. Chesterton had to remind himself again and again how cheerful a thing it was to become a Roman Catholic, so Barth seems obliged to repeat again and again: "Ye must believe! Ye must believe! Ye must believe!" Which is quite true, of course. But we do not believe willfully, but by acquiescing in God's will. Barth's temper is rationalistic, and he asserts faith rationalistically, albeit by the paradox of Neo-Kantian skepticism. His appeal to Reform theology is a dogmatic appeal: he seeks a certainty rationally; he understands God's relation to the world and men causally rather than existentially; he understands sin and grace legalistically rather than spiritually. He is therefore reactionary.[16]

The more obvious reaction, and that which our analysis of the Renaissance would seem to recommend, is the reaction into pre-Renaissance views of man and the world. This is a reaction based upon the view that since the Renaissance began as a break with the medieval viewpoint, and since it has failed in its experiment, it must therefore follow that we should revert to that which preceded it—the medieval synthesis.

There is much to be said for this. The unity of thought and life in the Middle Ages was unique in the history of the West. The blend of Christian, Greek, and Roman bequests into a unified Christendom was a majestic achievement on the part of the Christian thinkers. The absolute hierarchy of values, based upon a reasoned alliance between faith and reason, gave to men a system of order greatly to be desired in our own time. The ascent of the

[16] Emil Brunner, who was associated with Barth in the early stages of the crisis theology, opposes legalism, rebukes the causal interpretation of sin and the fall, and accepts the existentialist standpoint. His name must therefore be sharply separated from that of Barth. Brunner's use of Kierkegaard, Dostoevski, Scheler, Buber, Hamann, Pascal, Luther, Irenaeus, and others, qualifies his Protestantism quite out of relation to that of Barth.

mystics from the unrealities of this world to ecstatic union with God in the spirit is an attractive thought to men who are troubled by the spectacle of holocaust and death in the present world. The philosophical consistency of the Thomist synthesis gives to Catholic apologetics on all fronts an enviable coherence and unanimity, whether applied to politics, philosophy, art, or religion. There is at the surface of things much to commend the view that "the evils of the time can only be overcome in the end through the gradual education of Christians to that full conception of Christianity, religious and secular, which obtained in the Middle Ages but which was gradually lost after the Reformation." [17]

There are, however, two reasons why such a recovery is impossible. The first is that the so-called medieval synthesis was not, in fact, a true synthesis. It was an accommodation of Christian revelation to Greek metaphysics on the one hand and to the Roman imperium on the other. It contained within itself the seeds of its own disintegration. The second reason is that the crisis of our time renews the issue raised by the Renaissance as to the nature of man and his destiny; but it raises it in an absolute manner, as a question posed out of desperation, and posed *between* Christianity and paganism—of which medievalism was a blend. It requires not reaction but repentance. The alternative is paganism or repentance.

Wilhelm Dilthey has rightly shown how three great motifs were woven together in the medieval world view: [18]

The first was the Christian belief in the relationship between the soul of man and the living God. This motif had its origin in the biblical revelation.

The second was the formal defining of the European mind in accordance with the aesthetic-rationalistic unity of Greek metaphysics. This had the effect of suppressing individuality within a closed cosmos, a mathematical and harmonius ordering of the whole of actuality, under a highest Intelligence or World Reason

---

[17] Michael de la Bedoyere, *Christian Crisis* (New York: The Macmillan Co., 1942), pp. 110-11.

[18] *Weltanschauung und Analyse des Menschen seit Renaissance und Reformation, Gesammelte Schriften* (Leipzig and Berlin: B. G. Teubner, 1914), II, 1-17.

as the ground of the world and the link between human knowledge and existence. God is the supreme architect, the *formae substantiales,* the ultimate world soul. In this aesthetic-rationalistic world view there are already projected the ground lines of naturalistic metaphysics and science, which was later based upon the causal analysis of actuality. Platonic, Aristotelian, Neo-Platonic, and Stoical standpoints enter into this synthesis.

The third motif was based upon the Roman consciousness of order and power and the tendency to identify religion with the state. The Roman notions of freedom, order, justice, and duty were related intimately to the place of the will in Roman thinking. The will of the individual was subordinated to the will of the state. The emperors were divinized. The Roman imperium became the highest will, and the relation of rule and obedience obtained from the forum to the family, from the legions to the workers in the field.

The centuries of labor devoted by the great Christian thinkers to the fusing of these great bequests is a magnificent witness to their power and energy in subduing the pagan world to Christian faith. The issue must be faced, however. Their achievement was at bottom an accommodation of the Christian revelation to the Greek mind and the Roman will. In three respects this accommodation is most apparent.

The first, and most obvious, is the identification of the Church with the Roman imperium and the absorption thereby of the will to power into the Church itself. Theologically, this identification bound grace to the sacraments, which were mediated by the priests and controlled by the institution. Niebuhr has remarked of this identification that it is "an intolerable confinement of the freedom of God within human limits." [19] Combined with a covert will to power, this suppression of the individual under God became unendurable over a period of time.

The second and more important accommodation, however, is in the formal structure of the synthesis itself. The two-storied relation between faith and reason was an unstable relationship. It

[19] *The Nature and Destiny of Man,* II, 208.

was an accommodation of biblical revelation to the being-non-being framework of Greek speculation. An arbitrary distinction between the supernatural and the natural was introduced. Theology dealt with the things of faith and philosophy with the things of reason—without its being observed that the entire relationship was a triumph for the theoretical reason. This meant that the realities of spirit were thrust away into a realm of mystery and could only be known by a *via negativa*. On the other hand, the things of this world were scorned. The monastic struggle to retreat from the world and the ascetic effort to subdue the flesh are comparable to the Stoic's apathetic struggle to suppress the passions.[20] Thus to the institutional suppression of the indvidual under God there was added a metaphysical suppression implicit in the total world view.

Implicit in this canonized triumph of metaphysics over faith was the rationalist principle, which led on the one hand to intellectualism, or on the other to absorption in the Absolute One of the mystics. The sources may be either Neo-Platonic, as in the earlier centuries, or Aristotelian, as in the latter centuries. The dualism of world and spirit was not, at bottom, a dualism at all; for the whole was contained within the aesthetic-rationalistic unity of God as the world ground. This world ground is conceived as Being. Its perfect sphericity was bound, soon or late, to be broken by the content of Christian personalism and the Christian view of history.

It did, indeed, degenerate, as Gilson has indicated, into "logicism," as in Abelard, and into "theologism," as in Bernard of Clairvaux.[21] This taint of logicism was in reality a rationalistic taint. Its threat to the medieval world view was clearly stated by Petrarch: "Philosophy," he protested, "is so prostituted to the fancies of the vulgar that it aims only at hair-splitting on subtle distinctions and quibbles of words. . . . Truth is utterly lost sight of, sound practice is neglected, and the reality of things is despised." The true fault of the synthesis, however, was neither

[20] Cf. John MacMurray, *The Clue to History* (New York: Harper & Bros., 1939), pp. 155 ff.

[21] Cf. *The Unity of Philosophical Experience,* chaps. i-ii.

logicism nor theologism but ontologism, or the bringing of metaphysics into a relationship of immediacy with religious faith. It concentrates all in the notion of Being rather than in the person and work of Jesus Christ.

"He who believes no longer in God," wrote Paul Claudel, "believes no longer in Being; and he who hates Being, hates his own proper existence. Lord, I have found you!" [22] This is a sublime affirmation; but its avowal that by finding Being one has found the Lord is a misunderstanding. What he found was the principle of identity, which is, indeed, the cornerstone of Aristotelian metaphysics but is hardly to be identified with that stone which, in biblical terms, must become the head of the corner. This is not the God "of Abraham, Isaac, and Jacob, the God of Jesus Christ," to whom Pascal appealed in his memorial and which he distinguished so sharply from the God of "the philosophs and the savants."

The third accommodation resides in the suppression of the prophetic-apocalyptic view of history as God's activity in the world, in the interests of a notion of time already discredited by metaphysics. Time is at most "a moving image of eternity." This movement, however, is neither backwards nor forwards, but upwards and downwards. The mystical and analogical ladders of ascent are as near as the medieval world view comes to a notion of history. For history, as the Hebrews understood it, is suppressed. Again, the motion is not *into* the world, after the manner of the Hebrew prophets; it is *out* of the world into havens of retreat where God may be contemplated in his essence or imitated in his perfection. The medieval world view is devoid of historical teleology. There is no fullness of time in the prophetic sense; nor is there tragedy and comedy in the sense of Aeschylus or Aristophanes. The metaphysical significance of the moment in time is dissolved in a notional eternity.

For the Hebrew, God was not only a First Cause or Prime Mover: he was a Creator and a Worker. It was precisely through history that he made himself known. His will was brought to

---

[22] Epigraph to Jacques Maritain's essay *"Connaissance de l'Être"* in *Antimoderne,* p. 159.

bear as an eschatological demand upon men who were also doers and workers. God's purpose for the world was carried out in history. God was a worker, and men were workers also. "My Father worketh hitherto, and I work." The medieval view of the God-man relationship suppressed the creative responsibility of men under God, who requires that men should work with him in the fulfillment of his design.

Thus there was added to the institutional and the metaphysical suppression of medieval man this third suppression of his creative and historical significance. It is not surprising, therefore, that when the break came, it came precisely from within the synthesis itself. Joachim of Flores (1145?-1202?) was the first to oppose the static world view with a dynamic view of history.[23] He was the first to use the term *reformare*. Arnold of Brescia was burned in 1155 for preaching a return to the simplicity of the apostolic teaching. St. Francis represents not merely a fulfillment of the monastic ideal but a most important modification and qualification of the same. Luther arose out of the monasteries. Luther is the last in a grand succession of reformers whose aim was not to destroy the Church but to bring it to fulfillment. Jacopone da Todi, Wycliffe, Huss, Savonarola—all came before Luther.

When the break came, the medieval logicism flowed through. The deists asserted its causal law without the Christian revelation. The romanticists recovered the medieval piety, the mysticism, the ecstasy, within an immanental, pantheistic world view. Thus the medieval synthesis, shorn of the supernatural, triumphed none the less in its hegemony, which, applied in these latter centuries to the material order, empties into the new totalitarianisms, the rationalization of all mankind. There is a sense in which we experience today the end of the Renaissance heresy, and also the end of the medieval world view.

"To be deep in history," said Newman, "is to cease to be a Protestant." There was truth in this, considering that Newman believed he must choose between rationalism and authority. Protestantism had indeed congealed into a legalistic scholasticism of

---

[23] Cf. Spengler, *The Decline of the West*, I, 19; Niebuhr, *op. cit.*, II, 161; K. Burdach, *Reformation, Renaissance, Humanismus*, pp. 48 ff.

its own. But Newman "reacted" into the Roman Catholic Church, for he needed certainty. His faith required the support of authority. It is possible, however, in this form of the argument, that to be deeper in history is to cease to be a Catholic; for the reaction into the so-called synthesis leads to historical regress, or into the escape from faith and freedom by way of security through suppression, through the appeal to authority.

Reaction is an abridgment of the problem. It is partial. It would hurry us back to a point of refuge within the sources of our present sterility. Reaction in our time of crisis must be absolute. It must not stop within the progression but penetrate through it. As the turning of the soul inward upon itself stops its evasions and changes it to itself, so the retreat on history will thrust us out of history upon—the Cross.

iii

Let us consider now just where we stand.

We have seen how the present crisis has brought our Renaissance optimism to an end and how, by so doing, it has brought to light the concealed doubt which enervated its hopes and ventures from the beginning. Its experiments in thought form a remarkable parallel, therefore, to the attempts of decadent paganism to salvage its genius of wisdom and faith.

We have seen also how reaction into the world view which preceded the Renaissance would be an incomplete turning, since the elements which comprised it were never wholly fused.

The only point of appeal which seems to stand clear from all this retreat on history is the prophetic significance of Luther; yet he is so vulnerable in taste, in temper, in judgment, in pride, that we can only make him the focal point of the crisis with reluctance. It would seem much nearer the truth to say that the incarnation of Christ in the world was so stupendous a fact that it has taken two thousand years of historical experience to explore the arc of its possible accommodations.

It was necessary, after the resurrection, that the meaning of Christ for the world should be set forth in terms of the prevailing thought patterns of the time. It is therefore not surprising that the full height and depth of its significance—if, indeed, it were wholly understood even by the first Christians—should have been accommodated in part to the Greek patterns of thought. The dominantly Platonic acommodation by the Greek Church was succeeded by the Aristotelian and Latin accommodation of the Western Church. These were great achievements. The unity of the West was based upon them. The new Christian spirit in the world brought life to the dying civilizations of the classical world. Therefore we find in these syntheses Christian elements and humanistic elements side by side with the rationalistic and pagan elements we have just described. The Hebrew, Greek, and Roman bequests were organized and blended into a working whole—a compound of three world views, kneaded and modulated, pressed and forced into a fine amalgam—a serviceable alloy without the Cross. The Cross is indeed its *symbol;* but the Archimedean efficacy of the Cross as the fulcrum of historical determination, both temporal and eternal, is aesthetically displaced by the Greek world view.

The Reformation was an inevitable consequence of the leaven of Christian principles working within that static culture. The prophetic dimension appeared in Luther, who asserted once more the primacy of justification by faith. But here again the Cross was accommodated to causal and legal systems based upon a subtle determinism of God's·will as against human impotence.

The Humanists also were sound in their appeal to Greek wisdom. Their appeal to Greek and Christian wisdom brought back the seer and the sage, and displaced the power of the priests. Humanism diminished in direct ratio to its loss of faith in the Incarnation. It tended to become an eclectic moralism and lapsed eventually into the impoverished moralism of the humanitarians.

Curiously, the genius of the Renaissance lay in its recovery of biblical Christianity. That is, it appealed to the dignity of man, to the rights of the individual, to freedom, to man's creative responsibility in history, to brotherhood, and to the world as a tangible reality in space and time. These were all part of the Hebrew-Christian bequest. The Renaissance failed *because it did not recognize these notions as Christian.* Christianity had become identified with the medieval system. Therefore the Renaissance, in rejecting the pagan compromise of medievalism, rejected also the Christian root of its own ideas. It was driven into an experiment which was, and will continue to be, a fruitless experiment. It attempted to hold its Christian beliefs in a secular manner. Secularity was established by the antecedent doubt. By it the Renaissance sought to have the fruits of belief without the first premise of belief. *Unbelief,* therefore, is the silent sorites which has emptied the Renaissance of significance and reduced its courageous ventures to the absurd. The modern world has carried these aims to depletion.

The exegesis of history results, it is true, in a negative disclosure. It is also true that negatively the Renaissance and the Reformation were a revolt against authority. But they possess also a positive and a prophetic significance.

Both the Humanists and the Renaissance in general appealed from Scholasticism to wisdom. Erasmus' appeal to Christ and to Socrates had at least as much warrant as the medieval appeal to Christ and to Aristotle. The Scholastic appeal was superior in knowledge; Erasmus' appeal was superior in wisdom. Erasmus failed because his existentialism lacked the prophetic dimension. Similarly the Renaissance in general appealed to the curiosity and wonder of the Greek mind in the springtide of its power. They established thus the principle of free inquiry, which accords with God's creative intent for man in the world. The Renaissance age of discovery has lasted until the present time. But it has lost that elation of spirit which comes from recognizing in its discoveries God's way of discovering to us his secrets of wisdom and glory.

Luther supplied what was wanting in these turnings. He reasserted the primacy of faith. He recovered to man his personhood. Nature had heretofore been subtly ranked higher than personality. But Luther's man was a person of dignity precisely because he stood *before God* and had been spoken to by God through his Word. All thought for Luther was thereby personalized; and the relationship between God and man became necessarily dialectical, or more properly, dialogical. That is, it could not be thought logically, but must be thought existentially. Luther placed therein a greater demand upon man than the Medieval Church had done. Sin was an act and not a defect, and its source was not metaphysical but personal. The point on which it turned was the point of faith or unbelief. The focal point of faith was in a *"theologia crucis."* [24] Sin is "what one lives and does outside faith in Christ." [25]

This was also the focal point of Hebrew prophecy. God always stood over against man, and the relationship was one of willing and doing. The content of freedom, of history, of fellowship, all have reference to God. Luther's understanding of sin would have supplied to the Renaissance notion of history the sense of judgment and fulfillment which the Renaissance teleology did not have. But this prophetic possibility of faith miscarried and the Renaissance failed because, as Luther says, without faith the heart turns in upon itself.

The crisis in which we stand is, therefore, absolute. It cannot be solved by any retreat into history. It can only be solved by passing through the lost domain of Christian truth to the point of the Cross, for only so can it be revised possessively. This is a work of construction, of selection and rejection, of decision and remembrance. Until this renewal at the focal point of the Cross is made both by individual and compendious decisions in faith, we must live like the solitary men at the end of the classical decadence. Like Plutarch, we are syncretists of principles that have died. Like him, we would produce life from the union of bodies that are still. Apart from the Cross, we inhabit that arid declivity between a time dead and one powerless to be born. Of that parenthesis in antiquity Flaubert has said: "The gods being no more and Christ being not yet, there was between Cicero and Marcus Aurelius a unique moment in which man stood alone." [26] We have come full circle. The gods of our naturalisms being no more, and the recovery of faith only now being renewed, there is this moment of crisis in which man stands solitary and alone. The crisis of culture is, at bottom, our crisis of faith.

[24] WA, vol. 1, p. 362.
[25] EA, vol. 12, p. 111.
[26] *Correspondence*, 3rd series (1854-69), Paris, 1910.

Interlude

ALICE AND THE WHITE KNIGHT

or

REACTION AND THE PHILOSOPHY
OF HISTORY

An Experiment in Paraphrastics

EVERYONE KNOWS OF THE CHARACTER AND PURSUITS OF THAT CELE-brated gentleman and knight, Don Quixote de la Mancha—how he furbished his great-grandfather's armor; procured for himself a steed, not without blemishes; and found for himself a peasant lady to be in love with, whom he called Dulcinea del Toboso. The exploits of this doughty warrior are also well known, and are withal of so unique a character that one may safely say that in all the annals of knight-errantry there is none to be compared with him, none—save one! And that one is the redoubtable White Knight whom Alice encountered in the Seventh Square in her adventure through the Looking Glass.

Probably Alice was a very plain little lass and not one to be compared, therefore, with the fair Dulcinea; nevertheless the White Knight fought for Alice quite as heroically as ever Don Quixote did fight for his lady del Toboso. Nor could Don Quixote himself have been more courteous, more kind, more gentle, nor yet more chivalrous than was the White Knight when he led Alice into the Eighth Square, where she became a Queen.

In each there was something childlike, something bland and joyous, something pathetic and doleful. From the world's stand-point there was a certain "foolishness" in their aims and conduct. Each was a trifle mad, and each had a most remarkable facility for falling from his horse.

Don Quixote's madness took the form of beautiful absurdities

143

which he believed to be true, whereas the madness of the White Knight ran to wonderful inventions which he believed to be possible. Their aims were different. Don Quixote beheld everywhere dwarfs and giants and maidens in distress; whereas the White Knight's ingenuity ran to mousetraps, beehives, and ways of getting over fences. But they were equally bland, and neither was disillusioned by the rebuffs of the world or the rebukes of fact.

In the first of these likenesses there is perhaps nothing so very unusual. It is something that every man of faith can experience. There is doubtless something irrefragably absurd about every venture of faith when viewed from the standpoint of others who are presumed to be sane. We must recognize that truth which Pascal observed so adroitly, namely, that men are so necessarily mad that not to be mad would be another form of madness.[1] What is permitted us to say is that it is better to profess that foolishness whereby we are made to see clearly than to persist in that sobriety whereby we act foolishly. But inasmuch as this is a paradox which will seem foolish to those who act foolishly—seeing that they act so with great soberness—and will be seen clearly by those whose standpoint is the standpoint in faith only at the price of constant vigilance, we must agree now, for the sake of this issue on which everything depends, to undertake in all soberness an experiment, a thought project, in which we shall present this foolishness foolishly. For to present in all soberness this foolishness foolishly, and yet not to take foolishly what an author never intended anyone to take soberly, is surely as near an approach as it is possible for the mind to make, in a disinterested manner, to a problem which demands that we must choose—and that, a choice of decisive significance—between one foolishness and another.

In all of this there is nothing so very unusual. There is, however, something very uncommon about the second likeness between Don Quixote and the White Knight. A facility for falling from one's horse is, with knights-errant, not commonly considered an achievement. It inverts the true order. A skillful knight would not suffer himself to be unhorsed. And surely if this thing hap-

[1] *Pensées*, 414.

pened not once but time after time, the knight in question would scarcely expect to become immortal thereby. With the White Knight, perhaps, it did not so much matter; for he was living in a backwards world—Alice having passed *through* the mirror—and to some extent the order would be inverted or, at any rate, reversed. Don Quixote, however, had not this excuse.

He had, however, another, had he chosen to use it. His horse, Rosinante—"a name lofty, sonorous, and full of meaning"—not being accustomed to the demands of battle, stumbled and fell in his very first encounter, throwing his master into a field, where he rolled about for some time endeavoring to rise; but, discovering that his armor was so heavy that he could not, he at length lay still and recited epic poetry. Herein we behold a most admirable example of classic restraint and an effective sublimation of thoughts which must have bordered on the profane. Likewise, the White Knight kept on talking when, raising his hands too suddenly in his conversation with Alice, he pitched headlong out of his saddle and rolled into a ditch.

"How *can* you go on talking so quietly, head downwards?" Alice asked, as she dragged him out by the feet, and laid him in a heap on the bank.

The Knight looked surprised at the question. "What does it matter where my body happens to be?" he said. "My mind goes on working all the same. In fact, the more head-downwards I am, the more I keep inventing new things."

*　　　*　　　*　　　*　　　*

*　　　*　　　*　　　*

*　　　*　　　*　　　*　　　*

There is something very profound in this remark of the White Knight. He affirms the transcendental nature of the theoretical reason, which keeps on working irrespective of his physiological displacement and keeps on inventing all sorts of new things *ideally*—that is, in the abstract—so long as these new inventions are not embarrassed by being brought to the test of practical application. The White Knight affirms the abstract reasoning power, a theoretical mark of the intrinsic dignity of man. This faculty is quite unimpaired by his practical conditioning. Yet his condition is comical. And it is comical in direct ratio to the gap which exists between the facility of his abstract reasoning power and his failure to bring it into any sort of relation with his practical situation. For he is obviously in a state of crisis. He is bottom side up with his head in the mud. No matter how great the facility of his abstract reasoning power may be, the full dignity of this man is diminished in so far as he fails to bring it into relation with his practical situation. In short, it is not a mark of good sense to remain indefinitely bottom side up in a ditch.

Herein is a useful analogy with the human situation. Man in history reaches a situation of crisis in which the true order of things is inverted. To make everything depend upon the assertion of the abstract reasoning power as the true mark of the dignity of man at such a juncture is foolishness. It would be comical if the consequences were as simple as in the case of the White Knight, since it would only serve to set off more visibly the disparity between the claims we make for ourselves and the tangible results which should verify our claims. But the consequences are not simple. They issue in suffering and megalomania and collision and death. Which is possibly what Kierkegaard meant when he defined comedy as contradiction without suffering, and tragedy as contradiction with suffering.

What is important at the moment, however, is not the understanding of the White Knight as an essentially comic figure. It is rather that we should observe the entire series of difficulties which the White Knight would have to overcome in the event that he should become highly serious and genuinely wish to place himself right side up in his world. For it is quite clear that this philosophical narrative does not begin at the point where the White Knight fell into the ditch. The truth is, as everyone knows, that this pathetic fellow toppled many times. The real truth about the White Knight's world is that everything in it is backwards and topsy-turvy. But for the White Knight to understand this, or to see the real terms of the crisis toward which the narrative is moving, presents a problem of no mean difficulty. Or, to put the problem from our own perspective in history, the Renaissance-modern experiment is like Alice's adventure through the Looking Glass: at the surface of the narrative all is topsy-turvy and foolishness; but underneath (once the clue is provided) a problem in chess is unfolding and a checkmate is being brought to pass. Such is the dialectic of the spirit within a historical situation. In our time the checkmate is declared.

We know quite well, of course, that the Lewis Carroll story does not begin at the point where the White Knight toppled from his horse. It really begins at the point where Alice climbed up on the mantel, pressed her hands and forehead to the glass, and began seeing everything backwards! It is clear, then, that all we are obliged to do in tracing the historical antecedents of our spiritual distress is to go back along the pathway we have followed to the point where we first passed through the mirror, and the whole tale will become comprehensible at once.

*   *   *   *   *

*   *   *   *

*   *   *   *   *

Let us, however, take account at the very beginning of certain difficulties in this procedure.

It is easy enough for a reader of Lewis Carroll's little volume to say with conviction that the whole trouble began here where Alice passed through the Looking Glass; but would it have been so easy *for the White Knight to have said so,* or for the Queen who ran with Alice across the black and white fields so rapidly that Alice could scarcely breathe, or even for Alice herself to have found her way back to the mirror once she was implicated in the action? Did not the whole phantasmagoria impose its earnestness upon her to such a degree that she bowed soberly when formally presented to a leg of mutton she was about to eat? Should the White Knight, for example, undertake this little experiment of tracing his destiny backwards to the point where he first began to see all things backwards, might he not conclude that it was surely at that moment when he climbed on his horse backwards after having toppled off: surely he would be seeing the world backwards at just such a juncture, albeit his notion of backwards might overlook entirely the topsy-turviness of the world around him? How should the White Knight know that his world was topsy-turvy? Or, to apply an analogy so thorny and so disconcerting, since we are ourselves implicated in the complicity of events which have come suddenly to a climax, and since we have, in fact, arrived only lately on the scene and are perhaps no better informed than the leg of mutton that got up in its dish and bowed to Alice, since we inherit a world that has imposed its schedule of values upon us, *how are we to know* that it is topsy-turvy? Or how are we to discover the historical point at which we began seeing things backwards?

The time sequence in the analogy does not alter. The temporal series both before and after Alice passed through the glass remains constant. The clock goes backwards, truly enough; but life is lived forwards all the same. So also, the ground rules remain unchanged though comically transgressed at the surface. The chessboard remains constant, no matter how many times the Knight topples from his horse. The action is not even comical to the persons of the drama. It is not even comical to Alice, who is imposed on by their seriousness. It is only comical to *one who does not share their point of view*—to one, in short, who bears the same relation to the narrative as the Eternal bears to the temporal. But who in the story could bear such a relationship to the characters? Obviously no one but Alice, who, by acquiescing in their point of view, is more bewildered than amused and who, by being solicitous for the Queen's tears and impatient with the Queen's wrath, becomes comical herself. But comical for whom? Clearly, for the author or the reader—for those *who stand outside of the action*. In brief, there is no means whereby the topsy-turviness of a world in its absolute significance can be discovered apart from a petitioning of the principle of the *deus ex machina*.

But where, then, we ask, is such a principle discoverable in an action? It is present always at the beginning and at the resolution, and is present immanently as the condition of the plot's unfolding. Thus it might have revealed itself to anyone in that topsy-turvy world who witnessed Alice's coming through the mirror; or it might have been apprehended at the climax by the Queen, for example, had she perceived that she was such stuff as Alice's dreams were made of! It could have been seen by the White Knight, had he perceived that the ontological nature of the chessboard was such that it necessarily brought all purposive activity dialectically to a climax. In only one other way could it have been revealed, and that by Alice herself, who could have told the White Knight, for example, that he was nothing but a piece of wood that had broken its back and needed glueing together again.

Dame Folly plays this roll in Erasmus' masterpiece, saying to her audience: "And what is all this life but a kind of comedy, wherein men walk up and down in one another's disguises, and act their respective parts, till the property-man brings 'em back to the Trying House!" But who would believe Folly? And who would believe Alice? Yet the appropriation of such an understanding of himself would obviously depend wholly upon the White Knight's believing implicitly, and without reservation, what Alice should tell him.

In short, there is in the present situation no means whereby we may secure to ourselves the point of view of the Eternal save that of placing ourselves analogically at the beginning, or of being present at the end, or of believing implicitly an incarnate declaration of the Eternal from within our own plane of reference.

The first of these possibilities, the rational, we have observed already in the case of Hegel, who, in striving rationally to arrive at such an immediacy, arrived only at tautology. The reason which takes as its foothold its own self-sufficiency fails to secure its relation to existence; it projects the interminable dialectic of the ideal relations founded on the implicit analogy of itself. The principle that is immanent as the condition for the plot's unfolding is, as over against this, the constancy of the chessboard—the world ground. It is indeed a point of appeal. It validates the "logic of events in history"; but its disclosure is negative, as may be seen from its complicity with the second of these alternatives, the historical or eschatological. We have been considering this possibility with reference to the end of an era. Such a reference could serve our turn only in the event that the crisis were of such finality that all the options of cultural hope had been tried and had precipitated a crisis that was positive, not negative, in its prophetic significance. Or is it possible that the eschatological significance of every great historical crisis is a negation of false assumptions? An eschatology founded on faith may be said to yield a positive disclosure; but the eschatological disclosure which reveals an *absence* of faith and meaning can only be called *negative*. Hence the nihilism of Continental thinkers. The third alternative is the alternative of religious faith, but a faith of a particular kind—a faith in which somewhat has been revealed from without the plane of our action, a somewhat that is at once historical and of eternal significance. *Whenever this third alternative becomes consciously imperative either for an individual or for an epochal consciousness, that individual or that epochal consciousness has already abandoned the attitude of the period that provoked the crisis.* The fact of the crisis—the point of fevered suspension when everything hangs in doubt as to whether the disease or the life shall triumph —is itself the evidence that such a juncture has been reached. We have reached the point where a new decision in faith is an imperative.

   *   *   *   *   *

     *   *   *   *

   *   *   *   *   *

This disclosure presents, however, a problem of a different kind —the problem of the White Knight, the problem of reaction.

At the point of crisis it is inevitable that the consciousness shall turn back along the way it has come, in a desperate effort to recover itself. The White Knight will retrace his steps to discover at what point he began seeing the world backwards. Therein is the problem: if he concludes that his world became topsy-turvy at the point where he climbed on his horse backwards, his reaction will suffice nothing. It is partial. It is deceived. It resumes the topsy-turviness and is carried along by it, but from a slightly altered angle of reference. The White Knight may congratulate himself on having done something; but in reality he travels the same path, albeit everything appears differently since he now rides frontwards instead of backwards.

Communism, as in the Russian Revolution, is a reaction centering religiously in a naïve faith. It is, however, a reaction into paganism. At the same time it is a partial reaction, since it carries forward to logical completion the materialistic rationalism of the Renaissance-modern attitude and is, at the same time, carried forward by it. The path from Hegel to Feuerbach to Marx to Lenin is by this time a familiar one. To invert Hegel is to exchange an absolute idealistic monism for an absolute monism shorn of the protective coloration of the abstract ideality. So also German racism, which is a reaction into pre-Reformation Teutonism, is of a religious character. It nevertheless carries forward into violent fulfillment the latent implications of the "will-to-power" philosophies of the nineteenth century. Nietzsche's own eagerness that we should recover the zeal of the Renaissance was itself but a partial reaction, which would hurry us back into the presuppositions whose unfolding we have just witnessed and whose results we see about us.

This is true equally of those more genuinely Christian attempts to return to Reformation theocracy or to the Thomist medieval synthesis. There were elements in both of these accommodations of the Christian faith which prepared the way for the present crisis. *There is no return that is efficacious save a return to an absolute starting point.* In a time of crisis like our own, the surfaces of life are both complex and violent. The reactive tendency is easily pre-empted by the secondary cause—itself a result of the basic cause which lies concealed beneath. The crisis thunders about our ears. In desperation of our need we run to analyze the cause; but, underestimating what the basic terms in conflict are, we conclude too soon, or conclude within the momentum of the previous cause, the cause already in motion by virtue of the previous decision. Thus we offer split solutions which defeat our hope again. We resist the motion of the part, but suffer ourselves to be carried forward meanwhile by the stream of tendency implicit in the whole. In such wise all partisan solutions enter into a refined complicity with the events themselves and serve to aggravate the crisis. If a civilization is "sick unto death," we must not offer it a dialectical materialism, or a racial myth, or a utopian economy for the cure of its soul. This would be like saying: The man is sick at heart; therefore, when we operate, we must first remove the heart! Nor must we, on the other hand, expect to cure it by applying dogmatic systems, as authoritarian poultices, from the outside.

The pattern of reaction, meantime, goes forward apace. Our poets make new alliances. Our critics reconstruct the tradition. The age is intellectualist. Thinkers are eclectic, each one establishing a line of authority running back to Jeremiah, or to Aristotle, or to Thomas Aquinas. This in itself is prophetic of the end of the Renaissance attitude. It implies also that constructive critical thought in these days is "traversing the lost domain of thought in order to revise it possessively." But the real danger is that we shall conclude too soon and, like the White Knight, go back to the point where we mounted our horse backwards and assume that because we now view the world as we did before, we have therefore done something. The problem is much deeper than that. We must pass through the domain of perplexity in order that man may reach a decision concerning himself. We must strip off the trappings of the masquerade in such a way as to disclose the genuine that lies beneath. In short, there is nothing wrong with the White Knight's reason, his abstract reasoning power; there is something wrong with his *wisdom,* which has suffered itself to be imposed upon and deceived by a world whose practical notions have become topsy-turvy. Such a world requires the counteraction of a greater Folly. The nature of this greater Folly (the great Reasonableness) we can approach in principle if we go back briefly through this Looking Glass domain of perplexity and revise it possessively.

*　　*　　*　　*　　*

*　　*　　*　　*

*　　*　　*　　*　　*

What produces half the *non*sense in Lewis Carroll's blithesome philosophy of history is the fact that half the characters are altogether logical in their reasoning. But their reason overrides the practical and fails to take its purchase in the *common* sense. Thus pompously the persons of this little drama become most ludicrous when they, with dignity, do reason most exactly—geometrizing in a void which has no rootage in the practical, speaking truth but seldom deviating into sense. Alice asked:

"Do you think it's going to rain?"
Tweedledum spread a large umbrella over himself and his brother, and looked up into it. "No, I don't think it is," he said: "at least—not under *here*. Nohow."
"But it may rain *outside?*"
"It may—if it chooses," said Tweedledee: "we've no objection. Contrariwise."

Thus sense, so strictly held, becomes nonsense through carefully ignoring common sense, and through overlooking Kant's contention that the status of the speculative reason is *conditional* and that it is only in its practical employment that it completes itself.[2] "The reason alone does not suffice in order to be reasonable." [3]
Of course, the other half of all this nonsense is occasioned in just the opposite manner—through reason's doing what it ought to do, that is, taking its root in the common sense, but in a common sense that is itself perverted.

"I don't understand you," said Alice. "It's dreadfully confusing!"
"That's the effect of living backwards," the Queen said kindly: "it always makes one a little giddy at first ——"

[2] *Theory of Ethics*, III, 3.
[3] Pascal.

"Living backwards!" Alice repeated in great astonishment. "I never heard of such a thing!"

"—but there's one great advantage in it, that one's memory works both ways."

"I'm sure *mine* only works one way," Alice remarked. "I can't remember things before they happen."

"It's a poor sort of memory that only works backwards," the Queen remarked.

"What sort of things do *you* remember best?" Alice ventured to ask.

"Oh, things that happened the week after next," the Queen replied in a careless tone. "For instance, now," she went on, sticking a large piece of plaster on her finger as she spoke, "there's the King's Messenger. He's in prison now, being punished: and the trial doesn't even begin till next Wednesday: and of course the crime comes last of all."

"Suppose he never commits the crime?" said Alice.

"That would be all the better, wouldn't it?" the Queen said, as she bound the plaster round her finger with a bit of ribbon.

Thus the little dialogue runs on, the Queen both clear and lucid, spinning out the consequences of the premises, and Alice confused and discomfited because her common sense has been imposed on by a sense more common which contradicts with reason the reason she has been accustomed to. And all of this is nonsense, not to the Queen nor even to little Alice, but to the reader and to the author, to those who stand outside the action, to those who occupy the same relation to the action in the story that the Eternal bears to the temporal. It suggests that both reason and custom take their purchase in a reference both prior to and more ultimate than either of these in themselves. Or—to state the problem as before—when the common sense is itself perverted, how shall we secure to the White Knight or to the Red Queen or to Alice, who acquiesced in the perverted world view, the point of view of the Eternal?

This is a blow to confidence; for we have preened ourselves on rationality no matter how the follies of the world increase, and custom serves our turn when reason palls. Custom dignifies our errors through regarding that as sacred which has long been persisted in and has acquired thereby prestige of history. Thus, like Montaigne, we learn how little reason doth inform us and how "custom doth so bleare us that we cannot distinguish the true visage of things!"

The true visage of things will, all the same, exert its power over us. Philosophers of history aspire to comprehend it and to understand what men can do in the face of it. "It's a great huge game of chess that's being played," thought Alice, "all over the world" —which made her, or Lewis Carroll through her, a philosopher of history! Alice aspired, moreover, to become a Queen in the Eighth Square, just as men everywhere aspire to have their achievements crowned before the little game is played out. Alice, having acquiesced in the topsy-turviness of a world which is nevertheless laid out with all the underlying rigor of a chessboard, became implicated in a series of events which, both comically and pathetically, paraphrase the human situation. They are not parody, nor travesty, nor caricature, but *paraphrase*.[4]

Like other pawns in this singular contest of living, Alice found, in the pawn's square, that she had to run for all she was worth in order to keep in the same place. "And still the Queen kept crying 'Faster! Faster!'" The imperious masters of the workaday world command; and we obey, rushing pell-mell into the world's multiplicity, where "captains of industry," office boys, and subway trains scurry hither and thither, hurrying past one another, each one absorbed with his own pursuit, half the population hurrying east and half scurrying west, all immersing themselves in haste, in that spurious eternity of endless multiplicity, until exhaustion overtakes us where we tried so hard to keep in the same place! "Strange," said Emerson, "how the great masses of men worry themselves into nameless graves; while here and there some quiet soul forgets himself into immortality!"

Let us note in passing that this spurious eternity of endless multiplicity is, in reality, the spurious eternity of time and space, in which the sequence (the multiple coinsequence) of causal movement dominates our action. Men strive to build their aspirations on these space dimensions which flee before them into the infinite. The mythopoeic power of the Copernican world view imposed

[4] Παρα, by the side of; φράξω, to say, to tell—to tell alongside of.

this schedule of values, or of devaluation, upon us; the evolutionary hypothesis caught it up and projected it upon the future like
a movie film in terms of "process" and endless "progress"; now
the new science rises to refute this groundless optimism by raising the space-time myth to the nth power in its notion of expanding universes. The universe expands like stars upon a rubber balloon. The nebulae we see are scattering. By measuring the rate of
their recession we determine the rate of the world's expansion.
Today we see a million island universes, two million or so light
years apart, fleeing farther outward from each other at an ever-
increasing rate of speed. "Time's arrow" flies, and underscores
the "one-way property of time." [5] History is linear; it runs to overtake the stars. The stars recede, proportionately faster than our
history pursues. And this is ludicrous; for history cannot run fast
enough even to stay where it is, but turns in upon its own sphericity, its trifling provincialism of the earth, its ostracized spheroidal
lump that turns about a dying sun. Such a view is gloomy. The
law of entropy on which the view is built projects a final "chaotic
changelessness," a "heat-death" of the universe; for the energy
which is radiated is dissipated. The universe "is running down."
Heat moves from the object that is hot to the object that is cold;
but this motion, according to the laws of thermodynamics, is not
reversible. Dean Inge protested: This is "a painful stultification of
our belief in the values of life." To which Mr. Eddington replied,
with feigned surprise, "Since when has 'the heaven and earth shall
pass away' become unorthodox?" A strange inversion both of
scientific attitude and of early Hebrew consolation!

More disconcerting, however, is the fact that if the logic of the
law of entropy should be reversed—if the track of expansion be
followed backward ever nearer toward its source—a notion of
Creation in time is logically inescapable! Contemporary science
wheels us round precisely to that spot where the biblical account
in Genesis had placed us, and we see how great a deal of running
we have done to keep precisely in the same place.

[5] Eddington, *The Nature of the Physical World*, pp. 68, 69, 100, 75, *et al.*

ALICE AND THE WHITE KNIGHT

Emil Brunner writes:

Only the man who seeks his greatness in the spatial dimension has become a ludicrous figure—unspeakably ludicrous; and this is the comic element in our own day, that, while it perceives with consternation the hopeless disappearance of man in space, it seeks its triumphs mainly in the overcoming of spatial distances—like someone who has not caught the express train and runs after it for a bit, as if he could still catch it up.[6]

*　*　*　*　*

*　*　*　*

*　*　*　*　*

Alice, however, caught her train. She did it by sitting down to catch her breath. This is always the first step toward spiritual achievement—the motion toward collectedness. Then she got up, walked down the hill, stepped over the little brook into the Third Square, and suddenly she was on a train being whisked away into the Fourth Square.

The spirit always takes a bound when, through collectedness, it first defies the quantification of experience in terms of time and space, and glimpses the durability of transcendent virtues, values, ideas, or spiritual essences. It hurtles over Three and lands in Four, the leap from quantity to quality, from the temporal to the nontemporal, from the many to the one. But many pawns do not survive this leap; or else they bog down in Four, become lost in the woods there, or play the part of ubiquitous sentinels set out to guard the passages and so impede the march of those who venture more.

Before Alice came to Tweedledum and Tweedledee in the depth of the forest in this square, she had first to pass a section of the woods in which she could not recollect her own name. This initial anonymity of spirit, when the mind is disabused of that outward quantification of experience in terms of space and time and first turns inward on itself, is not uncommon in our world. In

---

[6] *Man in Revolt* (tr. Olive Wyon; New York: Charles Scribner's Sons, 1939), p. 422.

fact, it is much more common to encounter men who do not know their names. The Greek advice that we must come to know ourselves was not an idle moral maxim; it was a true necessity of coming into being, of becoming what we are. "I know who I am!" exclaimed that celebrated knight, Quixote de la Mancha, when his neighbor questioned whether he had lost his mind. By heroism he had come to know himself.

"I know who I am," answered Don Quixote; "and I know, too, that I am not only capable of being those I have mentioned, but all the twelve peers of France, yea, and the nine worthies, since my exploits will far exceed all that they have jointly or separately achieved."

"That is the hinge of all human life," comments Miguel de Unamuno, "to know what one wills to be." [7] Nevertheless, it is probably a much greater knowledge of the self to know what God wills that one should be than to know what one wills to be on one's own account. Don Quixote knew himself sufficiently to be a hero, a pathetic hero. He was capable, as Kierkegaard suggests, of losing his reason and with it the whole schedule of values of the finite world, "of which reason is the stockbroker." He had, that is, the capacity to make the "great dive from the spring-board which takes one into infinity" and so to "go through life standing on his head!" [8]

This is indeed a great achievement; but one which many have performed through being disabused of the finality of the spatio-temporal order of things. Don Quixote achieved it by donning his suit of armor one morning before dawn, mounting Rosinante, and sallying forth by the rear gate upon his high emprise. Socrates achieved it by reflection, by disabusing himself of confidence in spatiotemporality, cross-questioning himself into deliberate discovery of his own ignorance. This also was a great achievement. But to know one's self under God—to know one's self, that is, in terms of what God wills that we should be and do—this requires

[7] *The Life of Don Quixote and Sancho* (tr. H. P. Earle; New York: Alfred A. Knopf, 1927), p. 33.

[8] *Fear and Trembling* (tr. Robert Payne; New York: Oxford University Press, 1939), p. 44.

another motion. It is the miracle of faith and grace. In this miracle the finite world may be recovered, but *sub specie aeternitatis;* for we behold it as God wills it to be, and work upon it passionately to transfigure it in God's name.

It would be foolish to suppose that Alice, when she knew her name, knew it as Jacob came to know his, or Samuel, or Abraham, or even Don Quixote. For while her decision to pass through that wood in which she would not know her name was heroic (since she knew the danger beforehand, and also knew that to reach the Eighth Square she must pass through the wood), it was not heroic in either of these extended senses. For the Fourth Square everywhere reflects the first stage of these motions of the spirit. It is a Socratic movement, a reflective transition from naïveté into ignorance. It is a movement, nevertheless, that the pawns in Two and Three will never make. They will indeed be running errands all their lives and will not bound like Alice into either reflection or eternity. No, Alice is discovering merely that she is, and that she is what she is, and is not another nor at the behest of another. "I know my name now," she said; and then she encountered Tweedledum and Tweedledee.

Just who these two little gentlemen might be who look so much alike, and who stand together and erect like two pawns filed across a row, would be difficult to say. But there is a good deal of vociferous logic chopping going on between them which may supply a clue.

"I know what you're thinking about," said Tweedledum; "but it isn't so, nohow."

"Contrariwise," continued Tweedledee, "if it was so, it might be; and if it were so, it would be; but as it isn't, it ain't. That's logic."

Alice's reply is very pertinent: "I was thinking," she said, "which is the best way out of this wood"!

When one turns from the world of things to the world of the mind, it is very easy to mistake logic chopping for thinking, and cerebration for a knowledge of the self. In fact, if Alice hoped to find the way out of the wood by appealing to these little logic choppers, she was doomed to disappointment, for the mind can keep up this little game interminably. These little reasoners, whether they be called scientists, or philosophers, or Tweedledum and Tweedledee, can make game out of the Red King's snoring, or "The Walrus and the Carpenter," or a nice new rattle, and the result is the same: endless contention, endless parry and thrust of the reason reasoning—eristic. Plato, it is true, tried to show in his *Parmenides* how the mind might be disabused of these presumptions, by demonstrating that the same thing might be postulated of contraries and both identical and opposite conclusions drawn with equal justification. But for reasoners who reason for the sake of reasoning, this is but one more victory for reasoning, even if the victory be one of stultification. Tweedledum and Tweedledee will fight until six o'clock, even if they have nothing better than saucepans for helmets and umbrellas for weapons, and even if the occasion for the quarrel be nothing more than a rattle. This sort of thing, however, may be brought to an end in one of two ways: (1) by the concrete event's thrusting us out of the abstract, or (2) by the discovery that, in spite of the demands of logic, it is possible in actual life to be logically foolish without colliding with the actual. Fortunately for Alice, both of these things happened, almost simultaneously: the first, by the sudden appearance of a monstrous crow (the Rook?) which frightened the doughty, pettifogging fellows away; and the second, by the appearance of the White Queen, who had learned long since to believe "as many as six impossible things before breakfast" every morning. To put the same thing positively, rather than paradoxically, as the narrative requires, logic alone, however consistent with itself, has little practical value if its premises are not brought into relation with the actual. The premises of history are not ideal but actual.

One question, however, is raised by these reasoners which requires serious consideration. For, if we are disabused in history from being naïve realists, we ought to be warned against becoming, on the other hand, naïve idealists. When Alice and the Tweedles happened on the Red King snoring in the woods (how little worth the kings are in a chess game!), Tweedledee exclaimed: "He's dreaming now. And what do you think he's dreaming about?"

"Nobody can guess that," Alice replied.

"Why," replied Tweedledee in triumph, "about *you!*"

There is the little conundrum. For, said Tweedledee, "if he left off dreaming about you, where do you suppose you'd be?"

"Where I am now, of course," said Alice.

"Not you!" Tweedledee retorted contemptuously. "You'd be nowhere. Why, you're only a sort of thing in his dream!"

"If that there King was to awake," added Tweedledum, "you'd go out—bang!—just like a candle!"

Out, out, brief candle! Alice did not like this. Indignantly she cried, "I shouldn't!" But all the same she was impressed. And when they argued more loudly and more loudly, she had to caution them lest they should wake the King.

"Well, it's no use *your* talking about waking him," said Tweedledum, "when you're only one of the things in his dream. You know very well you're not real."

"I *am* real!" said Alice, and began to cry.

And then she had an inspiration! "If I wasn't real," she said, "I shouldn't be able to cry."

But Tweedledum was there with the appropriate rejoinder: "I hope you don't suppose that those are *real* tears?"

Are we ideas in the mind of God? Is our habitation here a passing fancy in his mental life? Are we only things in his dream? No. Indignantly the moral consciousness refuses to share in so extravagant a speculation. Whatever we are, we *are;* dependent, no doubt, and finite, but like unto the Power that created us. Most of all, we are what we are by his consent and by his will.

But here we can afford to hesitate a little. Whether *we* be waked or sleeping is still a question. For there are many kinds of sleeping—and possibly but one awareness?

> We are such stuff
> As dreams are made on, and our little life
> Is rounded with a sleep.

Or, as Sir William Hamilton affirmed, bestriding Shakespeare's utterance, "our dream of knowledge is a little light, rounded with a darkness." [9] Pascal too, himself a mathematical genius as great as Lewis Carroll, turned this matter over in his mind:

> If we dreamt the same thing every night, it would affect us as much as the objects we see every day. And if an artisan were sure to dream every night for twelve hours' duration that he was a king, I believe he would be almost as happy as a king who should dream every night for twelve hours on end that he was an artisan.[10]

Or again:

> As we often dream that we dream, heaping dream upon dream, may it not be that this half of our life, wherein we think ourselves awake, is itself only a dream on which the others are grafted, from which we wake at death? [11]

And since in dreams we have the sense of space and objectivity and motion, and since the dreams differ from reality only in being less stable and more diversified, ought we therefore when traveling to attach some special significance to our statement when we say, "It seems to me that I am dreaming"? Is it true that "life is a dream a little less constant"?

All this, of course, is the sheerest academicism and can be indulged interminably so long as there is no practical demand for a decisive act. The notion that the world and all its happenings are but phases in the divine thinking, or that the thinker and his thinkings are but sequences in the divine thinking, is barren of any real usefulness in the construction of experience; for all errors, evils, and dull blunderings would become God's errors, evils, and dull blunderings, or become themselves divine. Moreover, we should be automatons within the speculation. The speculation also would be deprived of *possibility*. In short, the problem of the validity of thought remains. For even if the world as we know it should be God's thought, it would still be necessary for me to

[9] *Discussions* (2nd London ed.), pp. 634-35.
[10] *Pensées*, 386.
[11] *Pensées*, 434.

think God's thought after him by the activity of my own mind; to build up his world, that is, in my own thinking, and to fit this thought into the system of God's thoughts in such a way that the validity of my thoughts might be valid in some abiding order which in a practical sense stands over against me and my thinking and which forms at the same time the necessary presupposition of my thinking.

Even Socrates got no further than this when he said to the young Theaetetus that "it remains that we should speak of dreams, diseases, and besides other things, of madness; and whatever else is called error of . . . perception." [12] Tweedledee's Walrus is the topsy-turvy Socrates!

> "The time has come" the Walrus said,
>   "To talk of many things:
> Of shoes—and ships—and sealing wax—
>   Of cabbages—and kings—"

Socrates raises Tweedledee's question: What proof are we able to give that we are not awake when we dream and dreaming when we are awake? For the standard of conscious experience to which we appeal in distinguishing between dream states and our waking experience must itself receive a validation from the ultimate nature of things and our real capacity to know it, and for this there is no adequate psychological criterion. [13]

The problem has, none the less, a practical significance, even though it is speculatively barren.

"It is not meet," said Heraclitus long ago, "to act and speak like men asleep." [14] It might be urged, for example, that Alice, had she been really awake, would not have allowed the Tweedles to impose the problem of the Red King's snoring upon her. She

[12] *Theaetetus* 158C.

[13] Negatively, this dialogue, the *Theaetetus,* is useful. It refutes the identification of knowledge with sensation, and with it the use of Protagoras' "Man is the measure" as a validation of each man's subjective right to measure apart from some objective reference or consensus. Pure relativism is untenable. No purely psychological criterion is possible. One may observe in passing that Plato's preoccupation with this formula of Protagoras completes itself at last in the *Laws,* where God becomes the Measure of all things and the end of man is to be strong unto measuredness.

[14] Fragment 94 (Burnet).

would have seen through the imposition at once and would have had no trouble in asserting her reality. But this merely doubles the difficulty. For if Alice was asleep and the whole phantasmagoria of the Looking Glass was but an associational play of the mind released from the corrective influences of the judgment, then we have the most curious involution of all. For now we have Alice dreaming that the Red King is dreaming and that she is a thing in his dream. And when she is told in her dream that she is but a thing in the Red King's dream and she indignantly replies that she is no such thing—that she is what she is, that she is real—the difficulty is that she affirms that she is real *when she is really dreaming!* And all this passionate conviction, this certainty, this righteous indignation, is therefore an illusion.

We often dream, as Pascal says, that we are dreaming; and in the dream that we are dreaming we are oftentimes amused at thinking that we are alive in the dream that we are dreaming; yet we do not always waken to perceive that the dreamer laughing at his dream is experiencing only an illusory wakefulness and is not awake at all. In short, in the Fourth Square of naïve rationality, where it is taken for granted that we know so much, it is possible that our spirits have not waked at all and that we possess neither that knowledge of reality which Plato called the forms nor that understanding of the true good which men of faith discover in the spirit. Like Plato's persons in the cave, who have lived in terms of shadows all their lives, the persons in the Fourth Square have yet to be turned away from appearances, released from bondage to the senses, taught that what they thought was knowledge was an ignorance, and so be led up from the shadows into the true light, when they shall see things as they really are. Idealism calls the world a sham, a shadow, an illusion, an unreality. Our good is not in it but in that world of ideal forms above it. We must waken from this prison house, this bondage of the sense world, to an intuition of the ultimate realities, the ideas and the essences.

But suppose that Alice had come to see this understandingly; not, of course, that at this stage she would understand that we are never certain apart from faith and the moral consciousness whether we are waking or asleep (for that is only possible when

things have reached the crisis), but that she has come to understand that temporality is the shadow of the real, that time and
space are but illusory, that tangibility comprises but the accidents
of reality. She could then have performed on her own account
the first motion of release: she could have made the great dive
from the springboard into the eternal, and so have gone through
the Looking Glass world standing on her head like Father William. She could have done it by way of the imagination, like Don
Quixote, or by way of poetry and mysticism, like William Butler
Yeats, taking Plato and Plotinus for her friends and gathering
herself into "the artifice of eternity." Or she could have done it in
the most dignified manner, by intellectualism, if she could have
found a Scholastic to teach her to distinguish between substances,
quiddities, and ecceities. Like the second-century Christians, she
could have denied the world and gone off into the desert to fast
and meditate; or she could have conducted her flight from the
world after the medieval pattern, fleeing from nature into super-
nature by way of a nunnery. Or she might have stalked off into
the wood to sit on a wall and commune with the infinite, like
Humpty Dumpty. In which event her achievement would have
been as great as that of the medieval scholar Alcuin, who refused
to have his studies interrupted even though his house was burning
down! [15]

One essential difference, however, between Alice and Humpty
Dumpty is to be remarked in such an eventuality: whereas Humpty Dumpty—and doubtless his cosmos too—was mostly all stom-
ach, Alice—and her cosmos too—would have been all mind;
idealism salvages eternity from time by sacrificing history. By
the selfsame stroke wherewith it severs man from bondage to the
world of time and space, it severs him from history.

This is very possibly the meaning of Ferdinand Ebner's claim
that the philosophical idealism of pre-Christian thinkers was but
"a dream of the mind" in which the thinker could never become

---

[15] A housemaid broke into the great scholar's study to tell him that the house was
on fire. She was rebuked for the interruption and told to find the scholar's wife, whose
business it was to manage the household affairs!

wholly conscious either of his dreams or of himself, the actual "I," in his dreams.[16]

This is the reason, no doubt, that the classical world view had no notion of destiny comparable to that of later Western culture, and why Spengler is partially justified in his claim that "the Greek who describes his ego as *soma* and who lacks all idea of an inner development" lacks also, therefore, "all real history, inward and outward." [17] The vital repose of the Greek temple, as against the infinite aspiration of the Gothic cathedral, the renunciation of the Stoics, the *ataraxia* of the schools, the concentration on the form in art, the being-nonbeing stratification in metaphysics, the ideal of contemplation through the *nous*—all these produced a static culture, which sought its meaning in the ideal present and projected no destiny in hope throughout the future. So far as theory of history was concerned—it matters little whether dominated by the upward and the downward way of Heraclitus; or Plato's time, the moving image of eternity; or the Parmenidean One—history was circular; and the various cycle views of history, in which events and men pass through eternal recurrences according to predetermined periodicities of historical reincarnation, were inevitable. The notion of the world as history, as destiny, did not emerge until the Christian point of view appeared. Augustine had still to refute these cyclic views, these wheels of recurrence, when he wrote his *City of God,* "the first real effort to produce a philosophy of history." Faith would smile, says he, at these argumentations, whereby the pagan mind would bedizen us to walk in a circle; and "even reason . . . shatters these revolving circles which conjecture frames." [18]

Thus the whole of Western history, apart from the Christian transfiguration of the ancient Hebrew and classical concepts, and apart from the new determination of historical meaning in the advent of Christ, presents to us this curious anomaly: that whereas our later history empties into an infinity, the spurious eternity of time and space, which flees before us proportionately faster than

---

[16] *Das Wort und die Geistigen Realitäten,* p. 112.
[17] *The Decline of the West,* I, 183.
[18] XII, xvii.

our linear achievements can pursue, our ancient history contained us in a static circularity, a monistic ὕλη covered by the One, in which history was shadow and endurance and a wise accession to the Fates. From the standpoint of history, which is per se the problem of the nature of man and his destiny, there is between these two a mathematical equivalence: zero equals the sign of the infinite! Abstraction has in each case triumphed over history. True history is always personal. The mind, in these *extra*-Christian instances, has performed a feat which would have been difficult even in the Looking Glass world (for it was only performed by the Cheshire Cat in Wonderland, it being able to abstract itself entirely from its smile)—the mind has swallowed itself. Or, more explicitly, the mind has swallowed its *self*.[19]

The quest for self-knowledge, then, is useful in two ways. First, it instructs us in the limits of our knowing, showing us how we begin from one ignorance, a naïve reliance on the world of things, and how we then philosophize to disabuse our minds of this naïveté, running over all that men can know,[20] concluding to a second ignorance, a "learned ignorance," the rational persuasion that the mind cannot transcend its limitations—and this is a useful knowledge of ourselves. Second, we are helped to understand Pascal's claim that "no person is certain, apart from faith, whether he is awake or sleeps"[21]—for in a spiritual sense this is doubtless very true; and history depends upon decision rather than reflection, which by its retreat upon the many or the One nullifies the action and depletes the sense of destiny. It was by intrusion of the concrete, monstrous crow that Alice saved herself from Tweedledum and Tweedledee.

[19] "Everything abstract," says Nicholas Berdyaev (*The Meaning of History*, p. 13), "is by its nature opposed to the historical." This is not, of course, to deny the legitimacy of reason in its proper sphere; but Emil Brunner's observation may on this point be taken as axiomatic: "The less a truth has to do with the centre of personality, the more autonomous is reason within it" (*Man in Revolt*, p. 544). In short, one must resolutely resist the depersonalization of the self, whether by its saturation in the spurious eternity of space-time sequence on the one hand, or by the abstract eternity of impersonal idealisms on the other.

[20] Cf. Pascal, *Pensées*, 4, 15.

[21] *Ibid.*, 434.

*　　*　　*　　*　　*

*　　*　　*　　*

*　　*　　*　　*　　*

We have no need, now, to linger over the Fifth and Sixth Squares; and we have, in fact, already considered the problem of the White Knight in the Seventh. The Fifth was "mostly water," as the Red Queen warned little Alice when first she set out; and in this Square all things were vague and blurred, with Alice alternately stretching out her arms for water lilies while riding in a rowboat with a female Sheep, and reaching out for objects in a dim and shadowy shop, exasperated by the way these objects on the shelves would vanish when she almost touched them, or would disappear through the ceiling when she stood upon a box. "Things flow about so here!" she said plaintively.

Philosophically, it is to be expected, I suppose, that when we fly from logic chopping and the discursive reason's idealization of its own powers after the pattern of the Parmenidean One, we should at once fall into the opposite extreme of the Heraclitean flux, where all is change and all things flow. Religiously, having transcended the spiritual limitations of the pettifogging reason, many persons lapse into an amorphous religiosity, an indistinguished mysticism or aesthetic "mystihood" of feeling. Here they spend their time stretching after water lilies that are always just a little out of reach, or pursuing phantom symbols worshipfully until they dissolve into the ceiling when the mind would seize them to fix them for their meaning. Alice quickly tired of this. But, being a determined lass, she fixed her eye upon an egg; and, though the egg moved further from her as she pursued it, she kept on walking until the egg grew bigger and bigger, led her across another little brook, and suddenly appeared upon a wall as Humpty Dumpty.

* * * * *

* * * *

* * * * *

It does not matter much who Humpty Dumpty was; but what he did instructs us. He was proud, cantankerous, and self-satisfied, like a person who has found all the answers and sits with conscious self-sufficiency upon his wall. At times he talks like an ecclesiastic (a Bishop?), particularly when he governs words by *ex cathedra* fiat, determining by his authority their meanings. This, however, is probably a misunderstanding.[22] Humpty Dumpty fell, and all the king's horses and all the king's men couldn't put him together again. This is instructive of our moral condition.

"Humpty Dumpty is more than a nursery rhyme," says the literary critic; "behind it is a cosmological myth." [23] It is a myth, indeed, which supports the literary critic's view, that "the truth about man is not to be found in his thought, but in his history." That is, the righteous unity of humankind under God is broken; the rectitude whereby man kept his precarious balance on the wall by having his mind and heart fixed upon God has been lost. The man whose mind was onetime stayed on God became self-sufficient, proud, and lost thereby his righteous poise. He fell— shattering the human image, man's unity in God, into "infinitely repellant particles" which all the king's poets and all the king's critics can't put together again. Four thousand two hundred and seven soldiers (that was the number the White King sent, so he told Alice) couldn't put him together again; and these were men in history, like the critics and the poets. "Though we reject the Christian interpretation of the Fall, the fall remains to be accounted for," remarks the critic.[24]

[22] Everyone knows that Lewis Carroll was a mathematician. Some know that he was lecturer at Christ Church, Oxford. But all seem to have forgotten that he was the son of a clergyman and received his deacon's orders in 1861.

[23] John Peale Bishop, "Finnegan's Wake," *The Southern Review,* V (1940), 451.

[24] *Ibid.*

The novelist (Mr. James Joyce) seems to suggest a new interpretation: Humpty Dumpty is a cosmological myth of the "earth
tumbling out of chaos"; for within the earth is a biological fact,
the creation of new life! But this is nonsense. Do things tumble
out of chaos? They do indeed tumble *into* chaos, as Humpty
tumbled from the wall; but this new fall would reverse the action.
The world, biologically, tumbles upward into newer life, it now
appears. Which implies, perhaps, that Humpty Dumpty was an
egg; and when he fell his shell was fractured, and a little red hen
jumped out as a new clucking creation in the world. And so, biologically, the little red hen was tumbled out of chaos. This is not
what the nursery rhyme says, of course. But the fall is still there
to be accounted for; and perhaps the novelist, as new theologian,
is hurrying us back to Orphic cosmology without knowing it?

> Before the creation of Aether and Light,
> Chaos and Night together were plight,
> In the dungeon of Erebus foully bedight . . .
> At length in the dreary chaotical closet
> Of Erebus old, was a privy deposit,
> By Night the primaeval in secrecy laid;
> A Mystical Egg, that in silence and shade
> Was brooded and hatched; till time came about:
> And Love, the delightful, in glory flew out.[25]

But even Aristophanes understood the fall better than this.

> Since time began
> The race of man
> Has ever been deceitful.[26]

That is the fact which remains to be accounted for. We do not
tumble biologically into righteous unity under God. That is nonsense. True it is that we need just such a nonsense, to tumble upward into God's truth. But this little miracle, this antinatural, anti-
gravitational leap, will not be accomplished by the running to and
fro of all the king's horses, men, poets, and critics, each one seeking horizontally his own; for, in terms of cosmological myth, all

[25] Aristophanes, *The Birds*.
[26] *Ibid.*

these are broken fragments of the image, each fragment assert-ing not the unity of the whole but itself at the expense of the whole. Such a miracle would be a redemptive miracle; it could be brought to pass by a gravitational tug from above, from beyond our means; but all the king's horses and all the king's men will not put the human image together again. They are themselves the shattered fragments of that image. This is a clue to the human situation.

Alice and the White King hurried on to where the Lion and the Unicorn were fighting for the crown. There they saw the Lion beat the Unicorn all around the town. The people, mean-while, put up with the nonsense for a time, and then, wearying of it, drummed them both out of town. It was during the drum-ming episode that Alice jumped across another little brook and found herself in the Seventh Square, where the White Knight, as truly chivalrous and foolish as the illustrious Don Quixote de la Mancha, escorted Alice safely into the Eighth Square.[27]

*   *   *   *   *

*   *   *   *

*   *   *   *   *

To recapitulate—which is always what must happen in a crisis —things reach the climax; forces long preparing meet at the point of ultimate significance where decision must be reached. The world as "given" sets bounds to our folly, compelling the infinite reflection, the endless retreat in thought and thinking to take ac-count of the results, the actuality, the point of crisis where the new decision must be reached. The checkmate is declared. Alice found herself a Queen, a *person*—no longer one more pawn in the im-personal hide-and-seek of circumstance—with the Red Queen and

---

[27] I refrain from commenting on the episode of the Lion and the Unicorn, though it is quite possible that the Lion is the State and the Unicorn the Church. The English Reformation is an important moment in the dialectical unfolding of our history; but it is doubtless true, as the rhyme suggests, that both Church and State suffered in prestige as a result of the contention.

the White Queen pressing her on either side. The fullness of time had come.

The world was topsy-turvy; the problem was to determine at what point it became topsy-turvy. It became so, we agreed, at the point where Alice first passed through the mirror, and Alice could have known this had she gone back through the mirror; but, as we saw, this was for her impossible because she acquiesced in the topsy-turviness and allowed the whole fantastic world view to impose its earnestness upon her. It was therefore quite as difficult for her as for the White Knight to track back through history to reach decision, for she was like one living in a dream who still supposed that she was quite awake; and the White Knight, as we saw, would have no means of knowing what the terms of topsy-turviness really were and would suppose that, if the world was backwards, it was so because he had mounted his horse backwards. Thus he would not cross the entire domain of lost truth in order to revise it possessively. He would revise his attitude by making an about-face, but not by making such an about-face as would turn the whole world upside down. No, Alice was a pawn, like all the rest of us, running hard to keep in the same place; and what she had to do was to strip the trappings off the masquerade in order to discover the genuine that lies beneath.

The Fourth Square of discursive reason was, therefore, an important move for her. At least it made her, like the moderns, "critical." She became, that is, a creature of "enlightenment"—a speculator trying to decide whether she could be or not—and so, by introspection, she was cheated of her practical belief in the world as a sphere of decision and in herself as a moral agent. Subjective idealism turned her to a dream; rationalistic empiricism made her doubt the dream; and all this earnest inconclusiveness took place in a topsy-turvy world where all was dream because the real was not disclosed.

A minor crisis thrust her out of this naïve reliance on the reason reasoning; and in the Fifth Square she lapsed into romantic reverie, the mystico-aesthetic world where all things flow together—pantheism and religiosity, where an appearance of the thing we hope for is before us ever as a symbol but where reality itself eludes our grasp. In the Sixth Square, then, she came upon our true condition—the shattered image of the Godhead in us. All our human effort does not mend it, for the dying do not live by pooling death. Then the bland knight came; and with his foolish faith and childlike, fumbling certainty he led her to herself, the Eighth Square, where she became a Queen, a person, one with power to command and barter kingdoms with the Kings and Queens.

This was a long way to herself. History for many hundred years may spend its time adorning folly or embellishing the masquerade until the generations mistake the mask for Truth itself. Then comes the crisis. All this long preparing of the masquerade is reflexively rehearsed in a moment, in the twinkling of an eye; and it is finished. The ass of Cortes may possibly have been twenty-one days in the dying; but the moment of death was but a moment, though the distance between death and life was infinite. Yet the masquerade was over, for the ass had died.

"Take care of yourself!" screamed the White Queen, seizing Alice's hair with both her hands. "Something's going to happen!" And it did happen, but in a certain way. Things began flying around in an unreasonable, malign confusion; and Alice cried, "I can't stand this any longer!" Then she saw the Red Queen, "whom she considered as the cause of all the mischief," and she seized her and began to shake her for all she was worth. "I'll shake you into a kitten, that I will!" she said. And sure enough the Red Queen became fatter, and softer, and rounder, and turned out to be a kitten after all—Alice's kitten. *Alice had wakened from her dream.* But how? By coming out from the sphere of reflection into the sphere of decision; by overcoming her defensive apathy, her acquiescence in the masquerade; by faith that she could be a Queen; and by believing to the point of action that untruth had triumphed long enough in this topsy-turvy world. All these things that had imposed on her with their little dignities and earnestness were dispelled in a moment, and an entire world of pretense turned into a kitten! That is the paradoxical denouement of history, when "not-being masquerading as life" is no longer permitted to triumph through "the incomprehensible configurations of sophistries."

But now we must distinguish, as the theologians used to say. For there are two analogies here, not one. If we mean by this denouement simply an analogy of horizontal history, and that our history has reached a crisis in which we have been thrust out of our reflective sophistries into the world as it really is—have been spewed out of our past pretensions, that is, like Jonah on the shore of the actual—it is all very simple. We are awake now; the dream is over; and we will set our house in order. It is true that we passed through the Looking Glass and everything reversed itself in value and reality, and it is true also that we have only reached the point of vexation and confusion in which we are shaking the Red Queen furiously. But she will presently turn into a kitten, and we shall all be awake again. We can adjust our human problem according to justice, fair play, and the rights of man. It is an immanent possibility, within our own powers. We have only to resume the point at which we first passed through the mirror—which occurred, doubtless, at the Treaty of Versailles, or at the French Revolution, or the Reformation, or the Renaissance, or perhaps in the Middle Age. . . ? No. The problem is still with us. It is with us because it is within us. We must recover the point of purchase *absolutely,* ground it in a considered view of the ultimate nature of things. We must revise our attitude. We must consider again what it is we live for, what we are, and how we may secure to ourselves the fruits appropriate to our proper being. In short, Alice awakened out of the dream; but the disclosure was a negative disclosure. It disclosed a world of things which were not; it did not disclose to her the nature of the world as it ought to be.

The second analogy is more difficult. For it presents the Looking Glass world as our world; and we are people not like Alice but like the White Knight and the Tweedles and the King's Men. We are in a topsy-turvy world, but unaware that it is topsy-turvy. Mr. Tweedle does not know that he is a thing in Alice's dream, though he was capable of telling *her* that she was a thing in the king's dream!

We are tempted in this second way of considering the narrative to think of Alice as the Representative Man, the Emersonian Adam (discounting gender) of our history, the Man who crossed the boundary between the world of true belief and right perception into this perverted world of sophistry and lucubration. This would mean that history would force her dialectically into a knowledge of herself, and she would recollect Socratically her former self and so recover true perception and right knowing at the climax. Here again the possibility lies within our power. This would presuppose a rational window open upon the absolute. We might concentrate ourselves into a Plotinian flight of the alone to the Alone, or climb the mystical ladders, or shuttle tripodwise from thesis to antithesis to synthesis until the Hegelian Absolute Idea had swallowed us. But history has shown no such denouement. On the contrary, it has clarified our impotence and thrust us out of the retreat upon reflection into the sphere of moral determination. So far as Alice is concerned, she did not waken by reflection at all, but by a miracle. She was wakened *by the author, who interposed* at this point and accounted her indignation unto her for righteousness!

For now we must observe what everybody knows quite well but seldom takes the trouble to observe: the story we have followed is a *comic* piece; it is humorous by being void of ethical significance. It is only two-dimensional. It is spatiotemporal, and it is intellectual—which corresponds, if the expression may be allowed, with the length, breadth, and *thickness* of human understanding. These are horizontal terms of reference. The vertical dimension, the dimension of eternal significance, the circumstance of tragedy and good and evil and eternal destiny is only played with in these little comedies, if, indeed, it appears at all. Alice's entire adventure began when she passed through the mirror into a garden. It was a garden of innocence, and it remains so till the end, when indignation thrusts her back into the world of good and evil.

Man's adventure is not a comedy; it reverses comedy. It begins when man is *thrust out* of the garden of innocence, and tragedy

175

and sin and evil attend him; then his folly is a wantonness and a persistent profanation. There is no return for him but in and by the Garden of Gethsemane, where the Representative Man is in agony. But the agony endures beyond the Garden and beyond the Cross. Here is indeed that real mirror which truly shows man to himself. Here man truly comes to know himself.

It is not merely that he comes to see in the mirror of that Goodness that he is not as good as he ought to be, and will resolve therefore to be better. That is the way we should like to have it. Then we could go on praising the "love" of Jesus and deny the Christ of faith. It is that in the mirror of the Cross we behold our depth of shame, our guilt, our defiance: we behold the deformities of soul, the leprous gnawing of defection eating at our hearts, the travesty of creaturehood defying infinite love in order to be little gods and Titanically striving to make the disobedience good until we fall exhausted, cursing God and the world for having damned us. We prefer this petty Titanism to the "humiliation" of surrender, though God himself in Jesus Christ has come the whole way into this our degradation in order that we might be recovered unto his eternal Truth. For Christ on the cross is indeed the Mirror which shows us to ourselves—a negative disclosure until we make the new decision, the new choice in faith. Christ is the Mirror through which we pass back to Reality. We must gather up our past and pass, as Brunner says, "through the Caudine Forks of the Cross." [28] This is not a movement backward. It is not a return to Paradise. It is not a recollection in the reflective sense. It is a step forward, *the* step. It is toward the New Jerusalem. This is the mo-

[28] *Man in Revolt,* p. 484. This startling metaphor of the Caudine Forks derives from a defeat suffered by the Romans in the second Samnite war (321 B.C.). The Romans were trapped between two gorges near the town of Caudium. They had either to fight through these gorges or surrender. As Livy tells it: "Amazement took possession of their minds, and a strange kind of numbness seized their limbs: they remained a long time motionless and silent, each looking to the other, as if each thought the other more capable of judging and advising than himself." (*The History of Rome,* IX 2). But the chief blow to the legions was the blow to Roman pride. There was no alternative but unconditional surrender. I take it that Brunner has this necessity in mind with reference to the Cross. We must pass through the Caudine Forks, which is an act, not merely a beholding; and we must surrender our pride in independent, self-sufficient autonomy. We must trust all to the power and magnanimity of the Conqueror.

ment of the new decision. This is the moment where the Eternal enters into time and gives to us what we could not supply ourselves, the point of view of the Eternal. For the only way in which we could come to know our true condition—to know that we are topsy-turvy, comical, and foolish—is by coming to stand outside the action, by bearing the same relation to our action as the Eternal bears to the temporal. This is impossible; we cannot stand outside the action for the reason, simply, that we are the action. But we have this point of view in Jesus Christ, in whom the Eternal Word is present absolutely. Thus in the crisis of our history when we are thrust out of our infinite evasions upon the actual, when history itself has pressed us dialectically with ontology of fact till we must choose again, we dare not disesteem the moment. For though the distance between believing and not believing is infinite, as infinite as that between death and life, the parenthesis of crisis in which the whole world teeters for the moment poised in doubt is but a brief one. Our temporal destiny depends upon it, as our eternal destiny depends upon each person's choosing to believe or disbelieve.

"Jesus will be in agony until the end of the world," said Pascal. "Do not be caught asleep then!" That is the present peril. Even Peter slept while Divinity agonized. We too can sleep—and in so many ways!—with piety, with reason, with the Law, with righteous indignation for secondary causes. Whatever prevents our passing through the Caudine Forks of the Cross becomes for us a form of sleeping while Christ agonizes in the Garden. How long, then, will the world pay tribute to the able men who teach us—that inestimable comfort that is also our pain—how to sleep?

Part Two

OUR HERITAGE OF FAITH

*Thou hast given a heritage
unto those that fear thy name
—Ps. 61:5 (A.R.V. m.)*

Chapter I

THE CHRISTIAN STANDPOINT

IT IS WELL KNOWN THAT ARCHIMEDES WOULD HAVE MOVED THE world, had he had a lever long enough and a fulcrum on which to place it. Sören Kierkegaard caught up this Archimedean vanity into a figure of speech to hurl at all the system builders. There is, said he, for every system of thought, an Archimedean point from which it would lift the whole world; and precisely because it would lift the whole world, it must therefore choose a point that lies outside the world, beyond the bounds of space and time. Every system of thought establishes this point by a choice, by a decision —a decision that is quite as much a volitional act as that of the believer saying, "I believe." The decision of the philosopher is a decision in the abstract, achieved by the positing of a premise; so long as the premise remains unchallenged, the system can spin out the web of its idea-structure indefinitely, protracting the implications.

The Christian standpoint is quite other than this: it is, in fact, just the opposite. For the Christian faith grounds itself, not in an abstract idea, but in an event—the *historical* Incarnation of Jesus Christ. With this belief as its Archimedean point, it proposes to lift the whole world; for the Incarnation—the explicit point of the Eternal in history, of God in time—that point, which by definition must lie outside the limitations of space and time (and was, therefore, not available to Archimedes or to the abstract philosopher) —has itself *come into time* and is itself the lever which, over the fulcrum of faith, can move the world.

This conceding to an event in history a character of eternal significance is indeed paradoxical—at least, to the reason. For all the systems—those of Plato, Aristotle, Hegel—have failed in their at-

181

tempts to bridge the gap between eternity and time, being and becoming, ideality and factuality. Indeed, it cannot be bridged in abstraction, nor by regarding God as the Absolute and man as merely a thinker. It can only be bridged in a personal world view, in a view which regards God as a Person and man as a doer, and which refutes the *stasis* of the mind thinking in precisely the same way that Diogenes refuted the Eleatic who argued that motion was impossible—*by walking.*

It is for this reason that Jesus Christ is the turning point of history. The Christian standpoint has always this advantage, that it starts from a historical fact and interprets all else in the light of this fact. It does indeed claim to decide in time the eternal happiness of the individual by relating it to something historical.[1]

It is doubtless desirable, however, that we should at this point proceed slowly. For to say in a single breath that God was in Christ reconciling the world unto himself and that therefore all determination of meaning of life in the world, of history, of culture, of personal destiny, is to be found here and nowhere else, is what is not tolerable to the soul cast up on the shoreline of the concrete. Being resolved unto ourselves by the dialectical denouement of our history, and being deprived like Proteus of our vast resources for evasion, we should like nevertheless a few paragraphs or chapters in which to consider whether there may be some other way out, or at least to secure to ourselves our dignity in the presence of the new demand, the absolute choice. As Augustine prayed for chastity and continency, so we would pray that God might make us Christians—*"but not yet."*

i

We should consider carefully what is involved in this deferment. For it means that, whereas our history has discovered to us our impotence apart from God, so now our reasoning must disclose it to us. The problem confronting ourselves and our world in a time of crisis is not a logical problem, a problem to be re-

[1] Cf. Kierkegaard, *Philosophical Fragments* (tr. D. F. Swenson; Princeton University Press, 1936), where the question is raised as to whether it is possible "to base an eternal happiness upon historical knowledge."

solved by further reflection or rational mediation or a higher synthesis; it is a problem of existence, of the Archimedean point by which we shall move the world. It is a matter of decision, and of faith. The problem with which we are dealing is *practical* and not *theoretical;* and by the same token the work of the reason is instrumental with regard to it, and not constitutive. A geometrician losing his balance on the side of an abyss does not rescue himself by reciting the theorems of Euclid, no matter how astutely he recites them. And if someone throws him a rope, he is not to debate ad infinitum whether it is made of hemp or cotton or whether it will hold him or not. He will not, in fact, know whether it will hold him until he has taken hold of it and thrown his weight upon it. This is what is arbitrary in the Christian standpoint; it is as arbitrary *as existence:* it is only a standpoint for those who will assume it, who will throw their weight upon it.

This is the *crux*—to use a Christian term—of the whole matter. All dogmas reduce to one dogma. It is only at the point of the crossing of the arms upon the Cross that one sees well. From this point of vantage we view things *sub specie Christi*—from the vantage point of the Eternal in time. But one does not gain this point of vantage by viewing the Cross as a symbol; it is necessary, as Paul says, to share in "the fellowship" of Christ's sufferings. Nor does one secure it by adopting the moral teachings of Jesus, nor by going into the desert, nor by any other external achievement. One must, by an initial act of belief, postulated in all inwardness, believe that he is what he said he was, and that what he said and did has about it, therefore, eternal significance, presenting in time the absolute clue to the meaning of life, history, and human destiny.

The secular mind, as well as the "purely philosophical" mind, will at once rebel at this, saying that such an act is arbitrary and that it runs counter to the "scientific spirit," which would prove all things and accept only that which has been proved to be true. Overlooking for the moment the fact that such a supposed pattern of acceptance is itself absurd—since all investigation of whatever kind is preceded by existence, and existence is that milieu in which we live *by faith* antecedently to our theorizings about it—the relationships here involved may be illustrated by the notorious case of Galileo and his telescope. The telescope revealed moons on Jupiter. But this revelation was counter to the prevailing beliefs of the day; so the Churchmen did not bother to look through his telescope to see whether there were moons on Jupiter, but proscribed Galileo and pronounced his findings blasphemous. "History" has made a good deal of this incident, showing how arbitrary and narrow was the medieval mind which would not look through Galileo's glass. And justly so; for this was to curtail the principle of free inquiry, which was of the very essence of the Renaissance and itself a derivative of the Christian notion of the infinite worth and creative responsibility of each individual soul. But now, when we reverse the situation and transfer the problem from physics to spiritual matters, the world refuses after the same pattern to look through the glass of the New Testament, and there is no one to raise the hue and cry. To see the world from the Christian standpoint implies simply that we must see it through the eyes of Christ, and that short of this we do not see it as it really is.

Many, of course, hold that Christ is the very image of our true humanity and that therefore he is that Glass in which we may see ourselves both as we really are and as we ought to be. But this does not always help us. For, while there is infinite merit in this notion if held in a Christian manner, it but shows us back to ourselves in an enhanced perspective (seeing ourselves as Christ) if viewed in the non-Christian, or almost Christian, fashion. Lichtenberg's remark is relevant: "Such works are mirrors: when a monkey peers into them, no Apostle can be seen looking out." To extend and soften the terms a little: Christ is a mirror; but when a speculator, or a "disinterested" investigator, or a faded Christian, peers into him, no Christ of the New Testament will be seen looking out. What we perceive is simply the reflex of our own egocentricity heightened a little.

It is often proposed as a third possibility that we should accept the Christian standpoint *as a working hypothesis*—that is, *provisionally,* until we see what the results are. But this is not to accept it at all. For it is evident that the believer still stands, in

184

this instance, <u>with one foot in speculation</u>; so that if all does not go right, or as he wants it to go, or if the Christianity should impose too much or demand too much, he can always step back into the speculative and so rescue himself from the infinite demand. For there is, between faith—faith that is decisive, that is absolute, that "goes the whole way"— and speculation about faith, a chasm. It is a gulf fixed, though not a great gulf fixed. It can, as a matter of fact, be crossed by a single step, provided the step is decisive— provided, that is, that the one who steps actually steps *from* the speculative and advances by faith. But in any other case, the distance between the two is infinite and is indeed a great gulf fixed. For speculation about faith is always existentially in retreat from faith, so that the two sides of the chasm are perpetually moving farther apart. The attempt to straddle the chasm, to have one foot in faith and one foot in speculation, would be ridiculous if it were possible (which, happily, by definition it is not); for in that case the speculative would retreat as before, and the supposed believer would fall between his own extremes. <u>Faith is *an act;* it is a total act, an act of the whole person.</u> As such it is a personal act, an act of the person-in-decision. It is a commitment, and that is why the contemporary dialectical thinkers refer to it as "a leap." It is a leap out of the abstract into the concrete, out of the categories of reflection into the categories of the personal-historical. It is a leap out of history as negation into the positive history of the creative purposes of God. *Therefore,* one must *pass through* the Caudine Forks of the Cross if one is to see well.

<u>That is why Christianity is so simple</u>—as simple as the <u>knowledge that "in His will is our peace"—which is itself a knowledge acquired by belief.</u> But <u>for this reason also it is so difficult, because there are so few simple people any more. Ours is an age of sophistication.</u> To pass therefore into the second, or higher, simplicity is no mean feat. One must be disabused of much supposed knowledge. One must be cross-questioned Socratically out of the presumptions of sophistication. <u>Experience may do this. Crises of cultures may do it if the violence of crisis thrusts the thinker upon the absolute boundaries of meaning.</u> But the cross-questioning, to be Christian, must deliver a man not merely into his igno-

rance but into an awareness of his alienation from God. The Socratism must be a Christian Socratism if the second simplicity is to be arrived at. The pathway lies beyond knowledge and ignorance: repentance and faith are requisite.

ii

In contrast to the several metaphysical gambits, the philosophical openings—Platonic, Aristotelian, Cartesian, Kantian, and so forth—that are available to the interpreter of life, the Christian standpoint offers an opening that is of a different order. It is, in the first place, not speculative at all, but postulates the event of the Incarnation of the Eternal in time; and, second, its starting point is concretely personal rather than reflective and mediational in the abstract. But this is precisely that starting point which answers to the need of man in a situation of crisis, the man who will not tolerate one more turn of reflective hare and hounds. Yet it is also that starting point which man will resist on behalf of his private autonomy.

We must therefore consider this curious dilemma: Whereas the Christian faith offers to man that standpoint which will permit him to move the whole world (which would certainly include the infinite movement of his own soul), it is a standpoint that is available to a man only in the categories of the personal-historical and only by a decision in faith; yet the very meaning of spiritual crisis implies that this is the decision which has not yet been made. Thus, while the Christian categories offer to man in his present crisis the *standpoint* from which he must interpret his nature and his destiny (his previous standpoints having turned out to be illusory), it is clear that his *starting point* lies on *this* side the Caudine Forks, and on this side of the decision in faith. This also is a paradox: for a crisis of culture is always, as we have argued, a crisis of faith; and the present situation is such that, by the extenuation and depletion of its own horizontal hopes, it has recoiled upon its own pseudo attitudes (its pseudo faiths), projecting thus, like the snake which swallowed itself, the infinite straight line perpendicular to the plane—the new dimension of the vertical, the dimension of absolute significance. Our history, that is, which has been in retreat from the Cross, has recoiled once more upon the Cross; and the final definition of the present crisis of history is that, whereas we have sought by every means to evade the Cross, we now confront it once more at the end of all our evasions. The Cross remains for us, even at the end of our consecutive refusals, the one point of contact with the Eternal, and that point through which our searchings for meaning are themselves illuminated and acquire meaning.

Our philosophers have sought, as we know, to start without this arbitrariness, without affirmation! They have sought for a starting point which would permit them to begin with the negative, with the determination to hold everything in abeyance. This, however, is a *human* impossibility. It is not possible for a human starting point to be found outside the human. The human being cannot hold *all* his conclusions in abeyance; for he is in the meanwhile obliged *to act,* and to act supposes both selection and commitment. Nor can he doubt everything; for in so doing he would have to doubt his own doubt, in which case he has said nothing, and he would have to doubt his own existence—which is absurd, for he could not do it without presupposing himself. The "suspension of judgment" is also something that is willed; it is consequently something that can be altered by a subsequent act of will—for example, by a decision of faith. Similarly, thought does not begin in negation. The so-called modern attempt to begin negatively by suspecting everything (though it has been tried many times before—by Sextus Empiricus, for example) has been a spurious attempt; it has managed so well for four hundred years only because it has not really been doing what it has pretended to be doing. It has been living off the accumulated power of previous beliefs. The "suspension of judgment" is supported by the previous judgments; the negations feed on the former affirmations. Contemporary doubt is parasitical; and if the parasite triumphs over the organism, both organism and parasite will die. The effort to be "realistic" and "empirical" and "practical" has been none of these: it has been a pipe dream of all of these indulged rationalistically at the expense of the practical. It is not practical to be "practical" if the whole question of meaning is ignored; nor is it realistic to be "realistic" if by doing so we beg the whole question as to what really is. The present crisis of history asserts nothing so clearly as it asserts the recall of reason to the practical starting point.

A poet, W. H. Auden, quotes from a philosopher, R. G. Collingwood:

> The ambition of "deductive" metaphysics is to present a constellation of absolute presuppositions as a strainless structure like a body of propositions in mathematics.
>
> That is all right in mathematics because mathematical propositions are not historical propositions. But it is all wrong in metaphysics. A *reformed metaphysics* will conceive any given constellation of absolute presuppositions as having in its structure, not the simplicity and calm that characterize the subject matter of mathematics, but the intricacy and restlessness that characterize the subject matter, say, of legal or constitutional history.[2]

The intricacies of "constitutional history" may still seem rather barren to the plain man, though it will come to him with some shock of relief to learn that even consitutional history reflects some elements of restlessness (for restlessness suggests, at the very least, a fringe of uncertainty open to human fallibility); but Professor Collingwood is suggesting, it would appear, that even metaphysics is in some sense subject to the priority of the personal and that therefore the philosopher must himself assert or assume in some form the primacy of the practical reason. It is appropriate, too, that a poet should be citing this; for surely the poet has learned that the "existence of a person consists always in an action, a suffering, and a transaction." [3] He is always, that is, the creature who must act. He is the creature who must say, "I suffer; therefore I am." He acts always in a world which he does not make, but which he finds. He acts always with reference to other persons and to personal meanings. He founds his destiny, in other words, upon belief. As de Lamennais has put it so incontestably, "Whether he likes it or not, he must believe, because he must act." [4]

[2] W. H. Auden, *The Double Man,* p. 112.
[3] Karl Heim, *Glaube und Denken,* p. 364.
[4] *Essai sur l'indifférence en matière de religion,* Part III, chap. lxvii.

We must affirm, therefore, the personal starting point within the human situation; and we must resist, with every critical device at our command, every attempt of the abstract reason, or of metaphysical reasoning, or of sociological or political or scientific thinking, yes, even of religious thinking, to depersonalize and dehumanize our understanding of ourselves and the world as these things are related to the problem of our nature as men and to the problem of our destinies. "There is," wrote Borden Parker Bowne, "an element of faith and volition latent in all our theorizing. Where we cannot prove, we believe. Where we cannot demonstrate, we choose sides. This element of faith cannot be escaped in any field of thought, and without it the mind is helpless and dumb." [5] This fact must be kept resolutely before the mind in every practical judgment; and, recognizing thereby the personal starting point within the human situation, we must consider (1) the manner in which this starting point serves as a method for clarifying the human situation and (2) what the human situation, so clarified, consists in.

As to the method, Karl Jaspers has proposed a useful partitioning of the possible methods employed by philosophers throughout the past. There are, he says, three fundamentally different methods. One of these is the familiar approach of metaphysical speculation. This is a purely formal method in which the philosopher aims by the discovery of first principles to transcend the world of appearance and arrive at Reality. In the foregoing chapters we have criticized the practitioners of this method in so far as they have applied it to the historical situation for the discovery of man's destiny and of religious truth. This method offers, nevertheless, a means for the formal comparison of initial attitudes and results; it is useful, that is, as a source for data in the exercise of the second method.

This second method aims at calling in question supposed fixed knowledge, and grounds itself in "world orientation." This orientation of man in the world is pursued and built up by the objective pursuit of knowledge, by the disinterested endeavor to know

[5] *Theism* (New York: American Book Co., 1902), p. iv.

scientifically the facts and potentialities that can be found in the world. The findings of these investigations come gradually to tyrannize over our thought and action and to assume the character of fixed knowledge—as does the Copernican world view, for example. They conspire to formulate for us our unconscious assumptions. They form at times a kind of corporate obstinacy whereby we sucessfully resist new truths. They become fixed, certain; and we rest in them. This calling into question of supposed fixed knowledge by confronting it with its long-term orientation in the world serves to remind the inductive and rational pursuit of objective truth of its limitations, disclosing the contradictions, limits, and incomprehensibilities with which such knowledge is fraught and thus calling into question our so-called fixed knowledge.

This method we have employed in the series of abridgments wherewith we have detailed the historical antecedents of our crisis—a knowledge so universally fixed, yet a knowledge, for all that, which has shattered against its long-term orientation in the world. The work of Wilhelm Dilthey illustrates the positive uses of this method.[6] Dilthey, improving on Kant, aimed at a "critique of historical reason" in which philosophy itself was brought to a kind of philosophical self-knowledge through having its relation to life and experience held up to it. This method of Dilthey's recognized that a *Weltanschauung,* or world view, was not susceptible of scientific proof. It appealed to a larger context. "Hitherto the whole of unmutilated experience has never been made the basis of philosophy."[7] Dilthey thus produced not merely an extensive critique of historical reason but a "philosophy of philosophy"!

The usefulness of such a critique is apparent in the liberating perspective it supplies with reference to the "modern" attitude. The "renaissential" world view which established itself when freedom and faith were severed gave rise to official and semiofficial philosophies which aimed to justify this contradictory attitude. Thus we come easily to understand T. E. Hulme's remark that

[6] See *Weltanschauung und Analyse des Menschen seit Renaissance und Reformation, Gesammelte Schriften,* Vol. II.

[7] *Gesammelte Schriften,* VIII, 175.

"men tried to make this new attitude necessary by giving it a philosophy." [8] Whether it is also true that systematic philosophy
comes at the *end* of such periods, as Hulme also held, a philosophy
of philosophy liberates us, at any rate, from the pedantry of supposing that an attitude must be true merely because it has been
systematized. What all these procedures suggest, in the last
analysis, is a "criticism of life" undertaken within the perspective
of the Christian standpoint, and incorporating in it all that Jaspers
would include in his third philosophical method, the "elucidation
of existence" (*Existenzerhellung*).

This elucidation of existence takes its point of purchase in the
conduct of life and in the pursuit of those satisfactions which will
answer to the deepest and ultimate needs of the soul. The method is not altogether original with Jaspers. Its Kierkegaardian
background is apparent. As Sainte-Beuve would say: "We track
him everywhere in Jasper's snow." Moreover, it was in some sense
practiced before Kierkegaard by Matthew Arnold, and by Erasmus, and by Pascal, and by Plutarch, and by Socrates; and it
forms the basis in method for a genuine "Christian Socratism." [9]
One aims by it to realize *"Existenz"* in life, to choose one's self
absolutely in freedom and responsibility under God and to resist
the soul's tendency to sag downward into objective knowledge,
or into the abstract, or into the subhuman. It aims at such a
criticism of life as shall provoke the self into a "being-oneself-as-
freedom"—or, more simply, being oneself as God would have us
be, becoming existing persons instead of subsisting individuals.
This contains, therefore, in method, an appeal to man's *original
freedom,* of such a kind as may be found in the very structure of
the human situation and may be held to be a clue of the most
far-reaching kind as to the final meaning of life and destiny.

iii

For the present, however, we must content ourselves with an
elucidation of the human situation under a simpler schedule, and
in such terms as our study of the crisis will thus far admit.

[8] *Speculations*, p. 26.
[9] See Chap. IV below.

Man's situation is, as we have seen, a mental situation. Man is mind—or, in the familiar parlance, a rational animal—and, as such, constructs his world and construes it. He is, indeed, a great deal more than this; but to speculate on what he would be without this, or what his situation would be apart from this is both absurd and contradictory. The fact that man exists and that he knows that he exists (the "I am, therefore I am a thinker" formula) is a primary datum and presupposition of all investigation. It is the assumed instrument of awareness whereby analysis of the human condition may be undertaken. The turning of the Greeks from the external world of things to the interiority of thought was a striking achievement in the history both of thought and of purposive action. The turning of the modern mind into itself is not wrong by virtue of the turning, but by virtue of presumptive turning—by virtue of its self-sufficiency. Man's situation is a mental situation, but it is more than a mental situation.

Mind "transcends," as we say, the world as it goes, abstracts from particulars to formulate general principles, and apprehends directly first principles—such as that a thing cannot both be and not be at one and the same time. But precisely because the mind has these powers we distinguish between the pure, or speculative, reason, which deals directly with these *formal* relationships and in which its function is *constitutive,* and the *practical* reason, which refers its activity to "actual (or moral) truth, as the fountain of ideas, and the light of the conscience." [10] Here the function of reason is *regulative*—working, that is, with reference to that which is given in life, history, and experience.[11] Already in these simple demarcations, with which every student of philosophy is familiar, our description of the human situation as a mental situation has transcended itself, and the man as thinker has been instructed in his "limit situation." That is, though the mind transcends the world, it must also discover its limitations. For just as the pure reason abstracts from particulars in order to universalize, so "life, history, and experience," the foothold of the

---

[10] Cf. S. T. Coleridge, "On the Difference in Kind of Reason and the Understanding," *Aids to Reflection.*

[11] Cf. Borden P. Bowne, *op. cit.,* pp. 320-21.

practical reason, personalizes in order to enforce decisions. Life is prior to our reasonings about it, even our "pure" reasonings about it. This means that in the ultimate relationships between these two the "living God" of religion must be held prior to the notional "God" of pure reason, and the primacy of the practical reason confirmed. Aristotle could get on very well with a division between the theoretical and practical sciences, and confer authority upon the theoretical (including metaphysics, mathematics, and the like) because his God was not a living God. He was a Prime Mover. He was Pure Act. He was the highest of the universals. He was a Notion. In Aristotle's view, the reason abstracts in order to universalize; religion personalizes in order to redeem.

The reason must come to know, therefore, the arc of its own limitations, and to confirm on its own account or by the instruction of its experience the saying of Pascal, that "the last proceeding of reason is to recognize that there is an infinity of things which are beyond it." By pressing with the mind and with the moral consciousness against the arc of possible knowledge we come gradually to know the true bounds and the proper sphere of the reasoning power.

The moment we attempt this "in all conscience," we discover that the human situation is a moral situation. In us is the knowledge of good and evil. And coincident with such knowledge is the fact of freedom and responsibility. Man is not merely the creature which thinks; he is also the creature that is free to accept or reject, to choose between alternate possibilities. By extension, he may become the creature that defies. And for his defiance he is responsible; and he knows it. He has, that is, a capacity for titanism, defiant action: he is, as Emerson has said, a god in ruins. Thus man's knowledge is qualified by his condition, and man is bent back upon his moral history; for he is the creature, in Dilthey's words, who "must make history."

This leads us to the third proposition. Man's situation is a *historical situation*. Man exists; but he exists in the world, and he expresses himself creatively in the world, and his consciousness is always a consciousness of existence in the world, no matter how greatly he transcends by reason and by spirit the elements of material particularity and flux which make up the "world as it goes."

iv

Let us consider this third factor in the human situation with some care. "I wish," said Coleridge, on behalf of his own system, "to connect by a moral *copula* natural history with political history, . . . to take from history its accidentality." [12] In the present instance we are connecting by a moral copula man as a rational animal with his cultural declaration of himself in a world which he does not make but which he finds. This implies that "history" derives its meaning not from the temporal successiveness of its natural "accidentalities" but from its moral significances. It is the arena in which man wrestles—with the world, with his fellow creatures, and with his God. It is the vicinity of relative self-determination in which he shall become a free person, or in which he shall submit to thing-ness, individuality, and accidentality. It is the arena in which man wrestles—with the world, with his fellow creatures, and with his God. It is the vicinity of relative self-determination in which he shall become a free person, or in which he shall submit to thingness, individuality, and accidentality. It is the sphere of moral and creative decision. It is the moment of dynamic suspension between oblivion and eternal life. It is a sphere of decision.

It should be clear in such a description that we are not emphasizing the terms "arena," "theater," and "sphere"—the passive continuum in which the historical takes place—but the fact, rather, of the "wrestling," the "self-determination," the "moral and creative acts of decision." The first terms belong to the impersonal ground of circumstance, or "accidentality," which attends upon the personal. This impersonal ground of circumstance has no "history," properly speaking. It has recurrence, returning upon itself perpetually after a fixed pattern. Water is gathered up into cloud formations; these concentrate to precipitate rain, which returns to the seas. The seed falls into the ground; the plant is produced, which in due course produces more seeds, which fall into

[12] *Table Talk.*

the ground. The seasons recur; the salmon return to their streams, the eels to the Rhine; the nebulae arise and die in the immense circularity of time as the moving image of eternity—such is the systole and diastole of impersonal recurrence. This is not history, properly speaking. It is what Berdyaev calls "degraded Reality"! It can become history only as it is related to ends of meaning, to the creative activity of the living God and to his purposes—in so far, that is, as it is an *act* of God, or the compound of the deliberated acts of free and responsible persons.

While the impersonality and perpetual repetitiousness of "the world order" is thus easily remarked, and is, in fact, a commonplace of speculation, the effect which it has upon history and upon culture and civilization is not always so easily remarked. For it acts as a negative gravitational tug, diminishing the personal and depriving the human of its creative significance by sucking events and meanings down into its "objectivity," its "order," its automatic circularity. Man's mind, it is true, transcends this order. Man is "a reed which thinks." We are able to build up for ourselves a second world, a world of the mind. But this world of the mind consummates itself in creative activity within and upon the spatiotemporal world. The mind choosing freely makes history, and by transfiguring the world it creates culture. The spatiotemporal order of impersonal repetitiousness is thus converted by decisive acts into an order of personal significance according to the cultural idea which is made to permeate it. Culture, therefore, as Jaspers has finely said, is "a form of life; its backbone is mental discipline, the ability to think; and its scope is an ordered knowledge." [13]

Clearly the place of the mind in building up its culture is paramount. Culture, as a notion, implies the constant exertion of the selective principle, determining by constant vigilance and creative assertiveness the priority and the order of that which is deemed good over that which is deemed bad. For this reason precisely the culture of the West owes to the classical world the determining elements in its culture consciousness. For here, in Greece primarily and later in Rome, the critical intelligence applied itself most res-

[13] *Man in the Modern Age*, p. 131.

olutely to the building up of wise life for men in the world, and in the creation of significant works giving to their cultural idea a character of permanence and concrete definition which has exercised a controlling influence in the entire history of the West.

Nevertheless, it will be noted that, however much we may owe to the cultural achievements of Greece and Rome, these cultural ideas have had significance for us only by way of a vital appropriation of their principles, an appropriation that is itself creative and critical and not on its own account a mere extenson in repetitiousness. For in that way lies the depersonalization of the culture-idea and the dehumanization of men living under the order of that idea; and culture itself is degraded into a mere shell of its former significance—into "objectivity," materiality, and "civilization."

It will be noted also that the appropriation for culture of the Greek passion for selection and representation has been modified in the West by the specifically Christian categories. The discovery of self-consciousness by way of the transcendent work of the mind has been qualified by the disclosure of God-consciousness through the Incarnation of Jesus Christ. The autonomy of the mind is here subordinated to the theonomy of God's will. Man ceases to be the measure of all things: God's will for man becomes the criterion, and man is the measured. Man remains, for all that, a measurer on his own level; but the autonomy of his measuring is displaced, and he is henceforth responsible under God. Man's work, his deeds, his creative acts, his cultural achievements, must coincide with the purposes of God; and it is through God that the transfiguration of the world into meaning of eternal significance is brought about.

The interjection, through Christ, of the Word of God into the world implies that "history" is not linear, but is, on the contrary, two-directional. It *is to* God and *from* God. Man flees God; he returns to God. His culture, as his acts, is defiant, or it is compliant. His culture is Promethean, or it is redemptive.

This is the reason why certain contemporary thinkers speak of history as "hamartiocentric." [14] The biblical notion of sin as

[14] See especially Helmut Thielicke, *Geschichte und Existenz, Grundlegung einer evangelischer Geschichtstheologie* (Gütersloh: C. Bertelsmann, 1935).

ἀμαρτία, as a missing of the mark, is here applied to history dialectically. This means that man projects by his cultural decisions a terrestrial destiny comparable to that which he projects by his individual moral acts, and that in so far as his cultural idea is wide of the mark—the mark of God's intention for man in the world—by so much is man's understanding of himself falsified and a dialectic of ultimate spiritual frustration begun. Such a cultural idea may be Promethean, as in the ancient world; or it may be utilitarian, or Faustian, or Nietzschean: in any case it distorts the image of God in man, is heretical to spiritual order under God, and projects its own decline.

Augustine wrestled with this idea in his *City of God.* "Two cities have been formed," he wrote, in the midst of the crisis of the Roman Empire, "by two loves: the earthly by the love of self, even to the contempt of God; the heavenly by the love of God, even to the contempt of self. The former . . . glories in itself, the latter in the Lord." [15] The rigor of this partitioning of the two cities was a little more than the Christian philosophy of history could stand; but as a clarification of the manifold ways in which anthropocentric cultures glory in themselves, it is incomparable. A culture idea dominated by the lust of power was immediately evident in Augustine's day, as it is in ours. "This lust of sovereignty disturbs and consumes the human race with frightful ills," he wrote; and he saw with irresistible incisiveness the critical necessity for stripping that culture of its "deceitful masks," its "deceitful whitewashes," in order that the basic truth of things might be seen "and scrutinized." [16] The Christian humanist ideal of the state made in the image of man, of a "duly proportioned arrangement of the parts," a "harmonious repose of the appetites, a harmony of knowledge and action, a peace of body and soul founded on a concord between man and God based on the well-ordered obedience of faith to the eternal law," was here precluded by manifold injustices and corruptions.[17] Kingdoms, wrote Augustine, become "brigandage on a colossal

[15] *De civ. Dei* XIV. xxviii.
[16] *Ibid.* III. xiv.
[17] *Ibid.* II. xx; XIX. xiii.

scale"; [18] and by virtue of magnificent piracies, "pride in its perversity apes God, and, instead of his rule, seeks to impose a rule of its own." [19]

The ease with which men acquiesce in terrestrial tyrannies of this kind is not as paradoxical as at first appears; it illustrates, rather, the manner in which two aspects of hamartiocentrism combine in the decline of the culture. Man is, as we have noted, in a historical situation. He "must make history." He seeks, by virtue of this fact, to realize himself and his spiritual meaning in history; and he has, therefore, a historical destiny. But the effort to realize spiritual meaning in the world is a strenuous one; and the elaboration of the new culture idea must be constant, as the effort to realize personality (personhood) and freedom must be constant. Creativity is of the essence of a culture, as it is the essence of self-realization. But whereas self-realization may be realized inwardly and in the spirit, culture must be produced outwardly, taking on tangibility and objectivity. Because of this very objectivity, which is necessary to culture, there is a tendency for all cultures to reach a point of *stasis,* a point of perfection in their kind, which paralyses or stops the creative urge of men living under their dominance. Thus the cultural idea may become fixed, lose its vitality, and lapse into a prolonged imitation of itself. Berdyaev has made much of this tendency, seeing in the necessary objectification of culture the causes of its necessary decline. He observes:

> Classical culture is the perfect form of man's objectified activity in the spheres of religion, morality, science, art and law. The ultimate effect of objective form is to extinguish man's creative fire and to weaken his creative urge, subjecting them both to the rule of law. It becomes a sort of stasis impeding the possibility of any transfiguration in the world.[20]

It is easy to see how this is true in the difference between the classical spirit and neo-classicism (or pseudo-classicism), which is a reduction of the spirit to the letter. But the reason that it is

[18] *Ibid.* IV. vi.
[19] *Ibid.* IV. iv; XIX. xii.
[20] *Solitude and Society,* p. 201.

so is surely traceable to another cause, a cause that is hamartio-centric and personal. It is personal in that it represents a tend-ency on the part of men to avoid the effort of self-realization and to escape from the responsibility of creating a world of spiritual significance. It betrays an eagerness to rest in previous achievements and so evade the necessity for re-creating the cul-tural idea perpetually. "What of old was great," says Jaspers, "lives on, so to say, as a mummy, and becomes an object of pilgrimage." [21] The effect of this acquiescence of men who must create history in the previous idea, or its tangible cultural counterpart, is to depersonalize and to dehumanize the image of God in man. For this also is a means of abstracting from himself, whereby he avoids the imperative of decisiveness in his own spiritual history. So the man whose dignity consists in the fact that he is created in the image of God avoids his re-sponsibility, sacrifices his freedom and his personhood, and comes to rest in an institution or a system or a fraternal order or a state, and so duplicates himself in error as his culture flies beside the mark.

Institutions, according to Emerson, are the lengthened shad-ows of men. And so men, ceasing to be men, come to rest in their own shadows! That is the paradox of hamartiocentric his-tory. "Cultural idolatry" sets in as easily as other forms of idolatry. And the difficulty is that—by virtue of our failure to maintain the re-creative idea in spirit and in truth—cultures, systems, institutions, become carcasses; and vast numbers of men and supposed thinkers crawl into the carcasses and hive there.

We must add then, finally, that man's situation is a tragic situation. For in history apart from God, man is overtaken by his self-projected dialectical fatality. He defies his destiny Faust-wise or Titanically, striving to be a person impersonally; or, projecting a culture-idea that is wide of the mark, he repeats himself in error, willful by the initial choosing, until by succes-sive abstractions from his own idea he submits to his own tyranny in death; or, avoiding altogether responsibility either for creatively transfiguring the world or for re-creating the moment that has transfigured the world, he lapses by default into vegetative anonymity. All this is tragic—or comic—for a creature whose dignity consists in his having been created in the image of God.

But, as de Lamennais said, it is not given to man to destroy himself! For, whereas history is hamartiocentrically dialectic toward death, a negative fatality, tragedy and comedy are dialectic toward crisis—toward thrusting men, through the conspiracy of their own decisions, upon the point of absolute decision. This may be brought to pass by the ontology of events themselves where we have refused to decide—as with *Hamlet* —or by the activity of an antagonist who, exploiting the previous errors, accelerates them to his own advantage, thus precipitating the crisis; or, as in a historical denouement where the outcome is impotence and negation, God himself may become the antagonist and clarify the action. This, at any rate, is the meaning of Christ in history; for every relative effort in the world which now goes wide of the mark is clarified in its flight from truth as righteousness by the absolute standard of the Cross.

"Paganism never gets nearer the truth than Pilate: What is truth? And with that crucifies it." [22] But, in a time of crisis, that is to get very near to the truth. What the exposition of history requires of us is that we should learn what Pilate did not see: that he propounded an academic question when he was confronted by the necessity for moral choice. So with us, our false history (*eine schlechte Unendlichkeit!*) abuts upon eternal history and clarifies the human *situation*.

Christianity, by virtue of the Incarnation, and by virtue of the new decision in faith, arrests all this. The stream of history which catapults toward agony and death is interrupted by the advent of the Eternal in time. The fatal plunge of hamartiocentric history is counterpoised and counteracted by the new

[22] Kierkegaard, *The Journals,* p. 146.

standpoint for human destiny. Man has offered to him within history a means whereby he may relate himself to the Eternal in time. The fulcrum for moving the world has been made available. The point which for Archimedes was hypothetical is for us actual. Christianity is the lever which over the fulcrum of faith will move the whole world. For it provides for man a new understanding of himself. It provides for history a τέλος and a goal. It provides for moral defection and corruption in the world a means of rectification and cleansing.

These are practical truths. They correspond to the four constants within the human situation. As man's situation is mental, moral, historical, and tragic, so the new standpoint makes available to man a true humanism, a true Socratism, a true personalism, and a means of reconciliation—four points of clarification and healing, interrelated and interdependent. It is not possible to have one without the others. It is not possible to have any apart from Christ.

Chapter II

CHRISTIAN HUMANISM

"In no time in history," says max scheler, "has man become so great a problem to himself." Men today are searching desperately for *man*. We speak of "primitive" man, "economic" man, "political" man, the hypostatized man of "humanity," the collective man of the "state," medieval man, modern man, and countless other products of the contemporary passion for scientific classification. That men should pursue this ideal of "objective" classification *passionately* may seem paradoxical. But it is not so; for man is the creature who must find himself at all costs, even though he lose himself in the process. He easily flatters himself with the supposition that if he classifies himself he has done something. Thus, in an age of "reason," when passion is discredited and scientific objectivity is prized, it is inevitable that man should pursue it *passionately*.

It is clear, however, that in the foregoing searches and researches, *man*, however desperate, will not find himself. The investigations are partial. They are "objective," leading outward from the soul. They do not clarify the man within. In direct ratio to the success of the objective enterprise, man is dehumanized and emptied into the abstract, or dissolved in the general class term. Thus man today searches desperately for himself; but, looking diligently for himself where he is certain not to be found, he prosecutes passionately the loss of himself.

Here and there, however, there are signs that this passionate pursuit of atomized man will shortly be countered. A crisis of history forces the consciousness inward upon the spirit, according to the degree of desperation. Thought itself is passing through a crisis. A crisis of the spirit challenges at the very center man's understanding of himself. Scheler holds that the problem of a philosophical anthropology stands today at the midpoint of all the philosophical problems.[1] Berdyaev goes further and asserts simply that philosophy is primarily the doctrine of man.[2] It is easy to see that ethics depends upon our understanding of the nature of man, and that the civilization of any particular period is largely determined by it. We also recognize that the so-called "ideologies" now contending for dominance in the world are at bottom anthropologies seeking to impose upon the world a new world view. All this implies that the process of dehumanization, which has gone forward for decades, has reached its moment of recoil. We are searching today for a new humanism—for the recovery of an understanding of man in his wholeness and completeness. In this larger and more intimate sense, we need desperately to be humanized.

Religiously speaking, this turning to man is a triumph for the spirit. It marks the return of philosophy from knowledge to wisdom. For the true paradox of man is that he is the creature who is forever searching for himself and at the same time forever fleeing from himself.[3] What we desire above all things is the true understanding of ourselves—not, indeed, in order to be wise, as the philosophers say, but in order to know our destinies—yet this true understanding of the self is what we would avoid at all costs precisely because it would confront us with our destinies.

This is a paradox which can only be understood religiously. Philosophers in recent times have seldom troubled themselves with this problem, perhaps for that very reason—that it would trouble them. Philosophy, as it has been practiced, has been one of the best ways of avoiding the issue. Philosophy also has aimed at "objective" truth. Philosophers have ceased to be Φιλοσοφίαε, lovers of wisdom in the ancient sense, and in so far have stunted their true work in the world through diminishing wisdom to science. Their work has become esoteric and detached. It touches the surfaces of life as little as possible, rebounding into the specu-

---

[1] Max Scheler, *Die Stellung des Menschen im Kosmos*, p. 11.
[2] *Solitude and Society*, p. 29.
[3] Cf. Brunner, *Man in Revolt*, p. 24.

lative the moment it does so, like a toy balloon. Life is severed from thought; and philosophers become specialists, men of science, men of one knowledge. They bear the same relevance to life as mathematicians or chiropractors. Philosophy has become what Nietzsche said it was—thought husbandry (*"Denkwirklich-schaft"*), a trade in thought.

This capitulation to the ideal of scientific knowledge was fatal for man's understanding of himself. Science was conceded the status of philosophy, and man agreed to understand himself in terms of objective analysis. He was steadily dehumanized and depersonalized. The attempt to understand ourselves in terms of segregation and classification was foredoomed to failure, no matter how passionately we might have undertaken the task of so understanding ourselves. For man is a person, a self, a conscious subject of experience. He does not *exist* in the categories of classification, no matter how desperately he tries. He is precisely that creature who must synthesize perpetually all the diverse elements of the objective and the abstract, and unite them vitally at the point of his own subjective interests. This is the point where his freedom and his critical intelligence meet, and where he fashions both his temporal and his eternal destiny. This is a creative act, and through these creative acts man comes to know himself as man. Its "process" is precisely the reverse of the ideal of scientific objectivity. It is a return inwardly to the human starting point.

This coerced return to the human starting point which we experience today makes it possible for a philosopher like Nicholas Berdyaev to say that "philosophers and scientists have done very little towards elucidating the problem of man"—and to say it with philosophical consistency! Bertrand Russell's description of men, for example, as "tiny lumps of impure carbons and water" has some scientific merit—particularly if it is considered that this is a view of man as seen from the star Betelgeuse. But if universalized, the definition would make for stark materialism. It is not merely partial; it attempts to explain the higher in terms of the lower, a logical impossibility. This would be true equally of Turgenev's description of men as "little two-legged beetles"—the ironic judgment of the Jungfrau as she watches the race of men arise on the planet and disappear over a period of a few million years. The two views have the merit of irony and effectively reduce man to his littleness, but the conclusions scarcely justify the imaginative effort required to achieve the perspective of Betelgeuse on the one hand or of an Alpine peak on the other. The definitions are transcended in the initial imaginative leap, which, in itself, tells more about man than the biochemical conclusions. But who, it may be urged, would conceivably be taken in by these little ironies —apart, that is, from Bertrand Russell and Turgenev. For is it not perfectly clear that Turgenev, for example, in order to prosecute his little irony, disguised himself as a mountain and brought forth wisdom even smaller than a mouse?

This effort to explain the higher in terms of the lower has been going on for decades. Hermann Lotze wrote:

Among all the errors of the human mind, it has always seemed to me the strangest, that it could come to doubt its own existence, of which alone it has direct experience; *or to take it at second hand* as the product of an external nature which is known only indirectly, only by means of the very mind to which we would fain deny existence.[4]

It is very strange. Nevertheless, when Feuerbach said, *"Der Mensch ist was er isst!"*—"Man is what he eats!"—he started a revolution which has become world wide in its passion to reduce man to an economic category.

There is, however, an explanation for this passionate eagerness wherewith the modern technician dissolves himself in detachment and objectivity. It is that he is searching desperately for man; but he is searching for something that does not exist, namely, *autonomous* man. The searching is presumptuous. It is grounded in self-sufficiency. It is grounded in the effort to find man by virtue of the analytical reason alone.

We have observed above, in our analysis of the Renaissance attitude, that this pursuit has made for the loss of self rather than for the discovery of self, and that it has made for the loss of the human image rather than for the recovery of it. The notion of auton-

[4] *Microcosmus* (Clark), I, 263.

omous man is an illusion. It is the great misunderstanding of man's nature which always ends in the dehumanizing of man.

i

The early humanism of the Greeks was relatively free of this presumption. It attained a view of man that was sane, balanced, and "human"—until it was itself overtaken by rationalism and an enlightenment comparable in many respects to the fate which overtook the Humanism of the Renaissance. This wholeness and health of the Greek perspective was grounded in wonder and in wisdom. The wonder of the modern world, said Chesterton, is that the wonder of the world has gone out of it. The beginnings of philosophy, both for Plato and for Aristotle, were in wonder— though Aristotle, perhaps, forgot it. Augustine renewed that fundamental wonder, which is at bottom a form of humility in the presence of the ultimate mysteries: "Others may reason and argue, but I *wonder*."

This sense of wonder arises early in Greek speculation. It is tied in intimately with the Greek view of man. There is the secret of its vitality. "Man is kindled and put out like a light in the night time," wrote Heraclitus in a line whose striking beauty unites the insight of poetry with the wistfulness of thought that is lost in wonder.[5] This image of man as a lantern lighting with his spirit the darkness of the infinite unknown contains the twofold wonder of the antique wisdom—the sense of living and abiding truth somehow surrounded by and caught within a flow of evanescence. With sure intuition the Greek mind turned to this element of permanence which everywhere transcends the flux or founds it, and established there its wisdom.

Wisdom, so defined, was something human, and as such common to all. In the later language of sophisticated speculation it was something which made for the notion of the universal man. It will be noted, however, that in this term there is already evident a loss of concreteness, of actuality. There is a loss of the

[5] Fr. 77 (Burnet).

particular in the general. There is no such *thing* as a universal man. The concept must be constantly referred to that which is common to all men. "Wisdom," said Heraclitus, "is common to all things. Those who speak with intelligence must hold fast to the common as a city holds fast to its law, and even more strongly." Like his contemporaries and successors, Heraclitus saw that in some fashion this wisdom was grounded in that which was above man. "For all human laws are fed by one thing, the divine." [6] He knew that though all those who speak with intelligence should reverence this wisdom, the intelligence was itself so constituted that it could presume against this wisdom. "Though wisdom is common, yet many live as if they had a wisdom of their own." [7]

Such attempts to live as from a wisdom of one's own were looked upon not merely as departures from "the norm;" they were departures from humility—from wisdom.

Later Greek and Roman thinking betrays the increase of this presumption. Nevertheless, from Solon down to Cicero, the antique wisdom is conserved; and it establishes the bounds which make man human. "What, in the name of heaven," wrote Cicero, "is more to be desired than wisdom? What is more to be prized? What is better for a man, what more worthy of his nature?" [8] In this oft-recurring theme, the Greek and the Roman were at one with the Hebrew: "Wisdom is the principal thing; therefore get wisdom." [9]

That which was most central to this wisdom was a certain view of man. The Greek regarded man as something intermediate between God and animals. He distinguished himself from what was above him and from that which was below him. He

> Neither made man too much a god,
> Nor God too much a man,

as Matthew Arnold said of Goethe; and he knew, from the conditioning of existence, that "man must begin . . . where

[6] Fr. 91 (Burnet).
[7] Fr. 92 (Burnet).
[8] *De officiis* ii. 2.
[9] Prov. 4:7.

Nature ends." These were distinctions which he held discretely. He did not permit himself to blur the distinctions by slurring over the practical discontinuity between these levels of experience. He did not rejoice, as we have done, in his "organic" relation to the cosmos. He did not consider it a point of pride or mark of distinction to leave off being human in order to become a vegetable, as Aristotle put it. He would not confuse the human with the subhuman, nor would he permit his fellow mortals to make themselves divine. To be sure, there were Greeks who tried to do both things—Empedocles, for instance, who climbed Etna and threw himself into the crater, thinking, by his mysterious disappearance, to deify himself and be worshiped as a god. But when he jumped, his slipper fell from his foot; and it was later found. What is significant about the story is that the Greeks retained it as an example of that conditioning by existence which ironically enforces our humanhood upon us at the very moment when we would overstep it. Such irony is always an adjunct of wisdom, qualifying every hope as *human*.

Irony and comedy and tragedy are all concomitants of wisdom, and with the Greeks they were an evidence that they "saw life steadily and saw it whole." Arnold spoke these words of Sophocles, whose drama is itself a wisdom and a "criticism of life," reflecting the wholeness of the classical perspective. It unites creative intelligence with critical discrimination and judgment; but it is an intelligence always critical of itself, as it is of life. The Greek would have been chagrined at the divorce which has existed since Descartes in Western thought between philosophy and science, thought and life, the practical and the theoretical. On the one hand, philosophy, as an acquisition of wisdom, was a thing greatly to be desired. But at the same time wisdom, once acquired, was ironically rebuked the moment it surpassed the human—either positively or negatively, either speculatively or practically. It is recorded of Antisthenes that he walked five miles to the city every day to hear Socrates. Zeno, when shipwrecked near Piraeus, went up to Athens. On picking up a copy of Xenophon's *Memorabilia* in a bookshop he was so pleased that he asked the bookseller where such men were to be found. The bookseller saw

Crates passing by and said, "Follow yonder man." That a common bookseller should have recognized at once the Cynic passing along the street is itself a witness to the native love of wisdom, just as the turning of the hundreds in the crowd at the
stadium to look at Plato as he came in to see the games was an
unconscious tribute to the lover of wisdom. "Follow that man,"
said the bookseller; and Zeno stayed with Crates twenty years.
On the other hand, wisdom was rebuked if it transgressed against
the human level. When Plato defined man as a two-legged feather-
less animal, Diogenes, with his usual resourcefulness, appeared on
the day following with a chicken from which all the feathers had
been plucked, and commented, "This is Plato's man."

The Greek, as if to remind himself that thinkers also were human beings, took note, by dint of a kind of Olympian imperti-
nence, that Aristotle had thin legs and lisped and that Plato was
overfond of olives. Even Socrates, when he presumed to know too
much about the ether, was suspended in a basket in the clouds and
thus held up to public ridicule by the comedian who believed the
thinker's thought had lost relations with existence. Yet how altogether impossible would it have been for Aristophanes to say of
Socrates what Heine said of Kant—that no life history of him
was possible because he had neither life nor history.

Socrates himself employed this irony against the Sophists, who,
presuming over wisdom, had lost the mind's humility. Irony became with him a philosophical instrument. It has been truly observed that "the use of the Socratic irony marks a new stage in the
life of civilized man." [10] For here we see the critical intelligence
disabusing men of supposed fixed knowledge, cross-questioning
the reason into the knowledge that it does not know. Kierkegaard
wrote:

Let us never forget (yet after all how many are there that ever have
known it or thought of it?)—let us never forget that the ignorance of
Socrates was a kind of godly fear and divine worship, that his ignorance
was the Greek rendering of the Jewish perception that the fear of God is
the beginning of wisdom. Let us never forget that precisely out of rever-

[10] Lynn Harold Hough, *The Christian Criticism of Life* (New York and Nashville:
Abingdon-Cokesbury Press, 1941), p. 31.

ence for the Deity he was ignorant, that, so far as a pagan could be, he kept watch as a *judge* on the border between God/and man, watching out to see that the deep gulf of qualitative distinction be firmly fixed between them, between God/and man, that God/and man may not in a way, *philosophice, poetice,* etc., coalesce into one. Lo, for this reason Socrates was the ignorant man, and for this reason the Deity recognized him as the most knowing.[11]

Thus Socrates prepared the way for his instruction in the "care of the soul." [12]

In Socrates himself the classical wisdom reached its apex, for in Socrates the criticism of life as wisdom led to the great revolutionary discovery of antiquity—the discovery of the soul. It is often held that the great discovery of the classical world was its discovery of man as a rational animal. This, however, is a misunderstanding and is, in fact, an emphasis of Greek rationalism rather than of Greek wisdom. This is not, indeed, to deny that man is a rational animal. The earlier Greek humanists understood this well enough—understood it much better, in fact, than the later rationalists. It is to say, rather, that the distinguishing mark of man rests in the fact that he is soul primarily and not merely a "mind imprisoned in a body."

In making the *psyche* the seat of the conscious life, and capable of being made both wise and good, Socrates went beyond the Orphic mysteries, which regarded the soul as a fallen god shut up in the prison house of the body and seeking release; he went beyond Anaxagoras and the Ionian philosophers, who thought of the self in terms of *nous* instead of *psyche* and who looked upon this *nous,* or mind, as corporeal; and he went beyond the Pythagoreans, who regarded the soul as a blend ($\kappa\rho\hat{a}\sigma\iota\varsigma$) or attunement ($\dot{a}\rho\mu o\nu\acute{\iota}a$) of the elements which make up the body. Socrates identified the soul with conscious personality. Burnet has expressed this very emphatically:

It is implied, we must observe, that there is something in us which is capable of attaining wisdom, and that this same thing is capable of attaining goodness and righteousness. This something Socrates called "soul"

---

[11] *The Sickness Unto Death* (tr. W. Lowrie; Princeton University Press, 1941), pp. 160-61.

[12] *Apology* 29D, 30A.

($\psi\nu\chi\acute{\eta}$). Now no one had ever said that before, in the sense in which Socrates meant it. Not only had the word $\psi\nu\chi\acute{\eta}$ never been used in this way, but the existence of what Socrates called by the *name* had never been realized.[13]

Thus the importance of Socrates resides not merely in the fact that "he must be regarded as inaugurating an entirely new period in the history of philosophy" [14] but, rather, in the fact that, as A. E. Taylor says, Socrates "created the intellectual and moral tradition by which Europe has ever since lived"; for it was Socrates who, "so far as can be seen, created the conception of the *soul,* which has ever since dominated European thinking." [15]

Now the importance of this for our present purpose lies in the fact that this discovery of the soul represents the antique wisdom becoming conscious of itself as *self.* This wisdom is basically *maieutic,* a criticism of life, teaching men that if they are to care rightly for their souls, as Socrates says, they must know what they are—what it is to be *human.* They must come to know their true condition; they must be made to recognize as their first task the task of existing as human beings. Apart from some such cross-questioning of ourselves into an understanding of our true nature and our true condition, we are sucked down into the impersonal sediment of the temporal order, where we suffer the loss of ourselves, our freedom, our existence as "human" beings, our vocations as persons. Pursuing ourselves where we are certain not to be found, we pervert the soul to *extra*human purposes, corrupting thus the human spirit and making it demonic. History, as we have seen, may perform this maieutic service by bringing before us in the "metapause" of crisis the ontological conditioning of historical experience and so become a dialectical instrument for the delivery of the self into itself, just as "experience," when criticized, performs this function for those who do not know history. The first step in the wisdom of Socrates was, therefore, a sound one, centering in his maieutic method.

[13] J. Burnet, *Essays and Addresses* (New York: The Macmillan Co., 1930), p. 140.
[14] *Ibid.,* p. 218.
[15] *Socrates* (New York: D. Appleton & Co., 1933), p. 123.

The second step, his positive mission in the world, was also sound; for it centered in the care of the soul and in the turning of the soul toward truth as goodness. Socrates committed this wisdom as a humanistic bequest to all subsequent Greek thought. And if it is true that neither his method nor his teaching understood sufficiently either the treachery of man or the demonic nature of the self-perverted soul, his identifications of virtue with knowledge had at least this merit, that it amounted to "a denial that there is any ultimate distinction between theory and practice." [16] The failure of later thinkers lay precisely in the fact that the thinkers forgot that the knower is an existing individual and that the task of existing is at all times the thinker's essential task.

Regarding Plato, two things may be noted: first, in his later work the doctrine of the soul was primary; and second, building on this doctrine of the soul, his thinking culminated in theology. As Burnet says, he "has left us the first systematic defence of Theism we know of, and it is based entirely on his doctrine of the soul as the self-moved mover." [17] This theology was in its turn grounded in mythology; so that we have in Plato, as Paul Elmer More observed, a system of thought which begins in philosophy and moves on to theology and thence to mythology, in which the claim to certainty becomes increasingly vague; whereas Christianity begins in mythology and moves to theology and thence to philosophy. It would appear that our ultimate choice, as between classical humanism and Christian humanism, is a choice at bottom between a view that begins intelligibly but ends in a mystery, and a view that begins in a Mystery (the Persons of the Godhead) and ends by making everything intelligible.

Which brings us to the fact we must consider—the fact, namely, that antique wisdom, for all its virtues, failed. What were the reasons for that failure? However we reply to this question, if we wish to understand ourselves, we dare not overlook the fact that in ancient Greece we find humanism, "that true subjectivism *con-*

[16] Burnet, *op. cit.,* p. 160.
[17] *Ibid.,* p. 220.

ditioned by existence which for us Westerners lies at the very heart of things." [18]

ii

Classical humanism failed in direct proportion as it came to rest in the notion of man as a rational animal—in proportion, that is, as it came to stress the reason rather than the soul as the distinguishing mark of man. Humanism, grounded in wisdom, was displaced by rationalism, grounded in knowledge. The humanism of Greek wisdom subordinated life to destiny; the later rationalistic humanism of Greek philosophy subordinated life to reason.

Four errors were consequent upon this turning: men came to regard the reason as autonomous; they identified the reason with the Divine; they assumed the essential goodness of reason, making matter by reflex the ground and source of evil; and the reason, in moral action, was looked upon as neutral.

To segregate these notions from the humanistic elements in the Greek and Latin thinkers is difficult, for two reasons: first, because the passion for Socratic self-knowledge and the notion of philosophy as the "love of wisdom" was retained from Socrates to Marcus Aurelius, so that humanistic wisdom is always present in, though subordinated to, the rationalist philosophies; and second, because there was an element of the rational immanent in Greek wisdom from the beginning. Thus Marcus Aurelius, for whom man is a rational animal in the rationalist sense, would have us retire into ourselves and there find tranquillity.[19] But the self into which he would have us retire is the mind, the intellectual part. Heraclitus, who very early urged the doctrine of self-knowledge,[20] also said, "Go hence; the limits of the soul thou canst not discover, though thou shouldst traverse every way; so profoundly is it rooted in the Logos." [21] We may, of course, regard this statement as Brunner does, as the self's discovery of its self-

---

[18] Theodor Haecker, *Virgil, Father of the West* (tr. A. W. Wheen; London: Sheed & Ward, 1934), p. 67.

[19] *Meditations* iv. 3; vii. 28; *et al.*

[20] Fr. 101 (Diels).

[21] Fr. 45 (Diels).

transcendence, thus preparing the way for the Socratic notion of the soul; [22] but it was easy in subsequent times to throw the weight of meaning upon the term *Logos* in such a way as to make the finite mind a fragment of the divine Mind, concluding all within monistic Reason. This, as a matter of fact, did happen; and the decadence of Greek culture followed.

The *locus classicus* of the notion of man as rational animal is found in Aristotle.[23] It is recurrent in all subsequent Greek and Latin thought, it was absorbed into patristic and medieval Christianity; it is recurrent everywhere, in fact, where man is self-regardfully eulogized as "the paragon of animals," "in apprehension how like a god." Aristotle himself was not consistent on the point; but his notion of the soul was in the main a development of Ionian theories, and for him the soul itself is mind. The *nous* is regarded as autonomous. It makes itself its own first principle.

The leap from *nous* to *Nous,* from *logos* to *Logos*—from reason to Reason, and from mind to Mind—is thus no leap at all. It is at bottom a motion of the mind deifying itself. For to make reason, as the immanent *nous* within us, the ultimate principle is to identify ourselves surreptitiously with the Divine. Aristotle did this through regarding *nous* as the distinctive element in man,[24] and through holding that the *Nous* was also the Divine.[25] Man, by virtue of his reason, possessed a scintilla of the divine essence, the mere possession of which "constitutes a prima-facie claim to divinity, lifting him above the natural order of which he forms a part." [26] The immanence of God disintegrates the boundary between the human and the divine, thus breaking the higher boundary which humanism had established between the soul and God. By taking one more step, that is, by regarding

---

[22] *Op. cit.,* p. 18. To this quality of transcendence we shall return. Meanwhile, note should be taken of Burnet's claim that "the word *Logos* did not mean Reason at all in early days." (*Early Greek Philosophy* [London: A. & C. Black, 1892], p. 133, n. 13.)

[23] *Nicomachaean ethics* 1177*b*26-78*a*7.

[24] *De anima* II. i. 2.

[25] *De generatione animalium* III. 736*b*

[26] Charles U. Cochrane, *Christianity and Classical Culture* (Oxford: The Clarendon Press, 1940), p. 406.

God as actuality and matter as potentiality (privation of being) the second boundary—the boundary between the human and sub-human—is dissolved and monism triumphs over wisdom. The idea of self-autonomy pre-empts the Godhead by projecting meta-physically a rational Deity. This Deity is not the Living God of religion. It is the abstract God of thought, concluding always to Pure Being, or the Intellectual Principle, or the Absolute, or to deism, pantheism, or some rationalist monism. This fact illustrates Brunner's claim that "the understanding of man always leads us ... either into the region of metaphysics or into that of faith." [27]

Aristotle, as is well known, was led by these necessities to postu-late his notion of the Prime Mover as the cause of all. This notion he pretended to deduce from experience, and from the evident principle that every moving object requires as its causal antece-dent a mover which is itself in motion. To break the indefinite regress herein implied Aristotle presupposed "an unmoved Mover whose immobility was not rest but a timeless activity which was not a process of change." [28] "This pretension," writes Paul Elmer More, "to lend the authority of physical fact, or scientific observa-tion to a theorem which is essentially contradictory to all our physical experience lies perdu in the very method of rationalism, and indeed in all so-called science which glides surreptitiously into metaphysical generalizations." [29] The *ratio scientiae* became the exclusive instrument of the real; and by it the identification of thought with being set forth by Parmenides was resumed, and a profound and far-reaching secular effort to discover in nature and in reason a rule for conduct and a means of knowledge was projected.

This ideal of scientific objectivity has its merits in its proper sphere, where its function is analytical and regulative, and where

---

[27] *Op. cit.,* p. 60.

[28] G. R. G. Mure, *Aristotle,* p. 88. Though Aristotle wished to avoid the Platonic "transcendentalism," he nevertheless was faced with a problem here and in one passage explained how this Prime Mover communicates motion to the world by saying, "It moves it like a thing beloved." We are left to make what we may of this. But medieval thought follows the same pattern, through trying to Platonize the Aristotelian meta-physics after this fashion. Hence Dante's Neo-Platonic-Aristotelian solution of the prob-lem in the *Paradise* (xxxiii, 52-63, 97-103, 124, 125).

[29] *Hellenistic Philosophies* (Princeton University Press, 1923), p. 211.

it is not given a metaphysical status—that is, where it is not made constitutive. Its tendency, however, is to depersonalize truth and to dehumanize man, reducing the former to abstract categories and the latter to impersonal objectivity. It overlooks the fact that, as Brunner puts it, "the question of man as subject is not one among many others; it is a new dimension of questioning, and the soul is an 'object' whose particular problems consist in the very fact that it is not an 'object' at all."[30] This new dimension is apparent, however, only to the thinker who regards man as soul in the sense of spirit primarily, and not to the man who regards man as reason primarily. The dehumanizing of the self is a consequence of the stipulated activity of the *ratio scientiae*—what Pascal called *"l'esprit de géométrie"*—which, by definition, directs the attention outwards and takes as its central task the ordering and organizing of the objects of the external world. Man soon becomes an object amongst other objects, and "the rationalization of mankind" such as we witness in the world today is a logical extension of this effort. This is the mind's central misunderstanding of itself, and the consequences of such misunderstanding are both morally and intellectually disastrous.

Intellectually, this notion of autonomous reason made for the barren disputations of the schools—the Academics, the dogmatists, the Cynics, the Skeptics. The skeptics came off best in this intellectual game, by using reason in such a thoroughly scientific way as to show that it was self-destructive as an instrument for knowing the ultimate nature of things. Thus the principle of understanding itself was lost. Augustine countered this systematic default of the understanding by appealing, through faith, from the *ratio scientiae* to the *ratio sapientiae*—which constituted once more a return to wisdom.

Morally, as Athanasius pointed out, the principle of life was lost. One has only to review the subsequent decay of humanist culture to see the path of depletion through the Greek decadence. A spiritual *phthisis,* a devitalization or wasting away of the life principle is everywhere apparent in the lapse of human dignity

---

[30] *Op. cit.,* p. 18.

in the direction of endurance, apathy, frustration, duty, and despair. "All things happen according to universal nature," said Marcus Aurelius; "everything which happens, always happened so and will happen so, and now happens so everywhere." [31] "Pyrrho used to say that there is no difference between dying and living: and a man said to him, Why then do you not die? Pyrrho replied, Because there is no difference." [32] As Pascal would say, who does not see the vanity of this must himself be very vain.

Epictetus and Marcus Aurelius are universally admired for their moral wisdom, but their wisdom is vitiated by a rationalist monism of such rigor that their wisdom is grounded in a state of suppressed spiritual desperation.

Since the mind was regarded, in all these schools, as a fragment of the Divine, it was only logical that it should distinguish itself from the body, as good is distinguished from evil. The body became a tomb ($\sigma\hat{\omega}\mu\alpha$, $\sigma\hat{\eta}\mu\alpha$). "You are a little soul carrying a dead body," said Epictetus.[33] Even Plato spoke of the body as "our prison which we bear about, shackled to it like an oyster to its shell." [34] And his Creator had always to work upon some metaphysical residuum of stuff, a necessity ($\dot{\alpha}\nu\dot{\alpha}\gamma\kappa\eta$), an intractable somewhat which threatened always to drag the soul down into eternal becoming. Aristotle, despite his underlying monism, was quite as dualistic on this point as Plato. His distinction between form ($\epsilon\hat{\iota}\delta o\varsigma$) and matter ($\tilde{\upsilon}\lambda\eta$) carries the same implications. His "substratum" ($\dot{\upsilon}\pi o\kappa\epsilon\dot{\iota}\mu\epsilon\nu o\nu$) is a "remnant, the non-existent, in itself unknowable and alien to reason." [35] It is pure potentiality as over against actuality; it is particularity as over against the universal; it is "privation" ($\sigma\tau\dot{\epsilon}\rho\eta\sigma\iota\varsigma$) as over against both being and the good. Reason is the divine principle, uniting man with the Divine; whereas the sojourn of the soul in the body is severe illness, limitation, particularity.

Reinhold Niebuhr is right in saying that the Bible knows

[31] *Meditations* xii. 26.
[32] Epictetus *Enchiridion* xciii.
[33] *Ench.* clxxvi.
[34] *Phaedrus* 150C.
[35] Werner Jaeger, *Aristotle* (tr. R. Robinson; New York: Oxford University Press, 1934), p. 382.

nothing of a good mind and an evil body. [36] Paul's "flesh" was nothing evil in itself. It was the acquiescence in the flesh that made for bondage. In this Paul was nearer to the Ciceronian wisdom, which distinguished the reason from the appetites, the former of which was meant to rule and the latter to obey. But Paul did not expect salvation by the reason! This reason did not counteract that other law in his members. It merely clarified as Law the bondage all mankind was under through the fact of sin. For the turning of the self in the act of sin was for him a total act, an act of the whole person, which did not leave the reason neutral in the choice but turned it with the self upon the evil end. The fatal misunderstanding of the self through the self-sufficiency of reason was held by Augustine to be a prostitution of the mind to its own fancies.

The neutrality of reason extended to the divine ideas, and both Platonic idealism and Aristotelian rationalism culminated in contemplation—a strenuous passivity whereby the mind contemplates the infinite projection of itself as the Absolute.[37]

If we consider now that later Greek thought retained from the time of Socrates its mission to save the world, the desperation of the schools will be more clearly understood. "That man," says Seneca, "is looking for salvation." Yet what the schools provided was not new life but willful persistence in the present death. Salvation was a work of the mind, and of the mind working willfully its own salvation. "From within comes ruin, and from within comes help," said Epictetus.[38] They aimed, as Berdyaev says, to "regenerate the soul through knowledge," and they "tended to regard philosophy as a means of salvation." [39] Such a wisdom maintained a noble turning on itself through Reason, Providence, Control, and Fate, as at the circumference of a cone. But its nobility, as it lost the centripetal force of its will to self-sufficiency, glided Stoically down the inside of the cone until it

---

[36] *The Nature and Destiny of Man*, I, 7.

[37] Plato is less subject to this criticism than is Aristotle, for his thought adheres more closely to experience. Moreover, his thinking is theistic, striving to arrive at a personalistic conception of ideas through a quasi-creative God.

[38] *Discourses* iv. 9.

[39] *Op. cit.*, p. 7.

reached the closed point of suspension between irony and despair, in which the humbler wisdom of the ancients narrowed to the point of pride. In Tacitus' fine epigram, "They make a solitude and call it peace."

iii

Christianity appeared when the vitality of Greek humanism had been taken captive in the concept. Therefore its "embodied Logos," its redemptive Word made manifest through the crucified God-Man, was a "foolishness" to the Greeks. On the other hand, it was a stumbling block to the Hebrew, whose religious tenacities had hardened monistically and moralistically into rites and legalism. Thus, a dual difficulty faced the early Christians. They had, on the one hand, to convey a "foolishness" to a world already thinking in the patterns of Greek sophistication; they had, on the other hand, to demarcate the Christian gospel, with its stumbling block of the Cross, from Judaism. This was a dilemma: Christianity had either to renounce the world or come to terms with it—to set forth, that is, a new humanism, a view of man, an ideology capable of becoming a world view of eternal significance. This it was able to do by virtue of its relationship to an event in history which had an absolute significance. By subordinating the problem of the finite and the infinite to the problem of sin, by abandoning the self-sufficient man (*autarkeia*) for revelation, by regarding man as the image of God, and by grounding virtue in faith instead of knowledge, a new world view was instituted. This world view marked a radical departure from classical ideology; yet at the same time it was a true fulfillment of the ancient wisdom, both of Greek and Jew.

Hebrew wisdom offered one great vantage point to Christianity. It had always been more personal, concrete, and actual. The Hebrew mind turned always from the abstract to the particular and moral. "Behold, the fear of the Lord, that is wisdom," said Job; "and to depart from evil is understanding." [40] This was the Hebrew standpoint. Wisdom was primarily moral rather than intel-

[40] Job 28:28.

219

lectual. Such wisdom took account, indeed, of the evanescent world of eternal change and becoming; but to pin one's destiny upon this panoramic flux and change was "vanity"—and all was vanity apart from God. All speculative efforts to deal causally with the finite and the infinite were, for the Hebrew, ethically barren. His thought began with the Creator God. For him, the question "What is man, that thou art mindful of him?" was primarily moral and religious, not metaphysical. Like Socrates, he practiced, in the presence of the metaphysical perplexities, a "divine abstinence." His thought was grounded in a *crede ut intelligas*—"believe, that you may know."

The supposition that this formula came late in Christian thought is a medieval superstition. Isaiah proclaimed it long before Anselm, and in a sense not vitiated by the medieval ontologism. "If ye will not believe, surely ye shall not be established." [41] The wordplay is preserved in Luther's German: *"Glaubt ihr nicht, so bleibt ihr nicht!"* This startling insight, addressed to Ahaz in the midst of a national crisis, had the force of revelation. History itself had posed the question as to ultimate meaning and allegiance. It had posed the very question of existence. Belief, in times of crisis, is an imperative demand. Not, indeed, that there is in it any compulsion, whether physical, psychical, or psychological. The compulsion is of another kind: it consists in the fact that that which has been pending in the historical situation can no longer be held in abeyance. Decision is required. The terms of temporal existence have been thrust upon the absolute requirement which must be acted on in terms of faith or unbelief. One stands on God's side or against him.

The academic doubt—"I do not know whether I can know God or not"—becomes, at the point of crisis, an obduracy. It is not a mere irrelevance; it is a willfulness. It is not a question of metaphysics, or privation, or predestination. It is psychologically and ethically grounded. For an obduracy of the mind which waits upon comprehension of the Absolute in a moment of historical crisis commits itself to a decision in unbelief, an unbelief

[41] Isa. 7:9.

informed with dialectical consequences. It is committed to a policy of rejection, with whatever penalties ensue. In brief, in the moment of historical crisis God and man stand over against each other in a relationship of infinite ethical demand.

Herein we have the eschatological crux of the human situation set forth in miniature. The prophetic word announced to Ahaz by Isaiah presents in the moment of Judah's crisis of history the same imperative that all of history beholds in Jesus Christ. Faith, as Otto Procksch has noted, is "the Archimedean point" which stands outside the dead weight of the world, and which secures historical existence which apart from faith falls downwards into ruin.[42]

Under "ordinary" circumstances—when things are "going smoothly" and there is no apparent transcendent demand—the faith question seems academic, a speculative dalliance, a whilom throwing of the dice, "a betting your life there is a God," while history itself seems to stand outside the sphere of this little game of chance. "But when the historical Moment itself puts the existence question" and the statesman or the individual confronts existence as a crisis which must issue either in life or death, then faith as a little bet made in a moment of speculative dalliance is beside the point, a superfluity. But this is not the case. In history outside of faith it never is the case. From our present standpoint Christ is always both the consummation of our probationary holding in abeyance *and* an absolute prophetic Demand. In a crisis, "what the prophet demands is itself the Wager *sub specie aeternitatis,* which the statesman . . . must fulfill. Through being bound to God in faith the Wager receives a moral character, and loses its accidental character." [43] Looked at backwards, neutrality also is a venture; it is also a wager. Ye must believe if ye would be established.

All of this suggests Pascal's notorious discussion of the "wager," [44] in which he calculates *sub specie aeternitatis* the increment of gain or loss according as we wager that God is or that God is

[42] See Procksch, *Kommentar zum Alten Testament,* Vol. IX, Isaiah 1-39, p. 118.
[43] *Ibid.*
[44] *Pensées,* 233.

221

not. By believing that he is, we stand to win all; by doubting that he is, we stand to lose everything. Pascal's computing of the odds stands nearer by a whole dimension to Isaiah than does the medieval *credo ut intelligam*—"I believe in order to know." The medieval formula remains a kind of notional consent, a propositional achievement within the framework of the theoretic reason: the calculus has passed from mathematics into metaphysics. Faith is not in being rooted like a pillar; it is a kind of abstract consent. Pascal's consent, however, passes from the calculus of mathematics into faith as the Hebrew understood it; for his decision is a risk, in which he stakes all, in the presence of an imperative: "Yes, but you must wager. It is not optional. *You are embarked.*" Here again, as with Isaiah, the decision is a dialectical result, grounded ethically and determining the life or death according as we reject or acquiesce in God's demand.

Pascal, it is true, is often charged with indulging his penchant for mathematics in the passage of the wager just referred to. This is to overlook, however, the dialectical fulcrum of the discussion, which is evident in the phrase "You are embarked." Pascal does not regard man statically, nor does he admit to thought any intellectualistic neutrality. Thought is for him like the pivot point between the pans of a balance-scale.[45] Because he thinks, man is able to know his misery; but to know oneself to be miserable is itself a greatness. The terms *greatness-thought-misery* must be thought integrally; and it is the unstable equilibrium of the terms which makes for man's restlessness and perpetual longing for escape. This understanding of the "wager" passage is further enforced by the warning with which it opens: "Our soul is cast into a body, where it finds number, time, dimension. Thereupon it reasons, and calls this nature, necessity, and can believe nothing else." That is, it *will* believe nothing else. It is an obduracy such as we have already noted in the case of Ahaz. Finally, as if to remove all question as to mathematical sportiveness, Pascal has concluded this *pensée* with

[45] Cf. Strowski's penetrating analysis of Pascal's *Pensées* in his *Les Pensées de Pascal* (Paris: Mellottée, 1930), pp. 119 f.

the solemn declaration that "it is made by a man who has knelt, both before and after it, in prayer."

What, then, has Pascal done, and wherein does its significance consist? He has turned the *esprit de géométrie,* the *ratio scientiae,* against itself. He has confronted it *on its own terms* with moral dialectic. The speculative calculus of probabilities is brought out of the abstract and thrust upon the concrete. The geometric reason is hoisted on its own petard. For the difference between the "man of reason" and the "man of faith" is not that one thinks and the other does not. It is that the reason takes its starting point within itself, in the one case, finding in its self-sufficiency the power and fulcrum and lever and weight to be moved, striving thus to make the infinite movement into certainty over the fulcrum of its own doubt; whereas, in the other case, it takes its starting point outside itself, through an act of faith, trusting thereby through Power not its own to move the world. Medieval systematics sought a compromise between the two. It ascribed some things to faith and some to reason. It was "two-storied," seeking to weld the discrepancy by the "hierarchical" principle —a purely metaphysical solution. This abridged the dialectical relation of God to man in faith or unbelief; and it tended to by-pass the integral unity of the terms *greatness-thought-misery,* so central to Pascal and Hebrew prophecy alike. Similarly, it produced a static culture, and left a Gothic longing reaching for the infinite. In this way the pagan problem of the finite-infinite survived the Christian emphasis on the wholly personalistic terms of sin and faith and emerged again in the aggravated longing of the German Romanticists.

All of which puts us in a position to see how wisdom with the Hebrews tends always to ground itself in the prophetic disclosure of God's will as over against man's intransigence, just as wisdom with the Greeks tended to move metaphysically into the problem of the finite and the infinite. Both problems present very real aspects of the human situation.

Nevertheless, it is in Hebrew wisdom that we see foreshadowed the outlines of the Christian principle. For it projects an understanding of man as he is known through God's requirement; the

223

problem of the finite and the evanescent is subordinated to the problem of the evil will; sin is referred from the body to the soul; and the conditions of wisdom are seen to be primarily moral rather than intellectual. The God who "searched the heart" was determinative for the Hebrew view of man.

When Augustine attempted, in his later works, to distinguish the uniquely Christian from the classical bequest, he resumed these points altogether, and arrived at a view of man which must be held distinct from all others. "From the soul and from the body, which are the parts of a man, we arrive at the totality which is man: accordingly, the life of the soul is not one thing, and that of the body another: but both are one and the same, i.e. the life of man as man." [46] This definition regards man as a unit, as a person, as a complex whole—of body, soul, and spirit. It is constant in the Christian view of man. But it is formal and structural, and its significance does not acquire its full import until this unit, man, is given a positive orientation toward God, the world, and his fellow man such as we find in the biblical view of man as an image of God.

This doctrine of the image must be regarded in a wholly personalistic manner. It is not related to the Aristotelian notion of man as a rational animal. And God said, "Let us make man in our image, after our likeness." [47] This means, in Emil Brunner's simple phrase, that "the nature of man . . . is not intelligible from itself, but . . . its ground of existence and of knowledge is in God." The Christian understanding of this doctrine becomes clear when the Old Testament view of man as created in God's image is referred to the New Testament for its definitive clarification. For here man is the creature who "images" God,

"an existence which points back or refers to something else. 'But we all, with unveiled face reflecting as in a mirror the glory of the Lord, are transformed into the same image from glory to glory.' Man's meaning and his intrinsic worth do not reside in himself, but in the One who stands 'over against' him, in Christ, the Primal Image, in the Word of God." [48]

[46] *De civ. Dei* XIV. iv.
[47] Gen. 3:26.
[48] *Op. cit.*, p. 96.

The tradition which views the reason as the seat of the image of God in man is thus shortsighted. It would be more to say that we are created like God by virtue of our being created as persons, endowed with primal freedom and a relative creative autonomy, endowed with a capacity for good and evil. But even this falls short of the unique diamond point of the *imago* doctrine, which consists in the fact that man is the creature who stands uniquely related to God in a relationship of response and responsibility. "Human nature, indeed, consists in the fact that we may and must remain in the hands of God." [49]

Concerning this doctrine three things must be noted:

First, man must be understood theologically, not ontologically. He must be understood from "above," according as he stands related to God's Word in purely personal relatedness. This relationship to God is the point of primary import. All else depends *from* this. "Man's relation to God is not to be understood from the point of view of reason, but reason is to be understood from the point of view of man's relation to God." [50] Or, as has been said more definitely by Augustine: "This trinity, then, of the mind is not therefore the image of God, because the mind remembers itself, and understands and loves itself; but because it can also remember, understand, and love Him by whom it was made. And in so doing it is made wise itself." [51]

From this a second point becomes clear, that a "true humanism"—that is, right wisdom—can only be secured through a renewal of the image of God, which has been perverted through sin. "Let it then remember its God!" as Augustine puts it. Here again the viewpoint is personal and is concerned with the problem of right-relatedness. This presupposes, on the one hand, a self that is capable of knowing God and, on the other, a maieutic discipline toward self-knowledge—a dialectic of life of such a sort as will deliver the self into its transcendent capacity for apprehending God together with the will to appropriate this wisdom. Thereby the true wisdom becomes God's wisdom, and the true lover of wisdom

[49] *Ibid.*, p. 97.
[50] *Ibid.*, p. 102.
[51] *De trinitate* XIV. xii. 15.

225

—the true philosopher—becomes the lover of God.[52] This wisdom is founded, therefore, neither on the Cartesian reason nor on the *esprit de géométrie,* nor on the *ratio scientiae* nor on the reason itself in any phase of its discursive activity but upon the *esprit de finesse,* the *ratio sapientiae* of Augustine, or, better still, upon a decision in faith which is the response of the whole man to God's declaration of himself.

But another matter also is clear, that this wisdom is intercepted by a fact of our condition—the condition of sin, the circumstance that man is not in point of fact living in terms of holiness and love under God. The psychological structure of man remains—his body, mind, and spirit. But it is perverted in its uses. Man's relation to God remains; man is always related to God. But the relation is perverted, and the perversion militates toward perversity in all man's acts. That is the stubborn fact of our condition. Therein is the clue to the explanation of the fact that man's true paradox is an existential paradox: he is the creature who is forever searching for himself yet forever fleeing from himself. For through his willfulness and his thirst for self-autonomy he shuns the decision of a return to God, wherein true wisdom and true humanhood consist. Christ is the way of this return. Outside of Christ there is no wisdom, properly speaking, but only knowledge yielding to the perverse will. Outside of Christ there is no humanism, properly speaking but only a perverse humanity. Knowledge is proud that it knows so much; humanity is "contrary" since it knows no more! Nevertheless, the true dignity of man consists precisely in his capacity to sin; and the fact of sin itself attests to the essentially theological nature of man.

iv

Looking back now briefly, we can see that as classical wisdom discovered through its discipline the soul, so Hebrew wisdom came to know man through the inmost searchings of the heart. Classical wisdom, too, through teaching men to know themselves, grounded wisdom in a theological understanding of man

[52] *De civ. Dei* VIII. i.

even as the Hebrew did. But whereas Socrates and Plato sought to disabuse men's souls of ignorance, of attachment to the world of flux and evanescent finitude, and to teach men how they might "mount upwards" by love of forms and essences until they might participate in God's eternal essence, Hebrew wisdom sought to disabuse men's souls of sin, teaching them to become obedient to God's Word.

Classical wisdom failed, through passing from Socratic abstinence and faith to knowledge; and the problem of the finite and the infinite passed over into rationalistic apposites of particular and universal, potency and act. Humanism—we have seen—can also be abstracted from itself and so cease to be human. There is a sense in which classical humanism ends the moment it reaches the sphere of the universal. The notion of the universal was a great achievement for the mind, but it was subtly a disaster for the soul. The category of the "universal" takes on a nominalistic character and acquires priority over persons as the mind acquires priority over spirit. From the religious standpoint—that is, from the human standpoint—the personal is always greater than the species: it is never anything *particular* as over against the *general*. As Berdyaev has indicated, "the 'general' category has no ontological validity." [53] The person is the principal category of religious knowledge. "The fatal error of rationalistic humanism," as Reinhold Niebuhr has said, "is its failure to recognize that reason is universal only in purely formal terms. . . . But no judgment which fills logical forms with material content is universal.[54]

How much more true is this of judgments filled with human content. What matters is man's relation to the absolute. It is man's relationship to God that determines his relation to the universal, as Kierkegaard has shown, and not his relation to the universal that determines his relation to the absolute.[55] Any humanism which comes to rest in the universal, will sooner or later become, like medieval Scholasticism, a parody of itself; and man will be dehumanized. *Christianity is the only point of view which offers*

[53] Berdyaev, *op. cit.*, pp. 33, 172.
[54] *Beyond Tragedy* (New York: Charles Scribner's Sons, 1938), p. 236.
[55] *Fear and Trembling*, p. 100.

a world ground that is at once Personal and Universal, and which recognizes at the same time that in man which is also personal and universal. For the *Logos* of Christianity asserts the primacy of Spirit rather than the primacy of Reason.

Mankind would be pleased if it could come to rest in the universal; for this would permit the self to rest in ethics, and so avoid the infinite demand of religious commitment. But ethics based on rationalist virtue becomes legalistic, barren, and duty-bound. The "salvation" of the later schools—the Stoics, the Epicureans—was of this kind. It was latent in Aristotle, in his failure to solve the hamartiocentric problem. It is all contained within the line from Terence—

> Since that cannot be which you will, will that which thou canst.[56]

As Augustine remarks, this "is aptly said, who denies? But it is advice given to the miserable man, that he may not be more miserable." [57]

It was precisely here that Hebrew wisdom failed. The Hebrew insights hardened into law. Judaism became legalistic and pharisaical. Yet it was also this Pharisaism, which was in truth the highest development of Hebrew religion, that Christ denounced throughout the Gospels. Pharisaism was but another form of the rationalistic escape from the personal confrontation of God in inwardness of spirit. Religion is always subject to this perversion. It was against the legalism of the Catholic Church that Luther rebelled, yet Protestantism became equally juridical and legalistic in its subsequent expressions. The Kantian appeal to duty is open to the same complaint. Wherever the ethics of grace and freedom in the love of God is universalized in the sense above indicated, legalism sets in, and the relationship of God to man becomes despiritualized, and man loses once more his true humanity.

Finally, all attempts to transcend the ethics of the law which

[56] *Andreia*, Act II, scene 1.
[57] *De trin*. XIII. vii. 10.

do not seek to transcend it through God's grace, become Promethean and defiant. The pantheon of Gods, whether Greek or Roman, represents not so much an effort to personalize the Godhead as an effort to divinize the human attributes. In the intercourse of gods with men, in their rivalries and machinations, we see the human spirit laying bare its contradictions. Defiance and revolt appear within their plots and counterplots, until one is oppressed, like Aeschylus, with a sense of the frustration of good and the fatal triumph of evil. Fatality here runs swiftly to overtake the god. Under Jove the peak point of human affirmation in the spirit is reached in a moment of Promethean defiance— which illustrates, rather than confutes, the ultimate futility of the ideal of human self-sufficiency. Prometheus, like the man of rebellious will, is the victim of his own egocentric obsessions, the rational obsessions of self-deifying reason. Greek religion, for want of a Creator God whose Word was self-sacrificing love and spirit, culminated in a Titanic self-justification. This was at bottom a mythological covering for the basic metaphysical solipsism which underlies the Greek world view. Nietzsche's Promethean projection of the private will to power in the apotheosis of self as the superman is not altogether unlike it —save that the Greek protest is primitive and Titanic, whereas Nietzsche's is pathological and pedantic. Man is the creature who must surpass himself! This, indeed, is true, and the Christian succeeds in this by way of the God-man. But Nietzsche would transcend the ethics of the law by the ludicrous device of having man leap over his own shoulders. It is of a piece with the Babel tower, which, by purely human effort, would coerce the heavens.

"Paganism," it has been well said, "is decentered religion—religion moving out from the midpoint." [58] It is a religion that turns outward into forms, or into legalisms, or strives to mount upwards into the willful infinite, instead of inward into spirit. Spirit only is creative, for it alone is wholly personal and free: through it man images the Godhead. Therefore culture must derive initially from spirit; and it must adhere, if it would pre-

---

[58] Theophil Spoerri, *Die Götter des Abendlandes* (Berlin, 1932), p. 9.

serve itself, to its spiritual center. Man and culture alike, apart from this center, lose their unity. Each establishes itself as its own center. "And instead of one God we create for ourselves a jumble of gods and demons." [59] Idolatry ensues. Man has either God or an idol. The sense of the divine ordering, the theological hierarchy of values, plummets into secularity. Idolatry becomes demonic, and—as in the present crisis of the West—all things human and divine become profaned. "At this point we stand to-day. The desecration of all things . . . is the true sickness unto death [*Todeskrankheit*] of our time." [60] Man has perverted the image of God in himself, and has lost himself and his cultural coherence in the fugitive pursuit of his own willfulness.

As Christianity is the only religion that offers a world ground that is both Personal and Universal, so it is the only religion that founds a humanism by an act of God. For the Incarnation confronts man with his inhumanity; and by its infinite requirement of total acquiescence in God's Word, it projects a world view that is both redemptive and creative through the renewal and the transformation of the human image from glory unto glory in the Lord.

Jacques Maritain is often cited for his felicitous distinction between anthropocentric humanism and theocentric humanism. The vice, says he, of "anthropocentric humanism has been that of being anthropocentric and not of being humanism." [61] This is a facile putting of the problem; but, in all truth, it obscures the fundamental difference. For all humanisms are, in a sense, anthropocentric. They are achieved by way of true self-knowledge and not by way of the analogy of being. For the self through coming properly to know itself founds itself transparently upon the Power that created it. And this it does through faith.

Thus there are only two "humanisms" at bottom—the one true, the other false. Pseudo humanism is the attempt of the self to

[59] *Ibid.,* p. 10.
[60] *Ibid.,* p. 11.
[61] *Humanisme integral,* p. 35.

found itself upon itself by virtue of its self-sufficiency. It believes naïvely, with Aristotle, that "happiness will be found in self-sufficiency." True humanism is the attempt of the self to found itself, by faith, upon the Power that created it. It believes naïvely, with Dante, that "in his will is our peace." In short, the basic opposition, in the understanding of man, is the opposition between self-sufficiency and faith. But this supposes a certain understanding of the nature of the self, and of its relation to the Eternal, which we must now examine.

Chapter III

CHRISTIAN PERSONALISM

THE JOURNEY TO THE SELF IS "A JOURNEY WITHOUT RETURN." IT is a journey of deliberate inwardness. It must end either in the choice of oneself absolutely or in a flight from oneself endlessly —endlessly inasmuch as the flight from oneself always presupposes itself. Such a flight can only be compared to a desperate pursuit of one's own shadow, which must culminate in weariness and tears. It will be noted, however, that the self, in order to cast its shadow, must have turned away from the Light. Thus, as the world turns, or as the self runs, the shadow lengthens, until at last the self pursues itself in infinite opaqueness. This is the condition of sin: man's dehumanization and despiritualization of himself. It is an act, a continuing act, a choice persisted in. To choose oneself absolutely, on the other hand, is to choose oneself totally, as a person; and it is to relate oneself totally to the absolute. But to the Christian this absolute is God—God considered as a Person. I relate myself to him, therefore, as person to Person. This supposes that I may come to know God in so far as God has chosen to make himself known, and this I do through believing that what God has told me of himself is true. There must be a place of meeting which is neither in him nor in me yet is at the same time in both of us together—that is, between us. Such a place of meeting is in the relationship, and the Truth is in the relationship. In the beginning was the Word, and the Word was the medium of the relationship.

The journey to the self, therefore, is decisive. "Thou lonesome one, thou goest the way to thyself! . . . Ready must thou be to burn thyself in thine own flame!" [1] The journey, that is, is pur-

---

[1] Nietzsche, *Thus Spake Zarathustra*, Pt. I, discourse xvii.

gative. It results in the infinite, solitary act of sinning in which the self consumes itself in its own flame; or it eventuates in an eternal fellowship with God in which God's fires burn brightly in the soul but it is not consumed. "Thou hast made us for thyself, O God; and our souls are restless until they find their rest in thee!"

Thus, as the ancients said of honey, the journey to the self is sweet to some and bitter to others.

i

We have seen above [2] how the notion of the self is presupposed in all human activity, whether speculative or active. The speculative *Cogito, ergo sum* of Descartes inverts itself when scrutinized and, as Augustine knew, is at bottom a tautology: it should read, *Sum, ergo cogito*. But Augustine saw further: he saw that the speculative doubt concludes to or presupposes an initial self-grasp—a consciousness of self as existing, living, thinking. In this initial self-grasp we discern the central clue to the understanding of the nature of the self. It consists in this initial capacity for self-transcendence.

To be sure, the self has not always been understood in this way. Our recent omnivorous passion for scientific objectivity has led us to pursue this self-transcendence at the terminal intersections of neurons and dendrons! But as Borden Parker Bowne, the first of American personalists, observed:

Personality can never be construed as a product or compound; it can only be experienced as a fact. It must be possible because it is given as actual. Whenever we attempt to go behind this fact we are trying to explain the explanation. We explain the objects before the mirror by the images which seem to exist behind it. *There is nothing behind the mirror.* . . . This self-conscious existence is the truly ultimate fact.[3]

There is a passage in Hume which Bowne employed to illustrate this tendency of the self to overlook itself as its own presupposition whenever it turns inward to examine itself. Hume

[2] Pp. 76-78.
[3] *Personalism* (Boston: Houghton Mifflin Co., 1908), pp. 264-65.

used the personal pronoun persistently in a passage which aims to question the fact of personal identity given in experience:

> For *my* part, when *I* enter most intimately into what *I* call *myself*, *I* always stumble on some particular perception or other, of heat or cold, light or shade, love or hatred, pain or pleasure. *I* never can catch *myself* at any time without a perception, and never can observe any thing but the perception. . . . If any one upon serious and unprejudic'd reflexion, thinks he has a different notion of *himself*, *I* must confess *I* can reason no longer with *him*. All *I* can allow *him* is, that *he* may be in the right as well as *I*, and that *we* are essentially different in this particular. *He* may perhaps, perceive something simple and continu'd, which *he* calls *himself*; tho' *I* am certain there is no such principle in *me*.[4]

Throughout the passage the assumptions of the language are perpetually reinstating what the theory denies.

Hume confessed his confusion on this point in an Appendix, in which he wrote that "upon a more strict review of the section concerning *personal identity*, I find myself involved in such a labyrinth, that, I must confess, I neither know how to correct my former opinions, nor how to render them consistent."[5] The whole effort is contradictory; for, in the very effort to scrutinize itself by objectifying itself as the sum total of its isolated perceptions, the self makes itself its own object—it looks away from itself. But this is precisely a witness to the soul's capacity for self-transcendence: it transcends itself in the very act of making itself its own object.

There is a sense in which this same perplexity enters into our attempts to construe the self in terms of reason, conscience, memory, freedom, and the like. Maine de Biran, who is sometimes regarded as the first philosophical personalist,[6] sought to define the word "person" as

an intelligent being which by the interior feeling [consciousness] of itself, a consciousness which is inseparable from thought, reflects, reasons, and considers itself as being the same in different times and places; it is in the

---

[4] *The Treatise of Human Nature*, Pt. IV, sec. 6 ("Of Personal Identity"). Italics are mine.

[5] *Ibid.*, Appendix.

[6] Cf. Berdyaev, *Solitude and Society*, p. 168, n.

conscience or the interior consciousness [*le sentiment interieur*] that the *I* resides, and it is precisely this consciousness which constitutes personal identity.[7]

This is serviceable, but it is not final. While it is customary to speak of the self in terms of reason, conscience, memory, and primal freedom; or to regard it as a self-conscious center of experience, or as that which distinguishes itself from all below itself by virtue of its capacity for rational choice, these several definitions, taken together, do not exhaust the feeling for itself as *self* which Maine de Biran has sought to define. To say that man is a "focal mirror of all *known* reality"[8] does not satisfy man's self-consciousness; for even this description, when examined, terminates in an absurd redundancy. We shall do well to say simply, with Bowne, that the self is *given,* or, with Berdyaev: "The Ego is primitive; it can be neither deduced from nor reduced to anything."[9]

Berdyaev means by this precisely what was suggested in the beginning: that although the self is incomprehensible apart from the reason, it is not, on the other hand, reducible to the reason in any aspect of its discursive activity. "It is not true to say, 'I think, therefore I am'; but rather, 'I am surrounded on all sides by impenetrable infinity."[10] The self is a synthesis of the finite and the infinite.

This, however, is not satisfactory either, for we must be infinitely cautious in our use of this term "infinite." Religion (which is the only point of view from which the quality of self-transcendence can, in the last analysis, be understood) has more than once been dissolved into the infinite—into a kind of galvanic aesthetics, a romantic exaltation of longing, "the primary position from which the whole view of life must be developed," as Friedrich Schlegel held.[11] The moment this happens the soul has merely made an object of its own *capacity* for self-transcendence, and so

---

[7] *Oeuvres de Maine de Biran* (ed. Pierre Tisserand; Paris: Felix Alcan), I, pp. 237-38.
[8] E. I. Watkin, *Men and Tendencies* (London: Sheed & Ward, 1937), p. 146.
[9] *Op. cit.,* p. 87.
[10] *Ibid.*
[11] *The Philosophy of Life,* p. 430.

commits itself transcendently to an infinite intensification of its own emptiness—its longing to be filled. This "bedazzlement with the infinite," as Amiel described it, is a snare and a delusion. "The *Henosis* of Plotinus," as he says again, "intoxicates me like a philtre" until extinction overtakes him—until "the coloured air-bubble has burst in the infinite space, and the misery of thought has sunk to rest in the changeless repose of all-embracing Nothing." [12] This always occurs—as in Romanticism, Plotinus, the concept of nirvana, the atman's dissolution in the Atman, the mystic's absorption in the "Divine"—whenever the self tries to relate itself to the ultimate by way of hypostatizing its own capacity for self-transcendence. These aberrations are instructive, however, and bear witness all the same to the capacity for self-transcendence; for, once the aberration is detected, we discover at least that it is possible for the self so to transcend itself as to know that the infinite projection of itself is not God. Which brings us back again to our starting point—to the point, namely, of the self as *given,* and to the fact that there is in this given an element that is unfathomable. This is the distinguishing mark of man.

ii

Augustine, whose researches into this reflexive conundrum posed in experience by the self to itself and whose meditations mark the watershed between the Neo-Platonic and the Christian views of man, approaches this problem by a self-imposed maieutic, cross-questioning himself Socratically from the outer to the inner world:

"And what is this?" I asked the earth; and it answered, "I am not He."
... I asked the sea and the deeps, and the creeping things that lived, and they replied, "We are not thy God, seek higher than we." ... I asked the heavens, the sun, moon, and stars: "Neither," say they, "are we the God whom thou seekest." And I answered unto all these things which stand about the door of my flesh, "Ye have told me concerning my God, that ye are not He; tell me something about Him." And with a loud voice they

[12] Cf. Matthew Arnold, *Essays: Second Series* (London: Macmillan & Co., 1888), pp. 310-11.

exclaimed, "He made us." My questioning was my observing of them; and their beauty was their reply. And I directed my thoughts to myself, and said, "Who art thou?" [13]

A striking parallel to this turning inward to the soul is afforded by the Forest Philosophers of India:

"Yajnavalkya," said Janaka, "what is the light of man?"

"The sun, O King," he replied; "for by the light of the sun he sits and moves about, does his work and returns."

"But when the sun has set, O Yajnavalkya, what is then the light of man?"

"The moon is then his light; for by the light of the moon he sits and moves about, does his work and returns."

"But, O Yajnavalkya, when the sun has set, and the moon has set, what is the light of man?"

"Fire is then his light. . . ."

"But, O Yajnavalkya, when the sun has set, and the moon has set, and the fire has gone out, what is then the light of man?"

"Speech is then his light . . . when one cannot see one's own hand, yet when a voice is heard, one goes towards it."

"But, O Yajnavalkya, when the sun has set, and the moon has set, and the fire has gone out, and no speech is heard, what is then the light of man?"

"The Self (Atman) is then his light; for by the light of Self he sits and moves about, does his work and returns."

"What is this Self?" [14]

That is the pivotal question. With the Forest Philosopher we have reached already the end of the quest; for he identifies the self with the infinite he gropes after: the Brahma and the atman are identified. But for Augustine the problem of the self has just begun. "I directed my thoughts to myself, and said, 'Who are thou?' And I answered, 'A man.' And lo, in me there appear both body and soul, the one without, the other within." [15]

Nevertheless, God was not to be found either in the body or in the soul, nor yet by the powers of mind or memory. "Great

[13] *Confessions* X. vi. 9.
[14] P. E. More, *Shelburne Essays, Sixth Series*, p. 30.
[15] *Loc. cit.*

is this power of memory, . . . O my God. . . . Who has plumbed the depths thereof? Yet it is a power of mine, and appertains unto my nature; nor do I myself grasp all that I am. Therefore is the mind too narrow to contain itself." [16] Augustine here fixed upon the vertical dimension of the soul, the capacity for self-transcendence whereby it is unfathomable in height and depth and by virtue of which it may relate itself to the eternal. "Of what nature am I? . . . Whatsoever is in the memory is also in the mind: through all these do I run to and fro, and fly; I dive on this side and that, as far as I am able, and nowhere is there an end." [17]

Now this stage of Augustine's thinking is doubtless reminiscent of the passage cited above [18] from Heraclitus: "Go hence; the limits of the soul thou canst not discover, though thou shouldst traverse every way; so profoundly is it rooted in the Logos." The resemblance is marked by the discovery in each of the soul's capacity for self-transcendence. But Heraclitus goes a step beyond Augustine, at this point: he roots the soul in the Logos. That is, he says something about this quality of self-transcendence that Augustine has not said. Yet it is also clear that precisely at this point something must be said. For the self cannot be grounded in its own transparency.

This is the point at which all thinkers who advance this far attempt to throw some kind of bridge betwixt themselves and the Absolute; and so religious philosophy is filled with "upward and downward ways" (Heraclitus), with flights of "the alone to the Alone" (Plotinus), and with "heavenly ladders" (Dionysius the Areopagite, and a thousand years of mysticism thereafter). But in these approaches we detect a kind of egoistic self-assertion, which attests, it is true, to the soul's need to ground itself in the Power that created it, but which indicates, on the other hand, its tendency to find that Power somehow in itself and so effect its own salvation. "Ye shall be as gods"—this was the temptation which, in the biblical account, led to man's first fall. In reality, it

[16] *Confess.* X. viii. 15.
[17] *Ibid.* X. xvii. 26.
[18] See p. 213.

is an endeavor of the self to ground itself in its own transparency —in its transcendent *capacity,* that is, apart from the positive content of God's love (ἀγάπη). All such attempts omit the strictures of our finitude, of creaturehood. They are all comparable, in some respect, to Nietzsche's eagerness to see himself beneath himself (which also attests to self-transcendence), but through the brain-bursting device of mounting upon one's own head!

There is a tendency of this kind in Augustine, as we should expect, indeed, from his neo-platonic background. He aspires to pass beyond his memory even, in order that he may proceed to God.[19] It is only in his later work, as he considers more deeply the problem of sin, that he sees the problem of self-transcendence and of God's transcendence in a more realistic fashion.

Let us not, however, press matters too rapidly lest we should appear overzealous, like the inquisitive woman whom Yajnavalkya was obliged to reprimand: "Do not ask too much, or your head will burst!" We must clarify the nature of this self-transcendence before we can speculate upon its good or evil uses. For, indeed, unless we do this, even the fact of self-transcendence is no guarantee against bursting one's head.

We can clarify its nature in three steps like the hop, skip, and jump of the child's play. For the steps are in a straight line, though they are not of the same kind, and all attempts of finite man to plumb the infinite are in some sense child's play.

The hop consists simply in the affirmation of self-transcendence as the primary mark of man: "Man alone," as Scheler says, "so far as he is a person, is able to soar above himself as a living organism [*Lebewesen*], and, from a center beyond the world of time and space, as it were, make everything—himself included—the object of his knowledge." [20] For Scheler, this transcendent capacity is already apparent in man's ability to distinguish between existence and nature. Irony and humor attest to it. Man is, as Bergson says, the creature that laughs. Irony, humor, laughter, always imply a perspective above one's own existence. Augustine obviously

---

[19] *Loc. cit.*
[20] *Die Stellung des Menschen im Kosmos,* p. 57.

had this "center" of transcendence in mind when he argued that when it is said to the mind, Know thyself, then the self knows itself by the very act whereby it understands the command to know itself—"and this for no other reason than that it is present to itself." [21] Moreover, there is always a gulf between this transcendent center and the objects of its knowledge. Augustine argued that the self is so constructed as to reflect the Holy Trinity; and the image of God is to be found in this total unity of whole mind—in the one mind "nowhere parted off"—and not in the activity of the discursive reason acting upon temporal objects, whereby the self is diverted from reflecting the Holy Trinity.[22]

Immanuel Kant, in his *Critique of Pure Reason,* referred to this primary self-transcendence as "the transcendental unity of apperception"—and thus baptized with formidable technological skill the fact that the self is an initial existential datum, and as such is prior to its consideration of other objects or to its consideration of itself as an object. It is, said he, "a condition which precedes all experience, and in fact renders it possible." [23]

The second step follows—the move, that is, from the hop to the skip. A hop is a kind of one-legged thinking, as by a determined effort to move by concepts in the abstract, just as it is a one-legged walking; whereas a skip begins in a hop but culminates positively by coming down on the other foot. Thus, beginning with the abstract affirmation of the fact of self-transcendence, we are now in a position to conclude this hop positively by defining this precondition to all experience as *spirit*.

Scheler, for example, following up his description of this "center" from which the person surveys the world, himself included, goes on to say that such a center, which seems to lie above man in the act of perception, and through which he is able to objectify his world, his own life, and his own "psyche," cannot itself be regarded as a "part" of the natural world. It cannot be assigned any particular place or time. It can only be situated in the highest possible ground of existence. This ground

---

[21] *De trin*. X. ix. 12.
[22] *Ibid*. XII. iv.
[23] "Transcendental Analytic," Bk. I, chap. ii; sec. 2, III.

is spirit; for spirit *("Geist")* is the only being which is incapable of being objectified.[24] The spirit, that is, is that part of the soul which objectifies all other things and orders them. It is by virtue of the spirit, then, that we become *persons*.

Man is a person, therefore, in so far as he has spirit, and in so far as he founds himself upon spirit. Spirit is the source of self-determination, of his relative autonomy in the finite world, of his *free* intelligence, of his essentially creative capacities. The category of the spirit is the distinctively Christian category.

Irenaeus phrased it simply. The perfect man, said he,

consists of these three, flesh, soul, and spirit. One of these saves and fashions—that is, the Spirit. Another is united and formed—that is, the flesh; while that which lies between the two is the soul, which sometimes follows the Spirit and is raised by it, but at other times sympathizes with the flesh and is drawn by it into earthly passions.[25]

Augustine also regarded man as a complex of body, soul, and spirit. The medieval notion of the soul, however, intercepts the understanding of man as primarily spirit with the Aristotelian notion of man as a rational substance. Boethius' definition of a person, so heartily approved throughout the medieval period [26] commits this despiritualization of the person: *"Persona est naturae rationalis individua substantia"*—"an individual substance of a rational nature." This divinizes the self, on the one hand, by virtue of reason; for reason as such, in this definition, cannot be perverted by an act in view of that which it already is by its nature. This precludes the Christian idea of sin. The notion of the self, moreover, is naturalistic and abstract. What is needed, as Bowne held, is the notion of the person as agent, not substance, if we are to understand the self personally and dynamically. It is for this reason that the medieval philosophy is intellectualist rather than personalist and precludes the development of a truly Christian personalist philosophy.[27]

---

[24] *Op. cit.,* p. 58 *passim.*

[25] *Adversus Haereses* V. ix. 1.

[26] Cf. Gilson, *The Spirit of Medieval Philosophy* (tr. A. H. C. Downes; New York: Charles Scribner's Sons, 1936), p. 201.

[27] Cf., e.g., Gilson's grounding of freedom in rationality, rather than rationality in

Christian personalism, grounded in spirit, reappears with the Renaissance and the Reformation, in Paracelsus, Pico della Mirandola, Sir Thomas More, Erasmus, Colet, and Luther. Erasmus, noting the self-transcendence of the spirit, says, "The spirit makes us gods; the flesh makes us beasts; the soul makes us men."[28] This view is humanist, and personalist, in the sense already noted; but it is Luther who gives to this view its full Christian accent and the point of view whereby the self as spirit reaches its true grounding. "The first part, the spirit, is the highest, the deepest, the noblest part of man, by which he is enabled to grasp incomprehensible, invisible and eternal things; and this is indeed the house in which there dwells faith and the Word of God."[29]

Here, however, we are thrust upon the third point, which is indeed a jump from the self considered formally as grounded in the spirit of the self regarded as a living, dynamic subject by virtue of its grounding in the spirit. For the self is itself an act. It is constantly and perpetually an act and in act. For man is man and not God. He is the created. He is, despite his capacity for self-transcendence, a finite creature. It is by virtue of his capacity for self-transcendence that he is the creature who may and must relate himself to that which is beyond himself.

Heidegger rightly defines the emphasis of the Christian understanding of man as comprised in the "idea of transcendence," implying that there is something in man which reaches beyond itself and by virtue of which he cannot be understood simply as a rational animal.[30] This need is universal. Man's reach beyond

---

spirit, which is also and at the same time the root of man's freedom. (*Ibid.*, p. 202.) Cf. also the conclusion to Gilson's otherwise admirable address on *Medieval Universalism and its Present Value* (Sheed & Ward, 1937), in which the person is constituted by the intellect instead of spirit, which is itself the root of free intelligence; and in which Gilson offers the formula "rationalism, realism, personalism" as the order of philosophical understanding. This supposes the priority of the rational over the personal, and gives the case away. Medieval spirituality is caught in this dilemma, which it inherits from Greek rationalism by way of Aristotle chiefly, and which culminates in a static understanding of the human situation and in a static philosophy and culture. Note also Brunner's protest against Boethius' definition (*Man in Revolt*, p. 551), in which he notes that evil on this basis is not personal but metaphysical.

[28] *Enchiridion*, v. 20-D.
[29] WA, vol. 8, p. 550.
[30] *Sein und Zeit*, p. 49.

himself is not confined to Christianity. "If there were gods," said
Nietzsche, with characteristic bravado of spirit, "how could I bear
not to be one." Whether gods or no, man for Nietzsche remained
the creature who must surpass himself. To be a person is to be a
total act, but it is to be an act with reference to an end beyond
ourselves. Man must choose his total end, and he must choose it
absolutely. This is a mystery which can be understood only from
the standpoint of Christian personalist philosophy, though it may
be observed universally. God *is* spirit; man *has* spirit, as Brunner
says. Which means that God constitutes man. Man does not con-
stitute himself. The spirit in man, therefore, is that transcendent
capacity whereby man, grasping himself totally in an act of decisive commitment, may relate himself to the Power that created
him. He may relate himself to God as person to Person. His failure
to do this commits him to the endless, futile attempt to relate himself to that which is not God, whereby his life is "bound in shal-
lows and in miseries." We must explore these possibilities a little.

iii

First of all, a man, by virtue of the spirit, may choose himself
in such a way as to relate himself to something outside himself,
but to something that is itself impersonal. In such a case the conditioning of existence is easily evident. He gradually depersonalizes himself, and loses himself in the object. He becomes like
Midas, who related himself so successfully to an object outside
himself that he turned to gold.

It is possible, however, to relate oneself to an object outside
oneself which has neither tangibility nor substance but is purely
a figment of the mind, a fantasy. This is, to be sure, an imaginative projection; but it is an objectification all the same. This is a
projection of make-believe, of Arabian Nights fantasies, of utopian
politics, of mystical Edens overlooking the sword which whirls
in every way to prevent so simple a return to ideality. Such men
are like the knight of the fairy tale of which Kierkegaard speaks,
who, perceiving a rare bird, supposed it to be an enchanted prin-
cess; so he ran after it, almost coming up to it, when it would sud-

denly fly off again, until finally, when night fell, he found himself in a deep wood, where he was lost and alone.[31]

There is a third possibility. Many men who are able to see
through these duperies of the tangible and the fanciful do not see
through the self's attempt to ground itself upon its own self objectively. Its interest in other persons is only interest in itself. It
seeks itself in all relationships and loves only whatever reflects itself back to itself. Like Narcissus, it loves its own reflection in the
pool of worldly circumstance. This narcissism has a multitude of
forms—forms which range from modern poetry to medieval flag-
ellation.[32]

Very much akin to this is the soul's attempt to ground itself
upon itself subjectively, save that here the self may choose to
ground itself upon its own capacity for relatedness, upon its own
transparency of spirit, thus attempting to ground itself upon its
power to relate itself! By this act it projects itself in a regression
which finds no end. Like a man between two mirrors, whose
image is reflected back and forth between the mirrors infinitely,
the soul pursues its own reflection into the infinite. It sees its image, and behind this image another image, and always a further
image beyond the last one, in infinite reduplication of itself; so
that to relate oneself to oneself subjectively is to suffer the progressive (retrogressive) loss of oneself through the infinite pursuit of
one's own power to relate oneself. This also is a "longing for the
infinite."

A prevalent form of this pursuit is the attempt of political ideal-

[31] I have borrowed this little parable from Kierkegaard, who has explored this
ground painstakingly. (Cf. *The Sickness Unto Death*, pp. 57 f.) It is perhaps not too much
to say that all these prophetic thinkers who have given thought to this problem—Jaspers,
Heidegger, Scheler, Berdyaev, Brunner, Niebuhr and others—have been influenced either
directly or indirectly by Kierkegaard. Augustine was not without insight into those areas,
and the New Testament is best of all; for does it not tell of a man who excelled in building barns—who pursued, that is, the phantom security of possessions—and whose
soul was required of him?

[32] Cf. Charlotte Wilder's *Phases of the Moon*: "I am the marble unappeased
undemonstrative statue of loneliness . . . and while I inflect my head with sympathetic
attention . . . feel vanity and pride in the hollow I face . . . without features,
without bulk; the terrible Narcissism of emotion, that—flung out into a place where
nothing reflects it—returns to itself, in self-passionate pity, and is secret." Its secret is
despair.

ists and social reformers to ground the self on an abstract idea, such as the idea of "Society" or of "Humanity." To relate oneself to humanity is laudable; but to relate oneself to Humanity is impossible. For it is an attempt to relate oneself to that which does not exist. It is difficult even to relate ourselves to humanity in the personal sense, outside of the antecedent relationship of God. For we thus attempt to ground ourselves on one another: which is to say, we ground ourselves on the universal necessity of all men to ground themselves. To ground ourselves on other people's needs to ground themselves is not to ground ourselves. It is to make a nuisance of ourselves.

But suppose a man chooses not to relate himself? What then? Why, then, he ceases to be a person. And the difficulty is not simply that he becomes, as Aristotle says, a vegetable. For he relates himself all the same—to the world as object. Only he relates himself passively, so as to be swept along by it; and he is, as a matter of fact, swept along by the "stream of history" or the "stream of consciousness" and catapulted over the cataract of time.

The attempt of the ego to ground itself on some other ego is far more desirable than any other relationship—if the other ego be significant enough. Isaiah related himself to himself by way of Uzziah, till that great king was smitten with leprosy and died. Isaiah was released from his illusion and sought to ground himself in God, in a Person of eternal significance—in the absolute Spirit. This was the proper turning; and it is the only turning by which the self can relate itself to itself without suffering the loss of itself.

That is, the total act whereby the self relates itself to Reality can have no other content than the love of God. Outside the love of God there is no true life in the spirit, no true personality, no true humanism, no true knowledge of the self as *self*. For God, as Spirit, is precisely that light whereby, when the soul chooses it by a total act, the "love of God is shed abroad in our hearts by the Holy Ghost;" [33] and, apart from that light, a man pursues the shadow which his soul casts. And since his soul is turned

[33] Rom. 5:5.

245

away from the true source of his being, his shadow lengthens as he follows after it, until the soul pursues itself in infinite opaqueness.

But this, as we have said, is the condition of sin. It is the delusion of self-sufficiency willfully persisted in. At the end of every infinite flight the soul becomes the Godforsaken. What has really happened is that it has forsaken God. And for such a soul there is no hope, for the deluded soul pursues with all its powers its own delusion—

> Only
> The fool fixed in his folly, may think
> He can turn the wheel on which he turns.[34]

There is no hope for it—unless its infinite delusion is shattered dialectically upon the ultimate ontology of things. This is the ontology of experience and history, impersonal and tragic, which out of all illusion and delusion precipitates despair. This is the negating eschatology of finite fact frustrating infinite delusion. It is not redemptive: in it are not found the issues of eternal life. It only ironizes at the expense of finite self-sufficiency. There is no hope for the soul caught in infinite delusion—unless beyond the eschatology of finite fact there is an eschatology of eternal hope, a point where at the end of every infinite opaqueness a shaft arises into eternal light.

The Cross of Christ is such a shaft. The crucifixion of the Son of God remains, from man's side, a deed of infinite opaqueness; but from God's side it is a shaft of eternal victory whereby the infinite (*die schlechte Unendlichkeit!*) is bent back upon the eternal. The Cross is personal; and it is historical. By it a man may found himself upon another person, upon a person in history who is nevertheless a Person of eternal significance. This relationship can be established through faith alone, for faith is the release from self-sufficiency. Faith *is* the victory. By it the autonomy of autarky is broken and the autonomy of spirit is renewed. By it we cease being individuals—the impersonal automatons of social inter-

---

[34] T. S. Eliot, *Murder in the Cathedral* (New York: Harcourt, Brace & Co., 1935), p. 24.

course, the Robinson Crusoes isolated in our little islands of flesh. We become persons, having fellowship with God and capable of fellowship with one another. By faith we ground ourselves transparently upon the Power that created us. Through ceasing to pursue ourselves in self-sufficiency we find ourselves in the spirit. We come to understand the paradox of faith whereby he who finds his life shall lose it and he who loses his life shall find it.

iv

It will be seen readily that certain corollaries follow—the first concerning man, the second concerning God.

Concerning man it will be seen that the true paradox of man is that he is "the little creature who is for ever seeking himself, and therefore also fleeing from himself; one who is for ever being drawn and attracted by something higher, and yet is ever seeking to release himself from this higher element; the creature who is both aware of his contradiction and yet at the same time denies it." [35]

By this it is not implied simply that man is a "split" personality, in the usual psychological sense, and that the "conflicts" in his personality are to be overcome through "adjustment" to his local environment. In this instance such diagnoses are of no value until they are pushed backward to include man's total environment. The understanding of man must be grounded both ontologically and dialectically in the spirit as the spirit stands related to God. The great merit of Kierkegaard is at this point, and the true secret of his present vogue resides in the fact that his study of man's condition in sin is "severely ontological" (von Hügel). It is also entirely dialectical.

The words of Brunner are also reminiscent of Pascal. "Description of man: dependency, desire of independence, need." [36] "Condition of man: inconstancy, weariness, unrest." [37] "It is in vain, O men, that you seek within yourselves the remedy for your ills. All your light can only reach the knowledge that not in yourselves

[35] Brunner, *Man in Revolt*, pp. 24-25.
[36] *Pensées*, 126.
[37] *Ibid.*, 127.

will you find truth or good." [38] We find our truth in God. Therefore the self was, to Pascal, "hateful;" and because the self was to him hateful, he was called the "sublime misanthropist." Such a judgment, however, is shortsighted. It sees merely that Pascal saw the "misery of man." What Pascal really saw was the "misery of man *without God*." Also, over and above this misery of man without God, Pascal saw man's true greatness. And in what did this greatness consist? In man's capacity to dilate horizontally upon the geometric reason of the Enlightenment? No. It consisted in the fact that man could know his misery. In short, Pascal affirmed in man that basic capacity antecedent to all self-affirmations, his capacity for self-transcendence. Did not Emerson say precisely the same thing? "Man may be base," said he, "but how does he know that he is base?" Yet Emerson has been called an optimist, because he offers us eternity upon our own terms instead of on God's terms—the spurious eternity of transcendentality instead of eternal communion with God through God's Word.

This distinction will be clearer if we consider that man, according to this understanding, is not a static somewhat to be comprehended formally—as intellect, feeling, will, and so forth—but that he must be understood dialectically, as a creature *in motion,* as already in course of action. He is a viator, a creature who must a way. He is, as Nietzsche says, "an arrow of longing," a "rope stretched over an abyss." He is like Karl Barth's Alpine climber who balances precariously upon an arête, and who must move forward in order to maintain his balance.

> . . . perched upon the sharp arête,
> When if we do not move we fall,
> Yet movement is heretical,
> Since over its ironic rocks
> No route is truly orthodox.[39]

Thus, essentially, his motion is toward God or away from God. But a motion from God is comparable to a fall from life in the spirit. It is a plunge into the infinite opaqueness.

[38] *Ibid.,* 430.
[39] W. H. Auden, *The Double Man* (New York: Random House, 1941), p. 47.

It is true formally, and structurally, that man may live his life on one of three levels: on the sub-human, the human, or the divine —below the level of the regulative control of reason, or within the regulative control of reason conditioned by existence, or under the regulative control of God's will. These levels of experience are conceived formally; but they are lived dialectically. Each level, when chosen, is a commitment to a total end. Each level has both dialectical and teleological implications. It is therefore possible to speak of the "dialectic of life" with philosophical consistency. The concrete results of such choices are observable, and subject to classification. For Pascal these levels are levels of the body, of the mind, and of charity. For Kierkegaard they become "spheres of existence"—"stages" on life's *way*. For Pascal the lower levels are "rivers of fire" which enflame rather than water, in which the lives of men are governed by the lust of the senses, the lust for power, or the lust for knowledge.[40] Men burn themselves in their own flame. For Kierkegaard they issue in despair, in irony, or in the tragicomic. For Pascal life on each level has its reward! but it is only on the third level, the life in the spirit, that we learn to see with the "eyes of the heart," which alone perceive wisdom.[41] For Pascal this was "wisdom"; for Voltaire this was "rigmarole."

Brunner has observed that ancient wisdom, founded upon the common-sense recognition of the discrete levels of existence, was naïve; it fell an easy prey to isms—realism, idealism, pantheism— which distort it through making some one element of human nature the principle for the interpretation of the whole life. "There seems to be only one exception to this rule. Where the poetic naïveté of this view of human nature has been combined with the Christian faith, there has arisen—for instance, in Pascal, Kierkegaard, Dostoevski, Gotthelf—a penetrating view of man which has no rival." [42] This is undoubtedly true, and highly significant. It seems to me that Brunner fails to follow up his insight. For all these views are based upon a Christian Socratism and imply that all self-knowledge is conditioned by existence in such a way that,

---

[40] *Pensées*, 458.
[41] *Ibid.*, 792.
[42] *Op. cit.*, p. 47.

followed through, it thrusts the inner self upon the Cross of Christ.

Turn the cylinder a little to obtain a clearer focus on these three existence levels, and it will become clear that, at bottom, there are two, not three. As between man and man, the three existence levels obtain; and, through the regulative power of the free intelligence, they make of history a sphere of decision and a realm of ends concretely modified by conduct. But as between man and God, there is existence in the spirit and subsistence apart from the spirit. But this subsistence is a fall, a plunge into the infinite opaqueness—a plunge which is supported, so to speak, by Spirit from behind. It is the plunge into Pascal's "abyss." This was why the infinite spaces frightened him. For he knew that the sense which most men have of feeling secure by virtue of the fact that they are standing on solid ground, was an illusion. Spiritually, we do not stand on solid ground. There is an infinite abyss beneath our feet. We are supported by nothing—save the hand of God. Yet God respects our "freedom." He leaves it up to us to take his hand or not. But men prefer, as Newman says, themselves and "the 'certainties' of time" to God and the "chance of eternity."

The world has contrived three ways of avoiding this issue. One is the device of divertisement (*divertissement*), whereby it prevents the self from considering its true condition by diverting it and preoccupying it, with amusement, work, travel, and the hundred other ingenuities in which we are adept.[43] Another is to call it "rigmarole" and foolishness. Another is to build a temple over it and house it in a shrine, to which we make our pilgrimage from time to time.

Such are the corollaries concerning man. Man is a viator, a traveler, one who must go a way. There is finally, then, "no human nature which is to be understood apart from man's relation

---

[43] *Divertissement* is Pascal's great category: "The struggle alone pleases us, not the victory. . . . We never seek things for themselves, but for the search." (*Pensées,* 135.) "Men spend their time in following a ball or a hare; it is the pleasure even of kings." (*Ibid.,* 141.) "The king is surrounded by persons whose only thought is to divert the king, and to prevent his thinking of self." "All the unhappiness of men arises from one single fact, that they cannot stay quietly in their own chamber." (*Ibid.,* 139.) Cf. Baudelaire: "It is necessary to work, if not by taste, at least by despair, since . . . to work is less boresome than to amuse oneself."

to God." [44] Man is what he is by virtue of his constitution in the spirit, which he has from God and which is the positive mark of his capacity for self-transcendence. This capacity is, therefore, a capacity for response to God's will. It possesses creative transparency when turned toward God in active, obedient responsiveness. When positively determined, therefore, it verifies Emerson's half-truth, that "we are here, not to work, but to be worked upon." The soul, so constituted in the spirit, knows the Psalmist's joy: "My cup runneth over." Negatively determined, the soul can know no such joy, for it is emptied of the influences of the Spirit. It is a cup inverted, containing nothing. Its transparency to spirit is forfeit, and opaqueness covers it. Man does not lose his constitution. By virtue of his capacity of self-transcendence he sets himself in opposition to his constitution. This is an act. It is a rejection. It is "original" in the sense that by virtue of this initial turning all man's acts become perverted, he suffers the loss of himself, and he no longer retains the wisdom of a true self-knowledge. His faculties are not impaired, but they participate in the turning and are carried along by it. They suffer the fundamental distortion of an alien will. Viewed psychologically, this condition is the "sickness unto death" (Kierkegaard); viewed ontologically, it is "existence unto death" (Heidegger); viewed religiously, it is sin, for which we are responsible.

v

Concerning God two things must be noted. First—as we have said already—God is Spirit, man has spirit. God is a Person whose personhood does not depend upon another; God is not grounded on anything except himself. But we are posited, created by him, and dependent on him. We are "human," he is God. We are relative to him, he is absolute—conditioned only by himself. We are finite, he is Infinite; by virtue of the self-transcendence of the spirit we have one window opening upon the infinite. By virtue of this open side we are "capable" of knowing God, of being related to him. But this capacity must not be understood as a power

[44] Brunner, op. cit., p. 111.

251

of ascent, whereby we climb into heaven; it is a power of response. We are capable of knowing God so far as God has chosen to make himself known to us. In brief, we understand God as that Person who stands "over against" us and who, in the very act of his communication of his Word to us, guarantees to us the discreteness of our personalities. This implies that, even in the moment of God's communication of himself, he remains what he is, and we remain what we are, and God is to be understood primarily in terms of the categories of personal relationship and not in the categories of metaphysical abstraction.

The second fact follows: God declares himself, "reveals" himself to us through his Word; and we apprehend him through our active response to his Word. This is clearly the truth that Heraclitus was feeling after. He saw that the self was firmly rooted in the Logos and that therefore we should not discover the limits of the self within ourselves. But the Greek Logos was never wholly personalized. It remained a metaphysical approach to God by way of the Idea divinized, or by way of Substance universalized. By virtue of the Idea immanent within us we could rise to the eternal Logos above us. Today this immanental hope persists in the hypostatization of "values," the "contemplation" of ideas, or of "essences," or even of "being." This is a hope which naïvely overlooks the prior alienation of our wills, supposing that the "reason" is existentially unimpaired by the decisions of the moral consciousness. It supposes that we can begin ideally from the beginning, before the passing through the Looking Glass. And, indeed, it can do all that metaphysics can do: it can conclude to the abstract God, the divinized Idea.[45] But religion bases apprehension upon the personal relationship, in which God remains the "Thou" in relation to the finite "I." Revelation is thus a communication of a highly personal kind.

Christian theologians have not always grasped this personal relationship in wholly personal terms. Hamann qualifies the Hera-

---

[45] Cf. Brunner: "It is of the essence of moral immanental thought that man possesses the power of judging for himself on the question of evil; thus man is both judge and accused criminal at the same moment. Hence it is impossible for him to believe in the seriousness of the breach between man and God." (*The Mediator* (tr. Olive Wyon; London: The Lutterworth Press, 1934), p. 210.)

clitean Logos but trespasses on the "otherness" of God in saying: "We see how necessarily our Self is rooted and grounded in Him who created it, so that the knowledge of our Self does not lie within our own power, but that in order to measure the extent of the same, we must press forward into the very heart of God Himself, who alone can determine and resolve the whole mystery of our nature." This is a penetrating utterance, and sound at all points save for the shadow of egoistic possessiveness which would press into the very heart of God himself. This is again ontologism, which is not permitted us. We must hear him in his Word, and are responsible for our response thereto.

Continental theology has been concerned in recent times with the metaphysical exploration of the terms of relatedness whereby God transcendently reveals himself. There is much discussion of the "I" and "Thou" and the "We" and the "It" and the way in which these planes of consciousness may intersect. Karl Heim in particular has done much to explore the "boundaries of content," the "dimensions" and "coexisting spaces" in which communication must consist. This is an intricate analogy devised after the pattern of the new physics with its "interpenetrating spaces" and "intensive manifolds" which overlap but still retain their own discrete identities. This analogy is useful and, apart from the special calculus of interpenetrating universes which none the less remain discrete, very simple. For it implies that in all personal relationships there is somewhat that is communicated and a somewhat that remains discrete. When "I" communicate with "You," the planes of our consciousness overlap at the point of the content of the symbol (the word) in so far as our understandings coincide. We "know" each other through this medium. Yet there is that in me which never is in you, and there is that in you which is over and above whatever I have understood of you. The planes of our consciousness both overlap and intersect yet remain discrete throughout. The same relationship exists between ourselves and God. God communicates his will to us, but God himself transcends infinitely the impartation of his will; He remains, that is, as we do, discretely other than the Word he speaks. The "place of meeting" between person and person, as between person and Person, remains the Word. Said Augustine:

> These words . . . are understood, and we understand. They are most manifest and most usual and the same things again lie hid too deeply, and the discovery of them is new.[46]
>
> Nor yet again as it is said, Know the will of that man: for this it is not within our reach to perceive at all, either by sense or understanding, unless by corporeal *signs* actually set forth; and this in such a way that *we rather believe than understand*.[47]

Appropriation, therefore, is a vital response, an act; and it is based upon belief and understanding, but an understanding which remains in a relationship of mutual otherness. Yet "all real living is a meeting," says Martin Buber, on whose work Karl Heim has obviously drawn, and God confronts us by his Word.[48]

But with reference to God, who has established us by virtue of the Spirit through his Word, the condition of this understanding is in belief that is also love. This love is not erotic love ($\check{\epsilon}\rho\omega\varsigma$). It is not desire of God which wishes to possess him. It is love which gives itself ($\dot{\alpha}\gamma\dot{\alpha}\pi\eta$) completely—a love that "seeketh not its own." For it aspires only to "know even as also it is known." [49] For it is known by the self-giving love of God, who by his Word creatively distinguished us, and established us as persons through calling us "by name." He "named us every one." Thus are we persons because God recognizes us—which fact we recognize through love. Christian personalism seeks to personalize truth at every point involving existential relationships. But man stands

---

[46] *Confess.* XI. xxii. 28.

[47] *De trin.* X. ix. 12.

[48] *I and Thou* (tr. R. G. Smith; Edinburgh: T. & T. Clark, 1941), p. 11.

[49] *Gnosis* puffeth up, but *agape* edifieth. (I Cor. 8:1.) Erotic love, in its longing to get beyond itself to the Divine, commits this gnostic presumption and remains within itself in spite of its "ascent." This contradiction Augustine saw when, in the Seventh Book of his *Confessions* he recognized the limitations of Neo-Platonism. Its results are described plainly in another passage (*In Joan. evang.* tract. ii. 4): "They [the philosophers] saw whither they must come; but ungrateful to Him who afforded them what they saw, they wished to ascribe to themselves what they saw; and having become proud, they lost what they saw, and were turned from it . . . to adore the creature and to despise the Creator." (Cf. Nygren, *Agape and Eros*, Part II, Vol. II, p. 252 ff., for a further discussion of this problem in Augustine.)

perpetually in existential relationship to God: he is the creature to whom God speaks.

God, we have said, is that Person who is also universal, and who, by virtue of his universality, must therefore validate our knowledge of him through our capacity for forming general concepts. But God is not an abstract generality. He is the Living Creator. He is to be understood, therefore, as Person rather than as Being. The Word of God is not the sign of the universal, but it resolves the difference between the personal and the abstract. It "breaks the barrier" between the personal and the impersonal. It brings the relationship out of the abstract and makes it actual through the concrete act of communication and response. By virtue of this act we become real—and, as such, persons.

There is, however, an apparent contradiction here. For we have said, on the one hand, that man is capable of response to God; on the other hand, we have held that man, by virtue of his previous response, is in the condition of sin—he clings, that is, to a spoke which turns in the wheel of time already rolling toward oblivion. This is true. Created by God with a capacity for free response in loving obedience to his Word, man's turning to himself is an act of "decisive significance," and an act for which he is somehow responsible. God is self-sufficient. Man is not. Self-sufficiency is the mark of God's divinity. But self-sufficiency is the mark of man's defection. It is the mark of the "fall," within which condition man can only fall forever deeper.

How, then, can man come to know his true condition? For if man is existentially within the precincts of his previous defiance, and if he is perverted through an alien will, how then can the endless flight into the infinite opaqueness be stayed? The answer is, It cannot be stayed unless the original relationship between God and man before the act of self-sufficiency can be restored, unless the true secret of our condition is made known to us. This adjustment cannot be effected by man upon his own account, for he is subject to his previous conditioning. It can only be effected by a Word which stands within our own condition and clarifies the height and depth of our defiance, yet a Word which both triumphs over it and has eternal significance. That

255

Word we find in Jesus Christ, who shows us to ourselves. He *is* that Word which is at one and the same time within us as our fall, historically, and above us through our faith, eternally. In Christ alone does man behold himself as he really is. Christ is therefore, the true Teacher; for not only does he show us to ourselves but he also is a Way—of restoration, of return, of victory.

Chapter IV

CHRISTIAN SOCRATISM

Heraclitus, before socrates, said "i have sought to know myself." [1] Socrates himself received the admonition "know thyself" from the oracle at Delphi. But Socrates was the first to make of self-knowledge a method and a teaching. Men of wisdom ever since have held that true self-knowledge is the clue to fullness of life.

Christian Socratism differs from Socratic self-knowledge in this respect: that whereas Socrates sought to know himself on his own terms and so discovered his ignorance, the Christian seeks to know himself by way of Jesus Christ and so discovers his "misery without God."

Guez de Balzac partially disclosed this difference; for in his *Socrate chrétien* (1652) he observed that this new Socrates has many traits in common with the old but that he has submitted his mind to the obedience of faith—which means that to the *"Je ne sais rien"* of Socrates is added the *"Je sais Jesus-Christ crucifié"* of the apostles, and through knowing this one thing he believes he may know all.

M. Étienne Gilson, the distinguished exponent of medieval philosophy, has recently revived this topic.[2] By virtue of this question we are brought to the very heart of the problem of Christian philosophy. Gilson notes, what is unquestionably true, that Balzac only hit upon the title of his book whereas it was actually Pascal who wrote it.

Certain it is that Pascal probed very deeply into the problem of a true self-knowledge as the Christian understands it. But then,

---

[1] Fr. 80 (Burnet).
[2] See *The Spirit of Medieval Philosophy*, chap. xi.

having come so far in his analysis of Christian Socratism, and quite as if he had not already said one of the most important things in all the world of criticism, M. Gilson, by a most extraordinary feat of transposition, accommodates the Socratism of Pascal to Cistercian mysticism. Gilson does this, quite as though Pascal had merely brought to light a discipline which medieval piety had understood quite well, and as though Pascal, in building possibly on St. Bernard and Nicholas of Cusa and Francis de Sales, had not made out of it all something new and altogether different. A meticulous critic might be tempted to observe that this accommodation is neither Socratic nor Christian. For on the one hand there is Socrates, who teaches us our ignorance; and on the other there is Christ, by knowing whom, as Pascal says, we come to know our misery. Then, suddenly, between the two is Gilson, thrusting the mystical ladder up whereby we climb to heaven, with Pascal and Socrates supporting it on either side!

This is very deft—to cover Pascal with the dust of St. Bernard and the Victorines, and thus persuade us that he looks like a medieval mystic—like Reynard when he fought with Isengrim the Wolf, whom he defeated easily by kicking such a dust into his eyes that Isengrim could never come to grips with his antagonist. Such a feat of transposition is as tactically adroit as was Eulenspiegel when sent up to the battlements to keep a lookout for the enemy: when the odor of the dishes from the great hall wafted up to him, he could not refrain from blowing on his trumpet, whereat the Count of Ambal and his knights rushed out in great alarm to battle, while Eulenspiegel descended to the great hall and ate his fill of all the victuals. Gilson blows the trumpet and draws us out to meet the problem; then, while we are searching, he substitutes himself for us and banquets on the mystic wisdom of the Victorines.

Nevertheless, Gilson is right in propounding the question of Christian Socratism as the primary question for Christian anthropology. This is all the more evident when the protective "culture" of man has been ruthlessly stripped away by the imperious demand of a culture crisis. Such a demand is at once historical and spiritual. Man must come to know himself. He must know himself "absolutely." He must know himself both inwardly and outwardly against the perspective of the ultimate meaning of things. He must know himself not merely as an object among other objects but as an immediate subject of experience occupying inwardly the precarious point of infinite commitment. This commitment, we have argued, is a decision in faith which is determinative for his total life. Everything depends on man's understanding of himself as he relates himself to the Absolute. But from the Christian standpoint the Absolute is God, and God is a Person. The relationship man seeks to establish through an understanding of himself absolutely is thus a personal relationship. Socratic self-knowledge, modified by the Christian understanding of the self as spirit, is the unique prerequisite to the desired relationship to God. Two questions thence arise: In what does this self-knowledge consist? and On what terms may the relationship to God be brought about?

i

Three classic answers to these questions have been given: (1) the Socratic answer, in which to know oneself is to know one's condition in ignorance, which ignorance is evil and is overcome through the inward act of *recollection* (ἀνάμνησις); (2) the mystical answer, in which to know oneself is to know one's condiiton as "privation," which condition is evil and is overcome through the inward act of *ascent* to oneness with God; (3) the Christian answer, in which to know oneself is to know one's condition in sin, which condition is evil and is overcome through the inward act of *repentance* and faith.

In these three views of the problem of self-knowledge we have three points of departure for self-recovery. Self-knowledge, in each case, reveals a need. From the classical standpoint, it would be ironical if it were not possible for the self to supply its own need out of its own resources. From the Christian standpoint, it would be just as ironical if, indeed, man *could* supply his own need from out of his own resources. From the mystical standpoint, either one unites oneself ecstatically with the Absolute and so possesses the Good, or he is simply deprived of it and no irony is possible—unless, indeed, the mystic were to trip into a well at the precise moment when he was ecstatically becoming uniate with the Divine in the All. But that, surely, would be to change one's standpoint?

The pathos of classical wisdom is subsumed in Diogenes—"a Socrates gone mad," as Plato called him. Diogenes went about in broad daylight carrying a lantern and saying that he was *looking for a man*. His light was the Socratic reason, ironically rarefied.

The pathos of Christian mysticism consists in its passage through the dark night of the soul to come upon the Light by way of ecstasy and the "inner light." Its light is the pure Eros—self-seeking deified. "It is I must be the sun, to give colour with my beams to . . . the Godhead entire." [3]

To the Christian, Christ is the light and the life and the truth and the way. He is the condition of our true self-knowledge. In him the Diogenic irony is transfigured. "Before one seeks for men, he must have found the Lantern." [4] Christ is the lantern by whose light men find themselves.

So much is involved, however, in these distinctions that we shall do well to hold them apart a little and consider them in order.

ii

Socratic self-knowledge begins with the wise admission that we do not know. This admission is laudable. Reason itself approves; for the admission is reasonable, and it gives the reason something to do! When the Delphic oracle pronounced Socrates the wisest of the Greeks, Socrates surpassed himself by saying that if this were true it must be because he knew that he did not know whereas others surmised that they possessed much certain knowledge. This consciousness of knowing nothing soon passed over, however, into a positive pursuit—the pursuit of knowledge of a certain kind. It became, that is, a method whereby Socrates, through "sifting men," brought them also to the knowledge that

[3] Angelus Silesius, quoted in Berdyaev (tr. G. Reavey; New York: Charles Scribner's Sons, 1939), p. 143.
[4] Nietzsche, "Modern Diogenes," *Human, All Too Human,* II, 7.

they did not know. This maieutic method dispossessed men of supposed fixed knowledge. Nevertheless, it did not stop here. By its second step it turned the mind away from those sense objects whereby its unity was "parted off" (Augustine) and turned it in upon itself. Men were thus delivered to themselves. In this fashion Socrates discovered, as we have seen, the self's divine constituent—the soul.

The "function" of the soul, however, was to know, to apprehend the true reality of things and to distinguish between the good and the evil. By virtue of this knowledge the soul could order life in the interests of the soul's "health," and so dispose itself toward virtue. From this it followed that no one erred or sinned willingly, for every man desires his own soul's health. We sin, therefore, through ignorance—an ignorance in which we stand through the outward pointing of the soul, whereby it suffers itself to be dominated by the things of sense and the objective world and to be drawn by them into the illusory reality of flux and finitude and evanescence. The soul, therefore, must be cross-questioned out of its ignorance and into itself, where, by virtue of a *recollection,* it will recall its divine origin and the true nature of things, and be virtuous.

Obviously, there is much involved in this. Aristotle credited Socrates [5] with the discovery of the inductive argument and the universal definition, in view of the fact that Socrates began with any commonplace of experience—a chair, a table—and reasoned to the general truth behind and beyond it. Plato grounded the Socratic method in the absolute ideas as the permanent, immutable essences which by recollection we can come to know. It is of these ultimate ideas that true knowledge must be said to consist; and, since both Truth and Goodness coincide in these, virtue may be said to be identical with knowledge. Thus, in overcoming ignorance we overcome evil, and the health of the soul is restored. This is a simple solution of a highly complicated matter.

The complication which the Socratic answer solves is brilliantly

[5] *Metaphysics* M. 1078b27.

stated by Plato in the *Meno*,[6] the question having been raised as to whether truth or virtue is something that can be learned. The difficulty is a "captious" one; for "it is impossible for a man to seek either what he does know, or what he does not know. For no one would seek what he knows, because he knows it already; and a man cannot seek for what he does not know, because he does not know what that is which he must seek." It is this "pugnacious proposition" that makes the Socratic solution such a brilliant one, for the soul is indeed in ignorance and must come to know the True. Socrates, presupposing the immortality of the soul, and supposing further that it must therefore have been born many times (and "cometh from afar . . . trailing clouds of glory"), held that the soul "should be able to call to remembrance all that she ever knew about virtue, . . . for all enquiry and all learning is but a recollection." [7]

From this it is clear that the "learner" possessed the truth already in his soul but that through "indolence" and wrong "opinion" he had fallen into error. The office of the "teacher," therefore is not an essential condition to his coming to know; the teacher is only the occasion by which the learner is delivered into himself. "Watch me," says Socrates, "if anywhere you can discover me teaching him or telling him anything, and not asking him rather his own opinions." For Socrates aims merely "to recover knowledge" for the learner himself, through himself, inasmuch as the teacher's function is merely to remind the learner of that which he possesses already. The movement of this teaching is thus self-contained. The "discovery" of truth is implied already in what the learner had known all along. Thus the truth does not come to the learner from without but is within him from the beginning. This became the starting point for the Platonic philosophy, whereby Plato, through identifying being with the forms, and through seeking to turn the "eye of the soul" from sense objects, the "shadows" of the Real, to the intuition of the One, the Real, sought to purge the soul of ignorance and evil and restore it to its proper health. This he could do by reason of the soul's perception of its

[6] *Meno* 80D.
[7] *Ibid.* 81.

262

own nature and by reason of the reason immanent within the universe, albeit Plato's forms remained in some sense transcendent to the world.

It is easy to see in this the latent rationalism of the Socratic quest, and one may easily object that Plato reduced the moral concern of Socrates to a metaphysical dualism which Socrates himself would not have sponsored. This development, however, is logically implicit in the rationalist identification of virtue with knowledge, which brings to the surface the hidden identification of the reason with the self and the corresponding tendency to view the Deity as Reason. One may tax this view, as Niebuhr does, with translating the moral paradox, "he that loseth his life . . . shall find it," into an ontological one;[8] for clearly the "redemptive" act with Plato is an act within our own powers and consists metaphysically in a turning from the "many" to the "One," from that which is always becoming and never is, to that which always is and never becomes. Nietzsche also complains of this rationalistic element when he sees in Socrates the "prototype of the theoretical optimist who with his belief in the explicability of the nature of things, attributes to knowledge and perception the power of a universal panacea, and in error sees evil in itself."[9]

The concluding clause contains the nub of the matter. For the identification of virtue and knowledge carries with it the converse identification of evil with ignorance. It is by no means clear that no man sins, or errs, willingly. Experience does not bear out the optimistic supposition that men would always do the virtuous thing if they were aware of all the consequences. Or, in Aristotle's plain words, "with all due respect to Socrates, his account of the matter is at variance with plain facts."[10]

These are brave words for a man who habitually lisped. There is, indeed, an internal logical lisp in Aristotle's challenge. For he scarcely improves on Socrates. He points out, none the less, that there are sins of incontinence, or lack of self-control, which con-

---

[8] *The Nature and Destiny of Man*, I, 77.

[9] *The Birth of Tragedy* (tr. Clifton P. Fadiman; New York: Modern Library, 1927), p. 267.

[10] *Eth. Nic.* VII. ii. 1145*b*.

tradict the Socratic understanding of the problem. By reason of incontinence (ἀκρασία), the ultimate principles become obscured, and the ensuing viciousness tends to destroy the moral principle.[11] And since "vice is destructive of the originative cause of action" it would appear that a man may become helplessly bound by the habit of moral incontinence. Such viciousness has, as a matter of plain fact, overtaken men everywhere. Aristotle thus confronts himself with a dilemma. On the one hand, he agrees with Socrates that only the virtuous can know the truth. But on the other hand, he attaches error not to ignorance but to that viciousness which obscures the ends of action; and the vicious man cannot know the truth. This viciousness may come to dominate and bind a man. How, then, will his "redemption" be effected? How can the man who is bound recover his "possession" of right reason?

The dilemma is only an apparent one. For Aristotle's man of incontinence is like a man intoxicated or asleep. He may recite the verses of Empedocles correctly, but the verses have no proper meaning for him. The universal meanings are obscured. The remedy for evils, then, is temperance, the practical "sobering up" of the incontinent, in order that the universal purposes of action may be held before him clearly.[12] So we return to the Socratic knowledge all the same.

 Now the objections to this "theoretical optimism" are three. First, it has not considered sufficiently the nature of sin, as Anselm would say—and that for the very reason that Aristotle himself assigns, that "vice is unconscious of itself."[13] The Greek self-knowledge was a partial wisdom never wholly conscious of itself. The starting point was wrong. The starting point of the entire inquiry is antecedently entrained in the self-sufficiency of reason, in the assumption that virtue is to be identified with knowledge. There is no place in this analysis for Dostoevski's prodigal confessor from the underworld:

[11] *Ibid*. VI. v. 1140*b*.

[12] *Ibid*. 1147*a-b*. "St. Thomas accepted unreservedly the theory of his master contained in the "syllogism of the incontinent." (P. Rousselot, *The Intellectualism of St. Thomas*, p. 203.)

[13] *Ibid*. 1150*b*36.

You may heap upon [man] every earthly blessing, you may submerge him in well-being until the bubbles shoot to the surface of his prosperity as though it were a pond, you may give him such economic success that nothing will be left for him to do but to sleep and eat dainties and to prate about the continuity of the world's history; yes, you may do all this, but none the less, out of sheer ingratitude, sheer devilment, he will end by playing you some dirty trick.[14]

Man, in other words, is "ornery," and it is the constantly recurring "dirty trick" that gives away the treachery in the heart of man. Dostoevski, it is true, is protesting against a rationalized society rather than against an intellectualized universe; but the interests of the person are very much the same. It was this same sense of ingratitude plus a thirst for self-sufficiency ("Ye shall be as gods . . . ") that led the first residents within the Garden to prefer the tree of knowledge to the tree of life. But the tree of knowledge does not suffice; man must have the tree of life. Lessing held that even the pursuit of knowledge is at bottom an attempt to have the tree of life willfully. He set forth, that is, an indiscreet and pugnacious alternative when he avowed that if God were to give him his choice between the whole of truth in His right hand and the infinite pursuit of truth in His left, he would choose the left hand. The *pursuit* of truth becomes a covert means of reassuring ourselves that we are; and if we have knowledge as the object of our pursuit these satisfactions of assurance can be concealed behind the ideal of detachment. Nietzsche pointed out very shrewdly that Lessing thus revealed the fundamental secret of science, "to the astonishment, and indeed, to the anger of scientists." [15] It is not the "disinterestedness" nor the prized "objectivity" of science that is the true secret of its power; rather, it is the passion in the pursuit that has led men to give all for science.

However that may be, the paradox is that the pursuit itself is an assurance. Man must "feel assured of the one thing with which he cannot dispense—namely, of the knowledge that men are still

[14] *Letters from the Underworld*, p. 36.
[15] *Op. cit.*, p. 265.

men, and not keyboards of pianos over which the hands of Nature may play at their own sweet will, and continue so to play until they threaten to deprive him of all volition." [16] Man may violate the whole business, and so assure himself of his "independence." That is the terrible secret. "Man alone is able to utter curses!" Man alone transcends all causes and has freedom to deny.

It was for this reason, no doubt, that Nietzsche regarded Socrates as the type of the theoretical man. Socrates wished, we may suppose, to assert the primacy of the practical reason through identifying virtue and knowledge. He wished, without doubt, to make right acting the condition of right knowing. But inasmuch as reason was the immanent means whereby right knowledge was to be attained, the scientific reason triumphed after all. This is the "imperturbable belief" of all intellectualist approaches to the moral problem. It is the belief that "with the clue of logic, thinking can reach to the nethermost depths of being, and that thinking can not only perceive being but even modify it." This, for Nietzsche, was the "sublime metaphysical illusion." [17]

Which brings us to the second objection. The solution offered by Socratic self-knowledge is ideal, or "theoretical." It omits the stubborn fact of human cantankerousness. Its identification of virtue and knowledge is a false reflection, since the medium in which the relationship is thought is not reality but ideality. The "irrational" fact of willfulness is deleted from the human situation and is overcome by reason through retreat upon itself. Evil, that is, is ignorance or error. But ignorance is overcome through an inward recollection of truth which is already possessed by virtue of reason; for reason is the soul's divine constituent, as it is also the principle immanent within the ultimate universe.

In the third place, the "moment in time." [18] has no decisive significance. The evil deed is not determinative. The act of recollection absorbs the temporal points of evil back into eternity. One cannot sin against the essences of things; one can only lapse

---

[16] Dostoevski, *loc. cit.*   [17] *Op. cit.,* pp. 265-66.

[18] See Kierkegaard, *Philosophical Fragments,* the shrewdest of all studies in "Christian Socratism" and a standing rebuke to all compromises on this point.

from them. Similarly, the teacher who is the occasion of my remembrance of the truth which I have known from all eternity is of no importance. The temporal incidents of error and of recollection have no genuinely metaphysical significance.

Greek tragedy is for this reason much more penetrating morally than subsequent rationalist philosophy. For tragedy by definition takes the moment in time seriously. The act is decisive, not only for my life, but for an indefinite succession of lives affected by my act. The impotence of man in tragedy is not an impotence of reason; it is an impotence of will, of power to recover the previous condition. Greek tragedy discovered sin as *hamartia;* and between *hamartia* (as the arrow which flies) and *akrasia* (as intoxication of perception which only waits on sobering) there is a radical disjunction. Tragedy dispels the optimism hidden at the heart of rationalism, which has formed the secret basis for the greater part of Western culture. Tragedy sought to reach a *reconciliation* at the point where impersonal destiny must overtake our guilt. But its rectification was one of eye for eye and tooth for tooth; it was not a salvation. It was one of fatal resignation, not of renewal and redemption. It was one of law, not of love. It advanced, that is, as far as men under the condition of hamartio-centric curtailment can advance: when men will not come to know God personally as the God of love, they must come to know him impersonally, as the God of fatality and justice. Tragedy thus contains more "metaphysical comfort" than does rationalist philosophy; for it at any rate confronts man with his destiny, albeit bitter like the fates, instead of with his reason, albeit optimistic—solving the problem totally but in the realm of ideality.

Nietzsche therefore was correct in preferring wisdom to science, and the metaphysical comfort of tragedy to the theoretic ethic of Euripides and Socrates. But Nietzsche also erred. For when he sought the metaphysical comforts of tragedy, he incarnated tragedy in Helen, and the self-sufficient individual (himself) in Faust. Thus with Faust he cried—

> And shall not I, by mightiest desire,
> In living shape that sole fair form acquire?

But what is this if it is not a kind of demonic Platonism after all? For in Goethe's *Faust* the forms are Helen; and Nietzsche, like Faust, would willfully acquire them by his mightiest desire.[19] This brings us round again full circle; for, as between the Nietzschean willfulness and the Platonic Socrates, we should at any rate appeal from the Teutonic inebriety of willfulness to the Platonic sobriety of Truth and Beauty and Goodness.

To recapitulate: Socratic self-knowledge was on firm ground so long as it cross-questioned men out of their supposed fixed knowledge in order to teach them that they did not know. This at least was wisdom. It taught men to be humble and renewed the fundamental wonder of the world. This was a preparation for a great belief. But Greek religion was not equal to faith's firm demands, and the Socratic method followed up its only clue: it turned more deeply to the self, absorbed the self into the reasoning power, and by an act of great transcendence thrust the mind into the universe and found its Truth and Goodness there. By inwardness it recollected what it had been from eternity. In three respects it erred: it disesteemed the fundamental nature of the fact of sin, it solved the problem of self-recovery ideally and not factually, and it overlooked the moment in time as ontologically decisive for man's eternal destiny.

iii

As a point of transition to the mystical solution this Nietzschean reduction of the Platonic self-knowledge to its possible Promethean pathos is not without its significance. For just as the Socratic starting point was the knowledge of the self as conditioned by ignorance, so the mystical starting point is the knowledge of the self as conditioned by privation of the good. The former solved its problem inwardly by recollection; the latter solves the problem inwardly by mystical ascent to God. Both movements are movements in immanence; both suppose a continuity betwixt ourselves and God; both view the problem as primarily metaphysical instead of moral. The mystical ascent

---

[19] See Nietzsche, *op. cit.*, pp. 291-92.

is a kind of Socratic rationalism baptized. The identification of virtue and knowledge is, so to speak, replaced by an identification of another kind—the identification of worshiping subject with its Object in essential coalescence.

The starting point, however, is Socratic. "Let everyone be the first to drink at his own well," said St. Bernard. "Begin by considering thyself." [20] Nothing could show to greater advantage the sanity and balance of the Christian Socratic aim than the passage cited by M. Gilson from Hugh of St. Victor: "To know his own condition and place, what he owes to things above him and beneath and to himself, to understand what he has been made, how he should conduct himself, what he should do and not do—in this for man consists self-knowledge." [21] Since, however, this is a starting point that is equally common to Epictetus, Erasmus, and to Matthew Arnold, the important question is the question as to how the self is to be understood and how the self relates itself thereafter to the truth.

It is here that the mystic's self-knowledge, like that of the rationalist, misunderstands itself through aspiring to lose itself—to possess and be possessed—in the object of its intuition. There is here a double motion, a coincidence of self-immolation and self-deification. God is everything and man and the world are nothing, in the one instance; through ecstatic union with God man becomes what God is, on the other. "I thank Thee, O God, that Thou, Who reignest over all, art now in very truth and unchangeably one spirit with me" (St. Simon, the Theologian). "But if I were not, God also would not be" (Eckhart). Medieval mysticism is often reproached, on this account, with being pantheistic; and it is unquestionably true that it rests back metaphysically upon a stringent monism. Its central misunderstanding of the religious problem is, in fact, primarily metaphysical. It commits "ontologism" in the sense already spoken of above.[22] This will become clear the moment we consider Christian mysticism in terms of its historical antecedents.

[20] Quoted by Gilson, *The Spirit of Modern Philosophy*, p. 215.
[21] *Op. cit.*, p. 216.
[22] See p. 134.

Christian mysticism is neither biblical nor Hebraic. It is a prismatic refraction of Alexandrian metaphysics through the glass of medieval sacramentalism. Plotinus is, in this sphere, determinative for medieval thought. In him the currents of Heraclitean, Platonic, and Aristotelian metaphysics are fused. The "upward and the downward way" is reduplicated in Plotinus' emanational view of God whereby the Deity flows over into a descending hierarchy of created orders, and by virtue of which there is a perpetual efflux and return of all things to and from the Divine Principle. His "flight of the alone to the Alone" is normative for monistic mysticisms. "Often," wrote Plotinus, "when I wake up to myself from the sleep of bodily life, and pass out from the outer world and enter into myself, I behold a wondrous beauty, and believe fully and firmly that I belong indeed to a higher world. Then I feel in myself a most glorious life, and I become one with the Divine."[23] At the end of his life he was still "striving to yield up the all in himself to the All in the world." The polarity of being and nonbeing governs the Plotinian world view and accounts for Plotinus' depreciation of the temporal order as "the sleep of bodily life."

We have noted already the infiltration of this Alexandrian world view into early Christianity by way of Augustine. But an even greater influence, perhaps, was that of the Pseudo-Dionysius, who lived about A.D. 500 but who passed himself off for an immediate disciple of Paul's—Dionysius the Areopagite mentioned in Acts 17:34. These works were regarded as genuine for a thousand years. Hugh of St. Victor wrote a commentary on them. Thomas Aquinas accepted them as semi-inspired. Not until Laurentius Valla, Erasmus, and Luther cast doubt upon their genuineness did they lose their hold on Christian thought. There was a notable increase of their influence in the twelfth century occurring simultaneously with the rise of Scholasticism; and there is certainly ground for holding, with Paul Elmer More, that this double development was not accidental but that these influences are complementary, expressing the affective and intellectual aspects

[23] *Enn.* IV. viii. 1.

270

of an identical movement toward a transcendental monism.[24]

The writings of the Pseudo-Dionysius are based directly upon Plotinus and Proclus coated with a thin veneer of Christian teaching. Here again is the erotic ascent consummating in ecstatic union with the Divine One. It is achieved through a disciplined dying to the sense world. Thus we have the *via negativa,* that process of denial whereby we arrive at the same goal as by the process of affirmation. Only in this case ignorance is knowledge, and darkness is light. In the absolute, both affirmation and negation are equally indistinguishable, if not identified. This is the pattern, basically, of subsequent mystical ascents to God, whether they be the "ways" of Bonaventura, the "twelve degrees of humility and pride" of St. Bernard, or the "dark night of the soul" of St. John of the Cross. These duplicate, each in its own idiom, the total interest of the medieval world view, which was a sytem of appetition grounded erotically upon the notion of metaphysical ascent to God. From the standpoint of works, there was ascent by way of the ladder of merit; from the standpoint of speculative theology, there was the analogical ladder of the degrees of knowledge; from the standpoint of the inner life, there was the ladder of mystical ascent to God. By these several means the problem of sin as a moral disjunction between God and man made actual by an act of defiance and disobedience was effectively sublimated into a metaphysical problem. It was solved by the purgation of the soul from its attachment to the world of sense, and through concentration on the transcendental essence of the Godhead. As Cyrano proposed to reach the moon by sitting on a plate of iron and hurling a magnet into the sky, which, when it drew him after, he would catch and throw again, so the mystic seated in his contemplative inwardness would throw his longing into the sky and be drawn after it to God. Both Cyrano and the mystic discount the centripetal mass on which they stand—with Cyrano, the earth; with the mystic, sin.

Again the objections are three.

First of all, the view is based upon the notion of evil as *defect,*

[24] *The Catholic Faith* (Princeton University Press, 1931), p. 241.

as "privation of the good" and thence as negative and illusory. It is something contrary to the good conceived as Being, instead of something that contradicts the Good conceived. Thus the nature of things, or ontology, triumphs systematically over the personal categories. In the same manner, privation of good is looked upon negatively, as the nonbeing of something rather than positively as an act: it is viewed, that is, metaphysically, not ethically. But from the biblical standpoint evil is an act, and thus a positive negation. Thus, for the mystic, the whole problem of guilt, so essential to the Christian standpoint, is effectively by-passed and sublimated from the reckoning. Christ becomes a "pattern" of ascent to God.[25]

Second, the mystical understanding of the self as conditioned by privation attempts to recover the true good through ecstatic union with God. This supposes that the soul can achieve this on its own account by virtue of its nature—that is, by passing from the outer to the inner world and by passing through itself, as it were, until the soul identifies itself with that which is like it in the ultimate universe. That which is most real in its own self-consciousness is in some sense identical with the being of God. Thus the quality of self-transcendence, which is the distinguishing mark of man, is hypostatized, and the soul effects a provisional deification of itself. The mystical aspiration for immediate union with God is thus a moral indiscretion. By it the "kingdom of the heavens suffers violence" and by the vehemence both of language and of passion the mystics become the "violent ones" who "seize upon it." [26]

In the third place, the entire mode, as a mode of Christian Socratism, is rationalistic instead of personalist. It is metaphysical instead of moral. "The command to know ourselves came down from heaven," Gilson paraphrases from Richard of St. Victor; "well, then, if we obey it, would not this be to ascend in spirit

---

[25] Nygren summarizes these views as follows: "To the question, 'Cur Deus homo?' (Why did Christ descend?), Bernard answers: by His descent (and subsequent ascent) Christ wished to teach us how we might ascend to heaven." (*Agape and Eros*, Part II, Vol. II, p. 418.)

[26] Matt. 11:12.

towards heaven?"[27] The answer is, No! From the moral standpoint it would not be to ascend towards heaven. The open continuity with God is broken by the act of sin, which establishes
a moral disjunction between God and man. Similarly, the creation of men as discrete centers of experience, relatively free and
responsible to God, precludes the coalescence of creature and
Creator in the immediacy of ecstatic "union." Biblical Christianity
repeats and heightens the clarity of common-sense experience.
The humanistic wisdom of all the ages is at one with it.

> We two must be twain,
> Although our undivided loves are one,

as Shakespeare says. The Psalmist also thirsts for God, but he
envisions his relationship to God both morally and personally:
"My soul thirsteth for God, for the living God: when shall I
come and appear before God?" The relationship maintains discreteness of the persons. It is true that certain mystics strive, upon
occasion, to guard against the final coalescence of persons in their
aspiration to be united with God. We must also make allowance
for all that is beautiful and poetic in the literature of their aspiration. But as Paul Elmer More has indicated, the end is a "swound
of oblivion wherein the conscious union of love fades off into
what is practically an unconscious unity of essence."[28] This may
seem excessive; but such a consummation is implicit in the whole
of medieval thought, possibly because of the fact that the

---

[27] *Op. cit.,* p. 221.

[28] Attention should be directed also to More's comment on the exposition of Heb.
11:6, as set forth by St. John of the Cross. "He that cometh to God must believe that
he is." The first deflection into mystical paraphrase appears in the substitution for
"faith" and "cometh to" of the phrases "draw near and unite himself," and "make
himself one with"—which implications, as More rightly says, would have been sheer
blasphemy to the Hebrew mind. The second has to do with the shading off of belief
"that he is" to belief in "his being"—which involves, as More claims, both a logical
and theological perversion, turning on "the old fallacy of distinguishing between the
copulative and the substantive force of the verb 'to be' in such wise as to draw therefrom the conception of pure Being as an entity that simply is without being anything."
This same criticism must be applied to the oft-cited Mosaic "I am that I am," which
contemporary Thomist apologists turn to the account of pure Being. For the Hebrew,
there was no such notion as τὸ ὄν of the Greeks. Or better, perhaps, the Hebrew had no
verb *sein* but only *geschehen*.

medievalist supposed that thought must oscillate between realism and nominalism, whereas there is the third possibility of Christian faith, which is personalist and "existentialist" and supplies a metaphysic of its own. The central flaw in medieval theology consists in its attempt to place the metaphysical in immediate relationship with the religious.

We conclude, therefore, that just as Socratic self-knowledge failed in its attempt to overcome our ignorance through its reflective reminiscence of the essences, so mystical self-knowledge fails through wishing to overcome ignorance and finitude by identification of the soul's essence with God's essence. The likeness which we intimated between Nietzsche's notion of the metaphysical comfort of tragedy and this metaphysical comfort of ecstatic union lies at this point: Nietzsche viewed the essences as Helen and became his own Faust who would willfully acquire them by his mightiest desire; in mysticism, the essences are God, and the mystic is the violent one who would willfully possess them by his mightiest desire.

iv

We come, then, to the third alternative, the way for self-recovery opened up to us by Christian Socratism. For Christian Socratism takes the moment in time seriously. It holds each man responsible to God in every moral act. There is no sublimation of the God-man relationship; it is not dissolved through self-knowledge either into the metaphysical comfort of contemplative knowledge or into the transcendental coalescence of mystical union. On the contrary, Christian Socratism forces us out of every nonmoral accommodation of God to ourselves. And how does it do this? Precisely by the maieutic method, by cross-questioning us into ourselves so that we may come to know ourselves as we really are before God. Wherein we discover not our closeness to him but our separateness from him, not our likeness to him but our defiance of him, not our capacity to ascend to him but our incapacity to recover the relationship apart from his grace and forgiveness. Christian Socratism is thus individualizing and personalizing. It closes off the will from its infinite resources for evasion. It isolates the self in its interiority of treachery and self-sufficiency. It affirms thereby both man's reason and his freedom, through pressing him into his final isolation as a free moral agent under God. So much is this the case that reason itself is deprived of its own preclusive prop in rationalism, and freedom is dignified to its highest pitch in this knowledge of ourselves as capable of defying God in a Titanic disobedience.

Gilson is right in holding that Pascal set forth this Christian Socratism; but he is wrong in trying to equate his teaching with the Cistercians and the Victorines, though they start equally in Socratism. For the mystic, self-knowledge is, in some sense, a means of immanent return to God. The purgation that he seeks through the "dark night of the soul" is compounded of aesthetic immediacy and a longing for the Infinite. The degree to which these elements may combine with the egocentric consciousness and ultimately invert the God-man relationship is clearly demonstrated in a recent poem:

> God is all naked,
> I am all incandescent.
> God must begin His ascent
> To me the Created.
>
> *   *   *
>
> God is my elected,
> Him have I chosen
> To be berosen.
> Him have I elected.[29]

This was not the case with Pascal. His God was always the God of Abraham, Isaac, and Jacob—of Jesus Christ. His Socratism centered in Christ.

Philosophers have said in vain, "Retire within yourselves, you will find your good there." We do not believe them, and those who believe them are the most empty and the most foolish.

The Stoics say: "Retire within yourselves; it is there you will find your rest." And that is not true. . . . Happiness is neither without us nor within us. It is in God both without us and within us.

Had Epictetus seen the way perfectly, he would have said to men, "You

[29] José García Villa, *Have Come; Am Here* (New York: The Viking Press, 1942).

follow a wrong road"; he shows that there is another, but he does not lead to it. It is the way of willing what God wills. Jesus Christ alone leads to it: *Via, veritas.*[30]

In these citations we see how constantly Pascal regarded man as a viator, as one who goes a way. His notion of truth is therefore dialectical. Apart from the true way, the self is delivered into emptiness and foolishness, or into whatever "rewards" the levels of sense, mind, and charity might hold. But only one way is the true way, and that is the Way which is also the Truth. We look therefore for that Teacher who is at once the Way and the Truth. By *conversion* we enter into this Way—by "annihilating self." And true self-knowledge consists in knowing that "there is an unconquerable opposition between us and God, and that without a mediator there can be no communion with Him." [31]

Not only is it not possible to equate Pascal with the mystics; it is not possible to equate him with Calvin either. There is no question here of sin as Calvin understood it. The incapacity of Calvin to think the God-man relationship dialectically reduces his understanding of the human situation to a kind of Stoic resignation after all.

Pascal is nearer, in fact, to Socrates!

There is a close proximity, as Paul Elmer More has noted, between the three Socratic theses and Pascal's basic principles.[32] Socrates held to an intellectual skepticism, a spiritual affirmation, and a belief in the identity of virtue and knowledge.[33] Pascal held that we must have three qualities—the skeptical, the geometrical, and Christian submission; and that we must learn accordingly where to doubt, where to be certain, and where to submit. These principles have a measure of correspondence; and they are held dialectically, not statically.

It does not follow from this that man is "intellectually impotent and morally responsible," as More elsewhere holds.[34] To Pascal, at

[30] *Pensées,* 464, 465, 466.
[31] *Ibid.,* 470.
[32] *Platonism* (Princeton University Press, 1931), p. 14.
[33] *Ibid.,* p. 2.
[34] *The Sceptical Approach to Religion* (Princeton University Press, 1934), p. 89.

276

any rate, submission itself is a use of the reason;[35] it is the reason itself which judges when it ought to submit.[36] It is quite true that "the practical paradox of ethics" precludes theoretical certainty and thrusts us forward upon religion, or faith, as a necessary decision of the will to convert the "probabilities of belief into truths of experience." This, however, is merely to reaffirm the primacy of the practical reason, and to confirm Pascal's claim that there are only two kinds of people who have a right to be called reasonable: those who love God with all their hearts because they have found him, and those who search for God with all their hearts because they have not found him. The question here is not one of intellectual capacity. It is a question of right affections. There is a vast difference, as Pascal knew, between knowing God and loving him. "Doubt," therefore, is not to be opposed to "reason." Doubt's true opposite is *faith*. And "sin" is not to be opposed to "virtue" —as something we achieve through moderation; but sin's true opposite is likewise faith. The crux of the difficulty is that we know all that we need to know but still we will not believe. We are, in short, both intellectually competent and morally responsible. These are the facts which give to sin its existential significance and preclude the possibility of its being treated legalistically. For legalism is also a form of skepticism. Sin is founded on belief. Its validity as a notion depends upon belief in the real presence of God.

Augustine's modification of Socrates' captious question in the *Meno* is therefore highly relevant. The mind, in seeking self-knowledge, is not really seeking to know itself.

> For the part which has been found, does not seek itself; nor yet does the part itself which has not yet been found, seek itself; since it is sought by that part which has been already found. Wherefore, since neither the mind as a whole seeks itself, nor does any part of it seek itself, the mind does not seek itself at all.[37]

That is very succinctly put; but it raises the question as to why the mind should be enjoined to know itself—the constant refrain of men of wisdom in all ages? To which Augustine replies:

---

[35] *Pensées*, 269.
[36] *Ibid.*, 270.
[37] *De trin*. X. iv. 6.

I suppose, in order that it may consider itself, and live according to its own nature; that is, seek to be regulated according to its own nature, namely, under Him to whom it ought to be subject, and above those things to which it is to be preferred; under Him by whom it ought to be ruled, above those things which it ought to rule.[38]

But this returns us precisely to the standpoint of Christian humanism, wherein the reason exercises its regulative function and the self, conditioned by existence, seeks to know itself—to know, that is, its true condition under God.

Under God, however, there is only one sublime alternative. There is the Way, and there are the ways. And these do intersect perpetually at every point where the conditioning of existence thrusts us on the point of choice. We choose the ways, and, being committed to the ways, we never find the Way but willfully pursue ourselves into the infinite opaqueness. We must therefore "stand in the ways" as Jeremiah says, "and ask for the eternal paths, what is the good way, and walk in it, and [so] find expiation for [our] souls." [39]

Sin, from this perspective, can only be construed as dialectical, though thought—which deletes existence to preserve its ideal circularity—can think of sin as one more term in the higher calculus of the divine economy. Sin, however, is an act; and, because it is a continuing act, it is also a condition. True self-knowledge is a coming to know that out of ourselves we cannot know our true condition, for the reason simply that we are in the condition. Christ becomes the *condition* of true self-knowledge. Through him we come to know our condition apart from him.

It is in vain, O men, that you seek within yourselves the remedy for your ills. All your light can only reach the knowledge that not in yourselves will you find truth or good.[40]

Know how much more than merely man is man, and learn from your Master, your true condition of which you are wholly ignorant. Listen to God.[41]

[38] *Ibid.* X. v. 7.
[39] Jer. 6:16.
[40] *Pensées,* 430.
[41] *Ibid.,* 434.

Everything depends in this distinction upon the radical difference between Christ as the *occasion* for our learning the truth and Christ as the *condition* for our learning; for, in the first instance, Christ is no more significant than Socrates, since the motion in either case is immanent within ourselves, whereas, in the second instance, the Teacher is himself the condition of our knowing.

Kierkegaard has analyzed with great thoroughness the difference between the teacher who is merely the occasion of our coming to know what was already within us and the Teacher who is the condition of our coming to know that the truth is not in us but must be brought to us.[42] Clement of Alexandria, however, had been over this ground before him and contrasted long ago the teacher, Socrates, with the Teacher, Jesus Christ.[43] Clement agrees that we must first of all be disabused of our supposed fixed knowledge, and that to know our ignorance is the first lesson in walking according to the Word. But "Know thyself"—a saying he attributes first to Chilon [44]—carries with it many implications: it teaches us that we are mortal, that we are human beings, that we are of no account because of fame or possessions; that we must come to know for *what we were born,* and *whose image we are,* and what is our essence, and what our creation, and what *our relation to God is.*[45] True knowledge is to know the object of our search.[46] True learning is obedience to God's commands.[47] True wisdom is the knowledge of the Son of God, for Christ himself is Wisdom.[48] Thus the mind itself is not the image of God. It is the image of the image. For man is made in the image of God; but the image of God is "the divine and royal Word, the impassible man"; and therein consists the divine correspondence.[49] Wisdom therefore implies a rectitude of soul and of reason, and purity of life.[50] It is founded on faith. It is God-given. It must be freely chosen. It is brought by the Teacher who is also

[42] *Philosophical Fragments, passim.*

[44] *Ibid.* I. xiv.

[46] *Ibid.* VI. xv.

[48] *Ibid.* VI. vii.

[50] *Ibid.* VI. vii.

[43] *Stromata* V. iii.

[45] *Ibid.* V. iv.

[47] *Ibid.* II. xi.

[49] *Ibid.* VI. xiv.

the Word. Three things follow: first, to "know one's self" is to find one's life"—which is brought to pass by losing it, by faith, by *conversion;* [51] second, the movement to conversion is by *repentance,* which is itself an effect of faith; [52] third, as belonging to all such wisdom, and as "supreme and essential," is the *Holy Spirit*—whose power follows and confirms true faith.[53]

There is, therefore, a profound sense in which obedience, as Frederick Robertson held, is the organ of spiritual knowledge, and disobedience is the original ground of our spiritual severance from God. The moment in time is decisive before God. Sin is an act, and it continues as an act. As such it is decisive, conditioning our relationship to God. It is like the branch cut off from the vine. The attempt of the branch to live out of itself is contradictory. Yet, conditioned by the antecedent choice in self-sufficiency, it must needs persist in self-sufficiency; it must wither and be fit only to be burned. The breach between the vine and the branch is a moral breach, though ontology obtains existentially (the branch must wither). The branch cannot restore itself to its previous condition. Only the Gardener's hand can perform that miracle.

Aristotle, in describing the man who has committed injustice voluntarily, compares him with the man who has thrown a stone. At one time he held the stone securely in his hand, and at such a time he might have helped himself; but now the stone is "out of his hand and [he] cannot recall it, though it [previously] rested with him to aim and throw it." [54] *The condition is changed* once the stone has left the hand and hurtles through the air. It is a continuing act and cannot be recalled, even though the person who has thrown it might wish that he had not done so. The choice to throw the stone was a choice of "decisive significance." [55]

Or we may think of the man who walks the "rope stretched over an abyss," and who maintains his balance through keeping his eye fixed in self-forgetting love upon the face of God at the far end of the rope. But, choosing to remove his gaze from that all-clarifying face in order to admire himself in his most estima-

---

[51] *Ibid*. IV. vi.   [52] *Ibid*. II. vi.
[53] *Ibid*. VI. xvii.   [54] *Eth. Nic*. III. 1114*a*.
[55] Cf. Kierkegaard, *Philosophical Fragments*, p. 11, n. 4.

ble balance, he loses that balance and suffers his fall into the infinite opaqueness. Such a fall is decisive, and the one who falls is subsequently conditioned by it. The moment he lost his balance is the antecedent moment. It is prior to and it conditions from behind, as it were, all his later actions. Self-knowledge consists in his coming to know that he is falling—which, indeed, is the knowledge that not in himself will he find truth or good, that is, rescue.

The moment in time is thus, for the Christian, significant. By it we condition ourselves. The Teacher, consequently, must also be of decisive significance; he must both clarify our true condition and bring to us the condition of recovery. In this respect Christ differs from all other teachers. He teaches us our true condition through becoming altogether what we are. He suffers himself to be conditioned by our condition, and our condition imposes its defiance upon him to the point of crucifixion. His truth accuses us. The world must rid itself of the accuser. Self-sufficiency would preserve itself at all costs. It would impale God and so be rid of the contradiction. It does impale him. But in so doing it only clarifies the contradiction.

> For thirty pieces Judas sold
> Himself, not Christ!

The stone which the builders rejected becomes the head of the corner. No edifice will stand without it. It confronts man with its cruciform clarification at the end of every human enterprise. It is the last word on man's side. No sin *can* prosecute its cause beyond the impaling of God! It has done its worst. To conceive a greater infamy is not possible to man. Christ is the first Word and the last from God's side; for in the resurrection the sin that worked its ultimate in perfidy is overcome and the way is opened for a "new Jerusalem," a "colony of heaven," whose citizens possess again the conditions of right relationship to God. Does this imply ascent to God? Not in the least. It implies *belief* that he who came was the Son of God, that he "came teaching," and that through faith in him we are renewed unto God in the fellowship of his Kingdom. It is the great "experiment," as Clement says—the

281.

founding of our knowledge on faith, on a Teacher who is both
the Truth and the Way.

Pascal was right, therefore, in teaching us that knowledge of
our true condition was to be found not in ourselves but in Christ.
The condition could not be found in ourselves because we ourselves are in the condition. There is no means, from the human
standpoint, whereby we may stand above ourselves to know our
condition. The capacity to transcend ourselves, to occupy a center
above ourselves from which we can make an object both of ourselves and the world, does not serve us. For, conditioned antecedently, we transcend ourselves in infinite opaqueness, which
waits upon illumination of the Spirit. We cannot stand upon our
own heads, as Nietzsche would have it; for we should only duplicate our own condition in a headstrong manner! Nor can we
transcend ourselves into salvation by way of the universality of
reason, for the antecedent condition of moral disjunction bears no
relation to particulars and universals. It is a question of the infinite particular—the individual's relationship to God. The capacity
for self-transcendence, which is the human characteristic, remains
to the end a *capacity*. From man's side, it is a capacity which
guarantees our personhood though it affirms our creaturehood;
it makes us human. From God's side, it is the means by which he
speaks to us and reveals to us his will—a revelation which does
not coerce us but leaves us freely responsible in our response to
him. It is a meeting place between God and ourselves. From God's
side, then, our condition can be explained to us; for he alone can
speak to us within our condition and yet from beyond it. His
Word can "make men aware of their own ruin"—a Socratic function, doubtless, but a Socratic motion with the dimension of the
Eternal added. "I mean to make them strike me," said Kierkegaard, "and in that way I all the same compel them through evil.
For if they once strike me they will be made aware." [56] What
Kierkegaard proposed to himself in imitation of Christ, Christ
had already revealed to him through having performed it beforehand infinitely. Through striking Christ men have been made

[56] *The Journals*, p. 638.

infinitely aware—of their own ruin. Christ is also that moment in time which has eternal significance—which means that he is the point of elevation by which, through faith, we may stand above ourselves and see our true condition.

This, of course, is what Pascal was seeking in his Socratic description of the misery of man without God. How foolish, indeed, of Montaigne to portray himself—a congeries of whims, reasons, and contradictions. But how foolish, also, of Epictetus to seek to know himself. For the one portrayed himself in pride, and the other knew himself in despair. Pascal discerned, beyond the rationalisms of Epictetus and Montaigne, the despair in the one and the pride in the other. It was not by putting the extremes of good in each of these philosophies together that we should achieve the ideal view of man; it was by assuming a perspective above them both that we should bring true knowledge to ourselves. In the case of Montaigne, speculative doubt moved dialectically to moral despair; and in the case of Epictetus, trust in the reasoning power led dialectically to extravagances of pride. The one did not know man's true dignity, while the other never knew his moral impotence. The Christian revelation supplies the missing terms. It transcends the partial grasp of each. It supplies the fulcrum for moving the world. Christ stands above the terms, yet stands within the human condition.

Gilson would have it that Pascal learned all this from St. Bernard, who explored the degrees of humility and pride. "To know God, and yet nothing of our wretched state, breeds pride," says Pascal; "to realize our misery and know nothing of God is mere despair; but if we come to the knowledge of Jesus Christ we find our true equilibrium, for there we find both human misery and God." There is no point in bending the insight of Pascal clean out of its orbit in order to recast it after the pattern of the mystics. Pascal understands man's situation dialectically, as a conditioning in sin requiring a conversion of its terms—of sin through faith, of moral impotence through grace. And such a transposition is God's act, not ours; for it is He who "has willed to redeem men, and to open salvation to those who seek it." [57] The true clue to the human

[57] *Pensées*, 430.

situation is not to be found in ignorance, understood rationalistically; nor is it privation of the good, understood ontologically. It is the moral disjunction between God and man produced by mankind's will to disbelieve, to which willfulness men become inured and "blame chance and the gods" or "lay their goatish dispositions to a star." Christian Socratism is that more thorough knowledge of ourselves whereby, through coming to know our ignorance as sin, we are thrust out of the Socratic refuge of retreat upon ourselves and thrown upon the Cross, which teaches us our wretchedness apart from God and provides the fulcrum and the power that will move the world.

Chapter V

ANALOGIA CRUCIS

Léon bloy was right in his claim that modern man has been brought to bay at the extremity of all things. The crisis of our history has indeed thrust us upon the true crux of the human situation. The true crux of the human situation consists in that precisely—in the fact, that is, of the *crux,* the Cross. At the end of every flight from the Cross the Cross is there awaiting us. At the end of every historical flight from man's original relationship to God the dialectical miscarriage of human hopes thrusts man once more upon the starting point. We are brought face to face with the redemptive problem, both for ourselves and for the world—the whole question as to the nature of man and his destiny, but in an absolute reference. Our thinking also suffers this recoil into the Christian truth.

This is true essentially of the culture of "the West," which culture now, the world around, is threatened with self-destruction. This is true for Western culture because the Cross is the unacknowledged (yet the secret) presupposition on which it rests. It is the supposition from which we flee; but it supports us in our flight. We therefore flee, like the man who has lost his bearings in the desert, in an elaborate circle back upon our starting point. It is, for us, either the stone which shall become the head of the corner or the rock that shall grind us all to powder.

For us, there is no means whereby we may rid ourselves of him. We crucified him, and thus made him the crux of all our free determination in the world. But death could not hold him. We exalted him, thinking to release ourselves from obligation through setting him so high above us that to reach him would be sacrilege. But he is the third one walking beside us on every road. He becomes what we are in order that we might become what he is. Christ is

> The strange man who little by little becomes
> my God and my Lord,
> Jesus more inward than shame, who shows to [me]
> and opens unto [me] His Heart.[1]

Therein lies the mystery. The Cross solicits me in every dereliction, pain, or agony by the analogy of its infinite suffering. The horizontal arms of the Cross reach out to encompass the whole earth. The Cross draws everything upon itself. And there, where the tragedy in the world is brought face to face with the tragedy of the world, and where we are brought face to face with the one true Image, the vertical shaft from heaven intercepts our pain; and we are healed.

This is, and remains, a mystery: what begins as an analogy, soliciting me at the extremities of faithlessness, ends as a singular redemptive fact. From it four things are clarified: (1) it reveals the nature of our basic human contradiction as a contradiction grounded in the *spirit;* (2) it clarifies the practical nature of truth as *personal* and *relational* rather than as ideal or abstract; (3) it discovers the inner forms of history as dialectically founded on the use of *human freedom;* and (4) it unveils *the way of victory* and shows itself to be the fulcrum over which, through faith, we may truly move the world.

i

The first of these clarifications is the most difficult to specify; yet it is the most intimate of all and lies nearest to the heart of every one of us—and for the very reason that it is a contradiction within, of the spirit. We are already "embarked," carried away by the policy of contradiction to which we have committed ourselves. We are up against the subtle complicity of our wills in willfulness, whereby we know quite well

[1] Paul Claudel, "Verlaine," *Morceaux choisis* (12th ed.; Paris: Librairie Gallimard, 1925), p. 174.

There is no vice so simple but assumes
Some mark of virtue on his outward parts.

We may, however, appeal from this complicity to our capacity for self-transcendence, whereby from a center above ourselves we can look down upon ourselves and contemplate our finiteness. By virtue of this self-transcendence we can exclaim with Shakespeare's Richard III, "Dive, thoughts, down to my soul," and there discover the discrepancy between our deformities of spirit and our desires. But also like Richard, we may content ourselves with this perspective and make of our deformities an excuse for further deformation:

> Why, I . . .
> Have no delight to pass away the time,
> Unless to spy my shadow in the sun
> And descant on mine own deformity:
> And therefore . . .
> I am determined to prove a villain.[2]

This does not argue any taint in the capacity for self-transcendence; it argues, rather, that human willfulness obscures its own capacity and perverts its knowledge to its own demands. Even though our good angel, beholding our folly, should suddenly swoop down in fury and, seizing us by the hair, beat us with his fists to teach us love and obedience, we should still be able to cry out of our willfulness: "I will not!" [3]

This refusal to be overruled, to be dependent, to acknowledge our finiteness and creaturehood, argues no taint in our capacity for self-transcendence. It reveals, however, how that capacity becomes for us a temptation. The temptation consists in our desire to overleap our creaturehood and universalize ourselves in terms of our capacity. Man is a synthesis of the finite and the infinite. By the one he is tied down to the necessary and the temporal; by the other he believes that he can rule the stars. This is in man his fundamental disproportion: he is "a Nothing in comparison with

[2] Act I, scene 1.
[3] See "Le rebelle" in Baudelaire's *Les fleurs du mal.*

the Infinite, an All in comparison with the Nothing, a mean between nothing and everything." [4]

Now the important thing for our present purpose is not the *duality* of finite and infinite in man, important as this is; rather, our interest is to note how man, by virtue of his capacity for the infinite, becomes presumptuous by wishing to overleap his finitude. He is not content to be what he is, a creature, being something but not everything, knowing something but not all. "I will speak of the whole," said Democritus.

Pascal understood this element of presumption very well. He saw that it was founded on our capacity for self-transcendence. Strange, said he, that men should wish to arrive "at a knowledge of the whole, with a presumption as infinite as their object. For surely this design cannot be formed without presumption or without a capacity infinite like nature." [5] It is presumptuous for the simple reason that we are "limited in every way" and that the intellect holds the same position in the world of thought that our bodies hold in the expanse of nature: it is a mean between the extremes. We are not capable of certain knowledge on the one hand nor of absolute ignorance on the other, and "nothing can fix the finite between the two Infinites [of littleness and greatness], which both enclose and fly from it." [6]

Implicit in this latter phrase is the entire dialectical impoverishment which the soul suffers when it suffers itself to be led out into either of these infinities and abandoned there. But we are not deceived: the impoverishment is not outside of us anywhere. It is inside, deeply buried within the spirit. Said Nietzsche:

Not the height, it is the declivity that is terrible!

The declivity, where the gaze shooteth *downwards,* and the hand graspeth *upwards.* There doth the heart become giddy through its double will.

Ah, friends, do ye divine also my heart's double will?

This, this, is *my* declivity and my danger, that my gaze shooteth towards the summit, and my hand would fain clutch and lean—on the depth! [7]

[4] Pascal, *Pensées*, 72.
[5] *Ibid.*, 72.
[6] *Ibid.*
[7] *Thus Spake Zarathustra*, II. xliii.

This confession carries us very far into that fatal dichotomy of
spirit created by the self when it would presumptuously leap over
its creaturehood by appeal to its capacity for the infinite. The "upward and the downward way," however it may fare for metaphysics, becomes for the spirit a way of imminent disaster. It
gives rise to "giddiness"—or, as Wesley somewhere says, "dizzi-
ness"—which is nothing more nor less than the mark of the
spirit's *anxiety* arising at the point where human freedom, founded on a fundamental trust in God, passes over into sin, founded on
an egoistic trust in ourselves. "It is," writes Reinhold Niebuhr in
a very happy simile, "the condition of the sailor, climbing the
mast ... with the abyss of the waves beneath him and the 'crow's
nest' above him. He is anxious about both the end toward which
he strives and the abyss of nothingness into which he may fall." [8]
Or, to return to Pascal: "We burn with desire to find solid ground
and an ultimate sure foundation whereon to build a tower reaching to the Infinite. But our whole groundwork cracks, and the
earth opens to abysses." [9] The abysses of nothingness are, fatally
enough, the depths on which Nietzsche's prophet would fain
clutch and lean.

The cracking of the foundations is due in part to the fact that
the infinities fly from us; but it is due inwardly to the nature of
the spirit which this fact reveals. When Jesus said to the disciples,
"Be not anxious" ($\mu\dot{\eta}\mu\epsilon\rho\iota\mu\nu\hat{\alpha}\tau\epsilon$), he used a word—it is repeated
four times in the passage—which implies being torn in pieces
through self-consuming care: "Be not in anxiety." [10] This interior
self-destruction of the spirit is the condition of that self which no
longer trusts in God's power but in its own powers. It is an anxiety
that leads to fear, a fear to which Pascal himself gave utterance
when he exclaimed: "The eternal silence of these infinite spaces
frightens me." [11] What is fearful in it is that, when we would
lean upon the depth, after the Nietzschean pattern, we lean upon
our own declivity of spirit, upon our capacity for the infinite,

---

[8] *The Nature and Destiny of Man*, I, p. 185.
[9] *Pensées*, 72.
[10] Matt. 6:25-34. Cf. Luke 12:29.
[11] *Pensées*, 206.

which infinite flies from us or cracks beneath us, opening upon an abyss of emptiness, because we have sought to lean upon a universalization of our capacity to universalize (to transcend ourselves).

In this experience, which is common to all men, we discover a double disproportion within our spirits: the disproportion between our finiteness and our capacity for the infinite, and the disproportion between our limited knowledge and our unlimited grasp.

Martin Heidegger, whose understanding of man is founded to a large degree upon the recognition of these disproportions and the anxiety of spirit which arises therefrom, presses this disproportion one degree further.[12] This fundamental anxiety, as an immediate datum of spirit, is a clue to man's possible perfection in so far as it reflects his freedom to become what it is possible for him to become. On the other hand, it reveals the fact that this very possibility is caught within, and circumscribed by, the world of contingency. Thus the basic structure of man is one of contingency and potentiality.[13]

We must, however, go further. Man is a synthesis of the finite and the infinite, of limited knowledge and unlimited capacity, of the contingent and the potential—which means that he is a creature on the one hand and has a capacity for God on the other. This initial discrepancy becomes a presumption of spirit whenever we, through anxiety, overleap our creaturehood in order to universalize our *capacity* for the infinite. "To leave the mean is to abandon humanity," said Pascal.

But to abandon humanity is to abandon the self by committing the self to a policy of self-destruction. This the self does through exalting itself as its own center; whereupon the self "turns in upon itself" and pursues the false universalization of its capacity for the infinite. This leads to "falsehood, duplicity, contradiction; we both conceal and disguise ourselves from ourselves." [14] It leads to what Pascal called the "hateful I"—*"Le moi est haïssable."* This

[12] See *Sein und Zeit* (1926). Cf. W. Tudor Jones, *Contemporary Thought of Germany*, II, 116-20. Note also Reinhold Niebuhr's use of this distinction in his penetrating chapter on "Man as Sinner," *The Nature and Destiny of Man*, I, 183. n. 4.

[13] *Sein und Zeit*, p. 199.

[14] Pascal, *Pensées*, 377.

saying has so often been misconstrued as a mark of morbidity in Pascal. But it is no morbidity. It is a result, observable both in ourselves and in the world: it is productive of spiritual and demonic injustices because "it makes itself the center of everything." [15] By virtue of this egocentricity the self tyrannizes outwardly over others, becoming hateful thereby; and it becomes hateful on its own account because it loves itself and no others, and is therefore not lovable. Such is the express condition of the world in which we now stand.

The true center of the self is not in itself but in God. True self-knowledge is to know that not in ourselves do we find truth. True wisdom consists in being rightly related to God. The presumptuousness of Pascal's *"moi"* consists in its demonic attempt to deny the relationship. Or, to recover our terms as above, the capacity for self-transcendence is to be understood only as "the *a priori* of relation." [16]

Relation, however, is an entirely personal and concrete matter. As between persons, it must be based initially upon a recognition of that sphere of discreteness whereby each individual in the world remains a conscious subject of experience. It must also recognize a relational event, whereby we communicate the experience of which we are conscious. As between men and God, it must also recognize that God is a "Thou"—a Person, *that* Person indeed who stands "over against" me. God must become to me a true "Thou" if my "I" is to exist in any proper sense of the pronoun. For the true "I" cannot exist apart from its relationship to God. And the "I" becomes an "I," a true subject of spiritual relatedness, the true "individual," the moment it becomes conscious of the fact that it exists in all actuality—*before God*. The *"moi"* of Pascal, the "self" that is hateful, the introverted, willful, self-consuming self, is the self that can never become a *self*. For it occupies the point of essential contradiction. Through its will to deny

---

[15] *Ibid.*, 455.

[16] Martin Buber, *I and Thou* (tr. R. G. Smith; New York: Charles Scribner's Sons, 1937), p. 27. Buber's analysis does not probe philosophically into the fact of self-transcendence; but this is the unacknowledged, though perhaps unrecognized, philosophical presupposition of his remarkable analysis of the God-man relationship.

the relationship (which it none the less presupposes, for the Spirit from God's side supports it even in its flight from itself) it seeks itself egocentrically through the pursuit of false infinites which flee before it ever faster than it runs. It squanders itself—that is, its self—in the compounded emptiness of its power to relate itself.

Clearly, what is required is something to stop the self in its flight from itself—something that is analogous with it in its flight, but which flies faster than the false infinities themselves, and which breaks them upon the Eternal. Such a one is Christ, who at once draws our flight upon him in such a way as to actualize it infinitely as the will to dispense with God, and who at the same time breaks the ideal infinities by bending the self back upon its creaturehood where it stands before God, before the Eternal in time. The self is brought back to existence. It stands in a concrete situation. It is confronted by a concrete Fact. It is actualized as the individual before God. The discrepancy between the self as an "I" rightly related to the "Thou," and the Pascalian "*moi*" destroying itself by anxiety, passing always deeper into its declivity of despair, is revealed as the will to dispense with God.[17]

But to will to dispense with God is presumption. And presumption against God is *sin*. And sin is the parting of the ways. But Christ also is the parting of the ways. In him, that which begins as an analogy, drawing us upon our creaturehood as we stand before him, ends as a fact—the confrontation of the "I" with the

---

[17] Cf. Ferdinand Ebner: *Das Wort und die Geistigen Realitäten,* p. 186, also pp. 15, 41, 54, 98, 113, etc., for an analysis of the Pascalian "*moi.*" This important work owes much to Pascal and to Kierkegaard; and it is the source also for subsequent works on the "I and Thou" theme which have carried the analysis of these relationships further. Cf. Martin Buber, *Ich und Du;* Brunner, *Man in Revolt;* Berdyaev, *Solitude and Society;* Karl Heim, *God Transcendent.* It seems to me that Reinhold Niebuhr, in his notable Gifford Lectures, in which he has availed himself so discriminatingly of the insights of Kierkegaard, Scheler, Heidegger, and others who disclose the dimension of self-transcendence, has seriously stunted his plan for Christian recovery by failing to follow up this appeal to the spirit. This means that, for all his incorporation of the existential and the historical, his own view must lapse from the religious sphere into the sphere of the ethical and the law.

On the element of presumption in the will to dispense with God, see Kierkegaard, *Christian Discourses* (tr. W. Lowrie; New York: Oxford University Press, 1940), pp. 63 ff.

"Thou." I am personalized. The "Thou" is personalized. But I am personalized in my guilt and confronted by his demand. We have reached the sphere of the personal, where all truth resides in the relation of my soul to God.

ii

The Cross is that event in history which speculative thought seeks earnestly to avoid, but upon which it nevertheless hangs. It is also that pivot of meaning which secular life would ignore, but by which it is nevertheless judged. Christianity becomes thereby a great embarrassment. It is a "scandal" and an offense to thought and life alike. It is an offense to thought because it conditions ideality by an event in time; to life because it brings to bear within the historical the judgment of the eternal.

For this very reason the Cross is the only true analogy of the human conditions, inasmuch as it clarifies the human condition from the standpoint of the eternal, yet does so as a theoretical reflection that always returns upon itself as an event in time. It stops the soul in its infinite flight from itself. It bends the human evasion back upon its fundamental freedom—the freedom we have freely sought to avoid—the freedom to choose God or not to choose him. It recovers to us the dimension of our creaturehood.

Men conceive God's relation to the world by some analogy with human experience. God's relation to the world has both theoretical and practical aspects. The relationship between God and man, however, is at all points practical. To treat the relationship as theoretical is to stop outside of the relationship; for the conditions of the relationship are, on the one side, God's communication of himself and, on the other, man's response to the communicated Word. This is a living relationship. It is essentially a communion.

The customary analogies—which conceive God as Poet or as Artisan or as Father or as King, or which relate the several degrees of reality to one another and to him by the analogy of being—are partial. They either (1) abstract from the relationship and so dissolve the actual within the universal, or (2) they bring the aesthetic or the physiological or the metaphysical into a relationship of immediacy with the religious. The *analogia entis* is the most evident example of this effort, since it both abstracts from the actual into the ideal and attempts to bring the metaphysical into a relationship of immediacy with the religious. It is based upon an alleged likeness (similitude) between God and his creation, yet a likeness which "even in this resemblance" declares their complete unlikeness.[18] By virtue of the imprint of God discernible everywhere in his works it is possible to argue a fortiori to the nature of ultimate being. Thereby we come to know the divine essence as that which is, though we cannot know what it is in itself.[19] The analogy of being is thus founded on the principle of identity—that which is, is. This is a logical postulate imbued with ontological implication. At the same time it conceives the relation between God and man in terms of causality, proceeding from the general principle that there is always discernible in the effect some likeness to the cause. God is that Cause. By detecting the "traces" of the divine in things and in ourselves we may rise to the contemplation of the divine essence. This is a *via causalitatis*; but it is also a *via negationis,* inasmuch as by it we shun the imperfections of the created world in order to rise to perfection in God.

This analogy, it is claimed, holds for thought on its own account: "There must therefore be a thought which will be Thought, and which will be the first cause of my thought."[20] The causal principle is thus related to the principle of identity in the further identification of thought with being. The relationship of man to God is conceived ontologically: man ascends speculatively to the contemplation of God in his divine essence. The ascent is made analogically through the "traces" of God in his creation, and in ourselves; but it is made negatively through shunning the imperfections of the sense world in order to fix upon the Perfect. The contemplation of the Perfect is, therefore, a contemplation in negation: it is a contemplation of That which is beyond our power to conceive. It is an ascent to God as "a like-

[18] Przywara, *Polarity* (tr. A. C. Bouquet; New York: Oxford University Press, 1935), p. 31.

[19] Maritain, *The Degrees of Knowledge*, p. 283.

[20] *Ibid.*, pp. 275-76.

ness which testifies from itself to a Deity who is *beyond simili-tude*." [21] By God's similitude we come to know him as beyond similitude! By contemplating his essence we know that he is in his essence infinitely beyond us!

The circumlocution of this "analogy" which turns and returns upon itself, and which by similitude teaches us that God is beyond similitude, is due to (1) the tautology resident in the attempt to ground everything in the principle of identity and (2) the attempt to put the metaphysical into immediate relationship with the religious. In the first instance, we have an attempt at metaphysical explanation which seeks to ground the particular in the universal by rising from existence to essence; but this it does through deserting existence, which is the one particular that has infinite significance, and with which we are infinitely concerned. It is not, therefore, a true analogy, since in rising from the known to the unknown it deletes the known (the fact that we exist and do not wish to be deleted) and reaches the unknown by tautology—as essence, as that which is identical with itself, which was pre-supposed ideally from the beginning. But the existent is the first term of the relationship; it is the term on behalf of which we seek to establish an analogy with the unknown. The "analogy" is therefore precedently or antecedently contained in the identification of thought with being; its movement is self-contained; it abstracts from particulars in order to arrive at the antecedent universal. It is a movement in the abstract. The movement is from one term to another within the previous definition. It is an analogy of pure thought, which, by definition, is identical with itself as being.

If it is objected that the movement obviously begins from the objective world of *things,* because it is in these things that we discern the traces of the Creator, it must be remembered that the principle of identity is there beforehand and that *things* have been emptied of existential significance: they are intermediate quiddities between potency and act. They are not decisive for God or man. Only God is Pure Act, as he is Pure Being. *Things* are not; they are only privation of being, to which God, as Pure Act, must

---

[21] Przywara, *op. cit.,* p. 30.

be indifferent; otherwise his Being would be corrupted by non-being. This was the dualism that intercepted Aristotelian thought. Aristotle could never bring the Prime Mover, the *Actus Purus,* into relations with the world. The attempt to solve the difficulty by a transcendental monism does not suffice. The analogy of being has profited from Plotinus, who, by importing the "upward and the downward way," erected a ladder between the poles of being and nonbeing. The ladder, however, is only apparent; it does not stand *in* existence, but beside it. The absence of relation still obtains. Or, as St. Thomas says, God's relation to the world is a relation with respect to the world but not with respect to God!

In short, the medium in which the analogy of being is thought is an ideal medium. It is not the medium of reality, in which existence separates thought from being; it is the medium of abstraction, of possibility, of ideality, which takes hold on actuality only by deleting it. It is like persuading the hungry boy that holes are as much a part of the essence of doughnuts as the circular cake ring which encloses them, and that therefore he should be satisfied with a bowl full of holes. This little game the boy will keep up so long as he sees the twinkle in your eye and knows that what you say you do not take seriously. But should he think for a moment that you are highly serious in your argument, even though you were to hold up to him (*via negationis*) the ideal doughnut as a subject for contemplation, and even if you were to argue further that the ideal doughnut can have no relationship with the boy and that therein lies its essential excellence, he would set up such a hue and cry as would get you both ejected from the pantry *cum celeritate.*

The question at issue here is not precisely one of metaphysics. The objection is not that the analogy of being regards the world of things as less real than the world of thought, or that the doughnut is not real in the same sense that God is real. Its fallacy as metaphysics lies in its *choice* of thought as its analogy, whereby it is led off into identifying thought with being instead of building on the *personal* analogy, as Augustine attempted to do his *De trinitate,* thus returning us to ourselves as conscious centers of experience standing in a relationship of apprehension and obedience

296

to God's will as the will of a Creative Agent. Metaphysically, only persons are real in any ultimate sense, and the phenomenal world is but the system of impediments that quarantines the spirit in its finitude and guarantees discreteness of finite experience. The objection is that the analogy of being abridges the distinction between the theoretical and the practical and attempts to put the metaphysical into immediate relationship with the religious.

What is legitimate in its own sphere (in the formal reasoning from particulars to universals and the like) becomes by this attempt a sophistry. We have seen how Matthew Arnold sought to substitute his "culture" for religion. This was an attempt to bring morality and art into a relationship of immediacy with the religious. The fault of Immanuel Kant was the same in kind, save that Kant attempted an ethical immediacy. By appeal to duty religion was reduced to ethics. Rousseau attempted a similar displacement by the immediacy of feeling. Similarly, by beginning with the metaphysical we do not arrive at the religious, for our interest in religion is replaced by metaphysics. There are sophistries of spirit which ignore or usurp the categories of religion. The "practical" is deleted, or the sphere of its interest is preempted by the metaphysical.

We therefore seek a new analogy—an analogy, indeed, which may not, in the first motion, be a way to God at all, but a way to ourselves and to a knowledge of our true condition under God. The Cross as tragedy is such a principle. The Cross as victory transcends the negative disclosure and completes God's declaration of himself to men. What begins as an analogy with human suffering leads us dialectically into our guilt and shame, and ends in the declaration, "This is my beloved Son; . . . hear ye him." In him God speaks to us; he communicates from the side of the Unknown what is not otherwise accessible from the side of the known. That is, the *analogia crucis* becomes the *theologia crucis*. It founds a metaphysic of its own.

The analogy of the Cross does not abstract into the universal— it shocks all things out of the universal and into the infinite particular. It brings all the categories into just subservience to the religious. It forces all particulars to stand *sub specie aeternitatis,* confronted by the eternal *as it stands in time.* The analogy of being, like the monk retreating from existence into the desert, retreats into metaphysical concepts that are ethically barren. At the end of every flight from existence the analogy of the Cross confronts one. It bends one back upon the starting point, the specifically religious problem of essential relationship to God. It overtakes the thief upon the cross, as it overtakes the saint in the desert. It sets a bound to every flight from God. The Cross is not, therefore, one more rung on the ladder of ascent to God, *via contemplativa;* the nearer one comes to the Cross, the sharper becomes one's sense of sin and guilt. This is indeed a *via negationis* since it negates our moral self-sufficiency and pride, and even negates thereby the *via negationis* itself. Such an awareness is always followed either by repentance or defiance. What happens beyond this choice is God's act, not ours.

It is true that the Cross may be viewed "objectively"—and be made an object amongst other objects having only relative significance. As such, the Cross would be the historical synthesis of the comic and the tragic principles. It would be comic as the great mistaken effort in which self-deification came suddenly to nought —came, indeed, to the palpable absurdity of a crucifixion. It would be tragic as symbolizing the end of human hope in irony and death. But from the religious standpoint, the Cross is that act of God whereby hope is reborn and creativity renewed and fellowship with God made possible again. What begins, therefore, as an analogy draws all the fugitive particulars upon the one Particular, the Fact that is pivotal both for thought and for history. And beyond these it reveals the Unknown as Redemptor and Sufferer, as Fulfillment and Judge. It is precisely that analogy whereby all things are led back from the fugitive misunderstanding of themselves in the false reflection of distorted relationships to see themselves as they really are.

From this two corollaries follow:

First, the distinction between the *analogia entis* and the *analogia crucis* as means to the knowledge of God throws an important light upon true self-knowledge. It implies that true self-knowledge can be secured only by that confrontation of the Eternal in time which the Cross supplies, and which thereby stops the soul in its flight from itself in such a way as to bend it back upon the choice of itself before God. Only so does it become truly a self or person. True self-knowledge lies precisely in the recognition of the discrepancy that exists between idea and actuality in one's self. Until this discrepancy is known and recognized, the relationship to God is not a possibility, since the soul is polemically in retreat from the relationship; and so long as the self is in retreat from the relationship, it does not become a true person, since to be a person one must be related to God through the hearing of his Word. The attempt to bring metaphysics into a relationship of immediacy with the religious is to invoke what Ebner calls that "dream of the spirit" whereby the self through its notion-making power "dreams from self" and so "projects itself" upon the universe.[22] We have seen already how difficult it is to distinguish between the dream and the actuality. "The world view of the metaphysicians is none other than such a projection. Actually it is none other than this: the ego puts itself in the place of God."[23] The Cross of Christ accentuates the discrepancy between idea and actuality, and it clarifies the nature of truth as personal.

The second corollary is implied in this. As truth is personal, so also it must be relational. "In the beginning is relation," as Martin Buber has insisted.[24] "All real living is meeting."[25] Between persons there must ever be a point of meeting. We come to know each other through our speech, through those symbols of meaning whereby we *address* each other. God also speaks to us. He has spoken to us in his creation. We, however, easily make an object of the world and reduce it to the "It" and see therein the causal sequence of impersonal dependability. In it there is no meeting with the Thou who created it. From it we learn, as Augustine learned, that it is not God, but that God created it.[26] We transcend it to the point where we can see that our true hopes are not to be fulfilled in it; or we perceive that the true purpose of this world is to make us seek for another, as Newman says. This, the

[22] *Op. cit.,* p. 113.
[23] *Ibid.*
[24] *Op. cit.,* p. 27.
[25] *Ibid.,* p. 11.
[26] *Confess.* X. ix.

sphere of natural revelation, reduces to law. It clarifies the fact that in the It-world we do not relate ourselves to God. Again the Cross supervenes and draws me to the point of meeting, to the one true *act* of my being—the act in which I address him as "Thou." For this is the act of faith whereby God's speech, his Word, is heard by me, and God meets me by grace through his Holy Spirit and communicates thereby the meanings I have sought elsewhere and failed to find.

Herein we see that the principle of the knowledge of God is not the principle of *mediation,* whereby we reason from our particulars to the more universal premise, and from that as a particular to the still more universal, and from that to the higher, until we reach the ultimate Universal. In all of this we stand not *in* the relationship but *beside* it; and by the same token we are "beside ourselves." The true principle is the opposite of this: it is the principle of *communication,* whereby God speaks to us. This communication requires a response, the condition of which is faith; but faith is also the turning point. It is the awakening, whereby the dream from the spirit is thrown off and we have eyes that see and ears that hear. The self, which otherwise is curved in upon itself, now finds that true center outside itself which it must find if it is truly to become an "I." All other centers prove to be false centers. The inmost core of the contradiction in the heart of man lies here—in his failure to meet God, that one Center outside himself which makes him a true person because he is addressed by his Creator. Apart from God, he seeks himself in centers of death. In Him are the issues of life.

iii

We have seen above that the a priori of relation resides in man's capacity for self-transcendence. Self-transcendence is also the a priori of human freedom. By self-transcendence man stands above himself and makes an object of himself, and so discovers that he can find no adequate measure for himself either in himself or in the world about him. If he seeks for such a criterion in the laws of the world about him, he fails to account for the self which discovers the laws; and if he seeks it in his reason, he must yet account for that capacity of judgment whereby he judges his own judgments.

This is true equally of the self when it seeks a center about which to organize its life. If it establishes its center in the world, its powers and its freedom will be sucked down into the impersonal sediment of the causal series. If it establishes its center within itself, it converts all value into egoism and by this fatal introversion exploits its power to relate itself. The only way in which the pathos of this impotence can be stayed is by relating the self to an other—an other, indeed, of such significance that the power to transcend oneself is stopped at the point of meeting. Such an other must be an Other of eternal significance.

This power to relate himself is man's initial freedom. But man, we must remember, is a creature in motion; he is a viator, one who goes a way. He lives in the moment in time, which is the moment in which decision is made. The power to relate oneself is therefore exercised already, and by this prior choice we are committed to the center we have chosen. The difficulty therefore comes when man, by virtue of his power to relate himself, has chosen that which is less than the Eternal and is committed to it. The Other, then, must enter into time to break the fatal mold in which the self continuously recasts itself. God through the Incarnation enters the mold—and shatters it beyond the tomb.

The Cross, therefore, reveals the nature of our basic human contradiction as a contradiction grounded in the spirit; it reveals therein the discrepancy between idea and actuality; but it reveals within that actuality the discrepancy between fate and destiny.

This is a view which must always remain antithetical to those who wish "to be merely spectators," as Nietzsche says, to those who "stand in the street and gape at the passers-by; who also wait, and gape at the thoughts which others have thought!" [27] For it recognizes the dialectical factor in experience, and sees that man is confronted at all times with an imperative of choice.

The gap between willing and thinking is closed in the existen-

[27] *Op. cit.*, II, xxxviii.

tial decision which we constantly face and perpetually enact. It is not that all men are philosophers, some good and some bad, as Aristotle held; it is that all philosophers are men, some good and some bad. The existential decision confronts one as a requirement which can neither be set aside nor deferred. It is at once a moral and an ontological demand, with teleological implications for fate or destiny. By it man "the composer, the riddle reader" may become a "redeemer of chance," a creator of destiny; or he may forfeit his relative autonomy in the spirit and succumb to temporality and fate. He is a destinated creature. Man is a "critical intelligence choosing among alternatives in the light of permanent standards." [28] What we must observe in this is that he is choosing and that his choices follow that policy of choice in which he has antecedently related himself to the will of God or in which he has failed so to relate himself. This is true in all respects, since the standards also, to be permanent, must be mediately grounded on the will of God. All ontology, in the last analysis, must be based upon the will of God. At bottom, then, all choices are decisions with respect to God. When determined positively by a willing obedience to God's will, the choice in God projects a destiny. When determined negatively by a disobedience, the choice becomes fatality and tightens like a Nessus-shirt with every struggle of our wills. In every act, therefore, we either (1) profane God's world or (2) hallow it.

The discrepancy between fate and destiny is first recognized as a discrepancy between necessity and possibility. The ordinary life of man is concentrated in the moment of time which is "here and now." We discover that our possibilities are surrounded by a Chinese Wall of finitude, of temporality, and of law. We seek to know what we are, and who, and why. We partition the moment into spatiotemporal units, divide it again between what has been and what is yet to be; we mark the barometric pressures of number, quantity, causality; we pin our findings firmly to the point upon the chart where nonbeing passes over into being. We are satisfied that much has been accomplished. But what we are and

---

[28] Hough, *The Christian Criticism of Life*, p. 165.

who and why remains. The living aspect of the moment slips between our reckonings; yet it remains to be accounted for.

We discover that the world which lies about us is unstable and illusory, that time is fleeting. Yet time enforces our mortality, and the illusory world absorbs us into its endless inexorabilities. *Destiny* is the category of all filled time—time filled full with creativity of spirit. Dead time—the interminable succession of depersonalized subsistence incidents—is the time in which most life is squandered. The self devoid of conscious relationship to God seeks its destiny in the world of dead time, where its word and its will to create cannot fructify. Its products are still-born. Dead time soaks up the "I" wherever the "I" would pour itself out upon the world. Dead time is a spilled eternity.

The Greeks especially were aware of this discrepancy. The world of flux contained for them a double fatality. On the one hand, it was that which is always becoming and never is (Plato, *Timaeus*); and on the other it was penetrated through and through with fate. This *fatum* was implacable. In the form of the Furies it pursued the evildoer with the stern impersonality of law, working soon or late a legal justice—an eye for an eye and a tooth for a tooth. This formed the basis for their tragedy, and the concept of tragedy was the nearest that the Greek mind came to a notion of history. The pathos of Greek tragedy was that history itself was tragic. The idea of the Fates applied in history; it did not apply in the realm of idea. Thus evil was identified with the world, and the mind was divorced from history. History was, so to speak, abolished by appeal to the mind. Art and thought in Greece shunned history increasingly. Art sought the perfection of ideal form, mind sought the eternal forms. They shunned the decision in time. Idealism resulted; and the Socratic standpoint with its resolution in the ethical, and the tragic standpoint with its ethical reversal, and the comic standpoint with its confrontation of idea with the practical, were obviated. Wisdom as the criticism of life was supplanted by ascetic rationalisms which sought their standpoint in the universal or the absolute.

What the Greek mind overlooked was that which Socrates had practiced so adroitly: the dialectical maieutic method whereby the mind is questioned back into existence. The Greek mind absorbed the moment in time into eternity, and history became a cycle as their thought became a sphere.

The supposed rational detachment, which eschews both decision and responsibility, nevertheless exercises its freedom responsibly in a fateful choice. It also has an elucidation in existence. Its refusal to acknowledge this attachment, together with the destiny which it projects, is therefore ludicrous or comic. This is the comic element which Aristophanes rightly seized upon when Socrates, as he supposed, sought by his "ideas" to shun the world. To hoist the philosopher in a basket amongst the clouds where he might lucubrate upon the ether without his thoughts' being corrupted by earth's dampness was an appropriate rebuke to thought's "detachment," however unjust to Socrates. Detachment as a way of life becomes a learning how to die.

The dialectic of life is the elucidation in existence of every commitment, even of that commitment which avoids commitment. It concentrates the pro and con of all hypotheses upon the fact of the decision in time; and time becomes history precisely because it is big with this decisiveness.[29] Had Greek thought not overlooked this existential factor, the static sphericity of the being-nonbeing world view might have been qualified by teleology understood as destiny. This implies a moral teleology. It shifts the axis of historical determination from the polarity of being and nonbeing to the polarity of faith and denial. Destiny is decision carried forward into action by the act of faith wherewith the self commits itself. Either commitment steps into the meeting place with God and so fills time with godly act and meaning, or it avoids

---

[29] There is also a sense in which thought in its relation to existence may be said to be dialectical in the Kantian sense. Kant proved the insufficiency both of rationalist and empiricist theories of knowledge yet recognized by his a priori synthesis what was valid in each. The synthesis of the rational categories and the data mediated by the senses was brought about by neither the one nor the other, but by a third term—the creative activity of thought. This view of thought as creatively active displaced the rigid logic of the static systems and made thought *dialectical*. Hegel, building on this insight, pursued this process immanently into the ultimate self-consciousness of the Absolute by the principle of "mediation." Christian dialectic, however, moves in just the opposite direction by qualifying all self-consciousness at the point of its discreteness. By this motion the transcendence of God is assured, and subjectivity is overcome in the dialectical relationship—the relationship, that is, in which "mediation" is supplanted by "communication."

p 49

$$\begin{array}{r} 18 \\ 20 \\ 2 \\ \hline 40 \end{array}$$

the meeting place and commits itself to fate in its impersonal implacabilities.

This alternative of initial human freedom is discovered from the Cross. The ambiguity of the Cross, as the historical moment where the Eternal stands in time, removes the ambiguity from life, history, and experience. It clarifies the choice of fate as willfulness and sin. Faith becomes our destiny. As sin is a continuing act, so faith—its contrary—is a continuing act. The decision in faith must be renewed at every parting of the ways. Christ is the parting of the ways, and the place where man stands is a parting of the ways. The one way slips off into the inertness of emptied time, where fate scratches away its meaningless recurrence, like the needle on a broken phonograph record; and the other way renews all things into the likeness of the image of God.

Understood theologically, destiny is related to Spirit, and fate is related to law. If we do not know God through the Spirit in the relatedness of grace and love, we encounter the opposition of his will as obstacle and penalty wherever we assert our independence in the world. The first gives life through personal relatedness; the second breeds death through the impersonal encounter with the Absolute. The law becomes a "curse," a "bondage," and the "wrath of God." Upon it we are ground to powder. By Spirit we are freed from the curse of the law: "If ye are led by the Spirit, ye are not under the law." But this is true not because of the law, for the law is still the will of God. It is true because of ourselves, who, because of our refusal to know him in the Spirit in creative fellowship, must know him as our Foe. By God's will we are either made or broken—but by the exercise of our initial freedom whereby we choose him or defy him. Which means that to deny relatedness to God in the Spirit is not merely to commit ourselves to a misunderstanding. It is an attempt at self-sufficiency and self-justification against God. It is a Titanism.

Titanism takes two forms. There is the Titanism of denial, and there is a Titanism of rebellion. The first is nihilistic in its forms; the second is demonic.

Nietzsche—the diminished Titan of the nineteenth century (a Titan, however, whose powers were augmented by the Christian teaching which he opposed)—foresaw the "rise of Nihilism" in the centuries ahead. Nietzsche's nihilism was a jubilant acceptance of the world as it appears, untrammeled by such notions as the Absolute, the Creator God, and the overruling providence of a transcendent Agent from beyond. The world existed on its own account, never beginning and never ending. "It lives on itself: it feeds on its own excrements." [30] It is to be coped with Titanically by man, who pits his strength against the world's strength and who will, by virtue of this overcoming, project at length the superman. This superman, however, was a desperate projection. Founded on a willful self, it returns upon its starting point interminably. It is a part of the disease it seeks to cure. It is the heart curved inward on itself, not choosing itself in despair, but choosing its despair. "Objection, evasion, joyous distrust, and love of irony, are signs of health; everything absolute belongs to pathology." The irony of denial that still would affirm itself overreaches itself: self-will, grounded in fate, confirmed by a nihilistic world view, plays a losing game. It transcends itself willfully in denying in the world the transcendent values of the Spirit while at the same time plunging the self into a pathology of self-transcendence. This is transcendence in infinite opaqueness.

"Have I—still a goal? A haven towards which my sail is set?
A good wind? . . .
What still remaineth to me? A heart weary and flippant; an unstable will; fluttering wings; a broken backbone.
This seeking for my home: O Zarathustra, dost thou know that this seeking hath been my home-sickening; it eateth me up.
'Where is—my home?' For it do I ask and seek, and have sought, but have not found it. O eternal everywhere, O eternal nowhere, O eternal—in-vain!" [31]

Herein we see how freedom freely binds itself. He is truly free who is able to will without arbitrarily willing self. History projected arbitrarily is self-will amplified; it reaches at length a point of stasis, the point where "the Eternal protests!" [32] It breaks

[30] *The Will to Power*, sec. 1066.
[31] *Thus Spake Zarathustra*, IV, lxix.
[32] Jer. 2:29 (Moffatt).

itself upon the "extremity of all things." The self, asserted so, reaches the point of recoil on itself through a curious deflection of itself as fate upon itself as self-will. For fate and self-will are incompatible. Fate is that which self-will cannot possibly endure, for self-will refuses to be bound by anything. Self-will is that which fate cannot endure, for fate binds everything. Self-will looks upon obedience to God as something which would bind it; sees it not as a relationship in living communion whereby we are empowered to realize God's idea of us, but sees God as law which bends us to his ultimate control.[33] Self-will, asserting thus its independence, delivers itself to fate. But self-will willfully refuses to acknowledge fate, and propogates its willfulness in deeds that willfully avoid the God relation. We avert our eyes from the eyes of Christ. We speedily move through the world, spending ourselves in the fullness of time's emptiness, thus avoiding the fullness of time, and trying to divert the mind from dwelling on the Crucified. Suddenly, around some corner of our choosing, fate confronts us; and in the shock of confrontation each declares the emptiness of other. This is the moment of recoil. Out of prodigality of denial the son comes to himself. Anguish fills him, as his desolation breaks the dikes of self-will and floods the consciousness.

Here again the defect of human willing confronts us in the curious fact that man, who wants God, nevertheless strives to avoid him—would, in fact, do away with him. Man who wishes to be autonomous, "on his own," wholly responsible, flies from the fact of his responsibility. But "Fear wist not to evade as Love wist to pursue." God overtakes us in Christ through becoming what we are, and in such a way that flight, evasion, and defiance are stayed—or are brought out into the open as rebellion and sin.

There is a greater form of Titanism than denial. It is the Titanism of defiance. Defiance easily becomes demonic where it would impose its will upon the world. Or it becomes lonely and Promethean where it asserts against the power of the world its essential divinity.

[33] Calvin's "grace" becomes a fate through his scholastic tendency to regard the God-relationship legalistically.

The outward similarity between Prometheus upon the rocks and Christ upon the Cross has often been remarked. The vultures gnawing in Prometheus' side, and the Messengers who come to heal his wounds each night, form a sober analogue to that wound in the side of Christ—the wound by which the wounds of the world are healed. But in the one there is defiance of the curse on behalf of human divinity; in the other there is redemption from the curse on behalf of all humanity.

The element of defiance is godlike. The Promethean pattern is refracted in Byron's *Manfred*—

> I do not combat against death, but thee
> And thy surrounding angels.[34]

It also appears in Milton's Satan, who

> . . . with ambitious aim
> Against the throne and monarchy of God,
> Raised impious war in Heaven.[35]

"Better to reign in Hell," said Satan; "Better to serve this rock," said Prometheus.

Here, however, is a difference. Satan defied the monarchy of Heaven. Prometheus defied the monarchy of law. For even Zeus could not avoid that which was destined. Necessity was over all. Destiny, therefore, he would endure, "knowing still how vain to take up arms against Necessity." The Greek mind knew there was that in it which was intrinsically greater than the overriding fate, and that in the conflict with necessity wisdom might be gained "through suffering." This faith was based, however, on a partial apprehension of the truth—an apprehension based upon the *ratio scientiae,* a closed cosmology of mind and matter constructed by the lonely "imperious thinking power." It is thereby oppressive, and enervated by a preordained defeat which makes its wisdom vanity. Through Christ these bonds are broken. Prometheus is unbound, and he is "revealed as the victim of nothing

---

[34] Act III, scene 4.
[35] *Paradise Lost.*

but his own obsessions, the obsessions of the 'scientific' understanding." [36]

Consequently, Titanism is that climax of tragedy to which our self-sufficiency and reason freely commit themselves through the tendency of thought as theoretical reason to deflect truth from life, freedom, history, and tragedy. On the other hand, the Cross recapitulates the whole to effect a reconciliation precisely at the point where life, history, freedom, and tragedy absolutely intersect. The dialectic of the law fulfills itself in Christ, for Christ fulfills "the demands of the law" [37] and yet through him we are released from bondage to the law through the Holy Spirit, since Christ is himself "the end of the law." It is for this reason that the Cross, as an analogy for God-consciousness, is necessarily historical and eschatological. It brings to bear upon every human choice, and upon history as the dialectical unfolding of the human complex of choices, the dimension of eternal judgment (the discrepancy between eternal fate and destiny), demanding and renewing the choice that is *crucial*.

iv

Time and eternity in all the systems are parallel lines, which, no matter how far extended, can never meet. We geometrize the ultimate relations. The Cross, however, is the meeting place in time. The lines of all relations intersect in it; and all the lines, no matter how extended, cannot avoid the meeting place.[38]

Therefore the Cross is crucial. Through it we enter into life. By it we pass between the extremes of fate and self-will and come to know ourselves as we are known, in destiny and freedom. Henceforth we live κατὰ πνεῦμα, after the Spirit. The body becomes a shrine for the Spirit's indwelling.[39] Spirit quickens: its gift is a consolation of power.[40] By it we are transformed into the

---

[36] Cochrane, *Christianity and Classical Culture,* p. 411.

[37] Rom. 8:4.

[38] Cf. Justin Martyr's *theologia crucis.* All things in the world show forth the likeness of the Cross. (*Dialogue with Trypho* xcvii; *The first apology* lv.)

[39] I Cor. 6:19-20.

[40] II Cor. 3:6.

likeness of Christ [41] who "for freedom set us free!" [42] By virtue of this fructifying in the Spirit we produce true values: "love, joy, peace, longsuffering, kindness, goodness, faithfulness, meekness, self-control"; for against these there is no law.[43]

(The Word was made flesh and dwelt among us.)

* * * * *

The Cross draws man upon himself to effect decision concerning himself by confronting him objectively with the ultimate consequences of his flight from himself. It also bends fate back upon his destiny in such a way that his freedom may be renewed in the will of God. This implies that man must go forward altogether into fate and there choose not despair but himself in despair apart from God. He must, that is to say, come to himself.

But how can he go forward into destiny when fate surrounds him with its laughing idols? Belief in fate is a form of willing, and it is binding only on those who will to believe in it. He must, therefore, enter like Childe Roland into that "ominous tract" of willed dubiety and there decide his destiny.

In much modern knighthood men have entered on a quest in which they no longer believe; or, rather, they believe that the object of their quest will not be found. But this itself leads to the ominous tract of dereliction, failure, and despair where each moves alone. It does not matter how many move thereto beside us, for the ominous tract—which may be the deep declivity of an aeon's despair—is within us. Once pledged to this all-fateful quest, there is no turning back.

> For mark! no sooner was I fairly found
> Pledged to the plain, after a pace or two,
> Than, pausing to throw backward a last view
> O'er the safe road, 'twas gone; . . .
>
> . . . .
>
> I might go on; naught else remained to do.

[41] I Cor. 12:13.
[42] Gal. 5:1.
[43] Gal. 5:16-22.

He who believes in destiny must enter step by step into his own aeon's despair, and into his own declivity, treading into the darkness of its perversity, until, surrounded by the hills of its Despond, the Dark Tower looms and his soul is brought to bay. This is the moment of decision, though mockery sits round to see the game at bay.

> There they stood, ranged along the hillsides, met
> To view the last of me, a living frame
> For one more picture! in a sheet of flame
> I saw them and I knew them all. And yet
> Dauntless the slug-horn to my lips I set,
> And blew. *"Childe Roland to the Dark Tower came."*

Whether he blows in resignation or repentance will decide his fate or destiny. He must be willing even to resign that demonic consolation which resignation itself provides when one goes down fighting against both the Word and the world.[44]

The Dark Tower must become for him the clarification of his basic apostasy, which is the denial of his relationship to God.

To as many as keep the love of God He gives His own communion. For the communion of God is life and light, and the enjoyment of the blessings that are with Him. But on as many as depart from God of their own free will He inflicts separation from Himself. But separation from God is death, and separation from light is darkness; and separation from God means a loss of the blessings that are with Him. But they who have lost these blessings through their apostasy, inasmuch as they are deprived of every good thing continue in every form of chastisement ($\kappa\delta\lambda\alpha\sigma\iota\varsigma$). But God Himself does not directly punish them, but their chastisement follows them in their deprivations.[45]

The fatality which this principle contains is clear, but men veil it or evade it. The hope which the principle involves is not discerned so readily. But Jeremiah saw it before Irenaeus, though Irenaeus

---

[44] Calvin's theology is oppressive because it sticks fast in resignation. Calvin required the certainties of legalism and of logic to assure his faith. His doctrine of the Holy Spirit is curtailed beforehand by the causal relation which he held to exist between God's will and ours. This also accounts for the fatalism in his notion of depravity. The true opposite of original sin (when held dialectically, not statically) is original freedom, not original righteousness understood as a legal demand.

[45] Irenaeus *Adv. haer.* V. xxvii. 2.

saw it after him.[46] "Thy apostasy shall reform thee." [47] The aban-
donment of God brings with it devastation and defeat. The return
is by the way of "quest" which is also "judgment." This is the way
to the last Dark Tower of existence in which is hid the final
secret of the spirit's ambiguity. We go the whole way, till comes
the "click as when a trap shuts" and all retreats are closed. This is
the point of infinite determination, the "terrible choice"—salvation, or damnation.

(*He descended into hell.*)

.*   *   *   *   *

The Cross is to history what "peripety" and "discovery" are for
tragedy. As such it cuts across our view of history as the causal unfolding of an infinite series of linear antecedents.[48] Peripety is the
sudden reversal whereby a tragic plot is suddenly transposed at
its climax into the opposite of what its events portend. The discovery is the change "from ignorance to knowledge" by which
the reversal is brought about. This means that in the drama there
is woven something concealed, a something which the plot itself
will in time reveal; and this revelation at the climax will work the
desired purgation of the plot's antagonism. In the drama of God's
dealing with the world, there is concealed in the Galilean Carpenter the fact that he is the Son of God who has come to take
upon himself the sins of the world and to reconcile the world unto
God. But the world does not know this. It seeks to do away with
him because his righteousness offends. It does away with him.
Yet he will not be bound, neither by sin, nor death, nor devil. He
rises from the tomb.

This is a reversal, an unexpected turn, a cataclysmic denouement
of "history." Christ stands at the point where the extremes meet.
In every crisis of history man spirals downwards in the whorl of
misery, contention, and destruction that his sin has wrought; and,
at the plunging vortex of despair, wherein he cries "My God, My
God, why hast thou forsaken me!" the first step of ascent begins.
The drama of historical conflict repeats the drama of the Cross,

[46] *Ibid.* IV. xxxvii. 7.
[47] Jer. 2:19.
[48] *Poetics* 1452*a-b*.

312

because it is thrust upon the Cross. Christ, "assuming the character of man, and fashioning Himself in flesh," as Clement says, "enacted the drama of human salvation: for He was a true champion and a fellow-champion with the creature." [49] The Cross is the point of cosmic and historical catharsis in which the antagonism of history as the efflux of human intransigency is resolved. It is *victory*. It is achieved through sacrifice and suffering, in which God himself becomes the protagonist who overthrows the antagonism of oppressive and demonic fate, the complication introduced into creation by man's defiant self-sufficiency and sin.

The fact of human freedom is thus revealed. Nothing is clearer from the Cross than this, that man is and remains free by the creative intent of God, even though by freedom man so circumscribes himself as to bind and destroy himself. He is free to love God or to defy him. He may have God or an idol. "Original sin" occurs always at the point where man exercises this initial freedom. All other sins are but the demonic extensions of this initial choosing. Thus cultures may become expanding universes of collective pride which burst at last from excess entropy of moral tension. Man freely thrusts himself and his idea of meaning into external works and deeds; but, having turned his spirit from the side open to God, he quickly empties himself and turns in upon himself and is bent backward on his emptiness. Only that cup runneth over which is open to God's freely given grace; the cup inverted cannot be filled, nor can it fill itself.

This tyranny of sinning could be broken, but only by a power potent to destroy it from within. The Word of God, therefore, confronts that apostasy and redeems therefrom his own. As Irenaeus wrote:

But this he did, not with violence, whereby the apostasy had originally obtained its power over us, greedily grasping at what was not its own, but by moral force, as it became God, by persuasion; . . . so that there might be no infringement of justice on the one side, and on the other that God's ancient handiwork should not perish.[50]

[49] *Exhortation to the heathen* x.
[50] *Adv. haer.* V. i. 1.

Thus from the beginning man is free to be free in God or to enslave himself; so also at the end, in the fullness of time, man is free to be free in God through Christ or to resume the fatal apostasy in one more aeon of melancholy willfulness.

Christ transforms. In the power of his creativeness man comes to know his destiny, which shatters all the causal circularities that self-will gives momentum to. Christ in us shatters every "framework," breaking through the complex congeries of bounds and bindings which that great chrysalis, the world, flings over us.

Apart from Christ, man is the little Gulliver who binds himself by Lilliputian cords of betrayal and self-will while his spirit sleeps.

(*Christ splits open every tomb.*)

* * * * *

By the way of the Cross we pass through our little Gethsemanes of tragedy and dereliction. There is a "beyond good and evil," but it is to be arrived at by the redemptive way. The real is thus tied up with history, as history is tied up with freedom. "Recapitulating all things in himself," as Irenaeus said, Christ reconciled the world to God. What begins as an analogy, declaring to man the cruciform nature of reality under God, concludes, therefore, as a fact, as *the* fact, as that pivotal Fact by which the absolute terms of our history and the world are declared to us. On this side of good and evil, the Cross appears as an eschatological confrontation, as the Last Word, whereby the masks are removed from off our willfulness. Beyond good and evil, Christ is Emmanuel, God with us.

There is in this no way of return to Paradise. Christ offers no retreat into a hermetic isolation of the spirit, whether by asceticism, mysticism, metaphysics, or aesthetics. The way is forward into history, toward the Kingdom and toward the New Jerusalem. The way is *through* the Caudine Forks into creative destiny. The isms which the mind creates are all retreats from freedom—romanticisms, pacifisms, monasticisms, totalitarianisms, rationalisms, scientisms. They all lead, each by an inner dialectic of its own, to the depersonalization of our relationship to God and to each other. They dehumanize. Christ humanizes because he personalizes. The way is forward, through the Cross, and into free-dom under God and the destiny that lies between us. All else is a betrayal of our heritage of faith.

We reach today, therefore, the crisis of our faith. It is not that crises have not been reached before. It is that each reduplication of apostasy is more pathetic and absurd. It is also much more ter-rible; it cuts more sharply through the masquerade. It is not simply that each new generation repeats the errors and mistakes of previous generations. It carries forward in its own catastrophe the unresolved evils that have gone before: its guilt is multiplied. Says Martin Buber:

In each new aeon fate becomes more oppressive, reversal more shatter-ing. And the theophany becomes ever *nearer,* increasingly near to the sphere that lies *between beings,* to the Kingdom that is hidden in our midst, there between us. History is a mysterious approach. Every spiral of its way leads us both into profounder perversion and more fundamental reversal. But the event that from the side of the world is called reversal is from God's side called salvation.[51]

V

There remains, however, from the standpoint of culture, a point where reversal from man's side and salvation from God's side must meet in a continuing transfiguration of the world. The work of Christ was indeed to reconcile men to God. It was indeed to bring to men the means of salvation. But it was also to renew the world, and to renew through man the power of the Spirit in the world. The renewal of the image of God in man is the renewal also of man's creative freedom.

There is nothing in the New Testament more constant than this emphasis upon the new—the new covenant, the new hope, the new Jerusalem, the new *life.* "Learn," wrote Irenaeus, "that he brought every new thing, bringing himself." [52] For it had been proclaimed that "newness would come to renew and revive man." And such is the power of this renewal that through it man may renew the world. Through Christ not merely are we called into

---

[51] *I and Thou,* p. 120.
[52] *Adv. haer.* IV. xxxiv. 1.

that salvation whereby we are caught up out of the world, but we are called equally to participate in the transfiguration of the world. "Behold, I make all things new." That is the compendious transfiguration which attends upon the power of renewal in the Spirit.

A new spirituality is coming to birth in the world. The travail and agony of these times marks the slow return of our civilization up the dolorous slopes of Golgotha. The "metaphysical crisis" through which we are passing is one that thrusts the individual upon the primary terms of human freedom, upon the primacy of faith. The prophetic possibility of our hour is nothing less than a religious transfiguration of humanity in the world.

Transfiguration of the world, when all things have reached a climax of entropy and tension, implies that none are exempt and all are called and the destiny of the world is in the balance. Transfiguration begins, it is true, on the mountain top. It begins with the vision of God, at the point where God makes himself manifest. But it descends to the plain. Its primary aim is not to build tabernacles in which to enshrine the vision; it is to go down into the valley where the demoniac lad is waiting to be healed. Today also Christianity must go down into the valleys to touch and to heal the demoniac world. It is a way of compassion and sacrifice.

It is also the way of creativeness. It is a way of victory and beauty, transfiguring the world into the wonder and splendor of God. Our creative acts in the world bear witness to our true vocation. The image of God is the image of the Creator. Through us he extends his power. Such creative acts are also acts of freedom, for through them we secure that liberation into spirit which is at once a victory over "time" and over that lethargy of death which creeps over all souls that deny God's power. The tragedy of the modern world has been that it has tried to create from that lethargy of death a new world fructified by a Spirit in which it no longer believes. Therefore our works are stillborn and our souls without true power to transform the world.

There is, therefore, no analogy quite so appropriate to our time as that Apocryphal story according to which Jesus, when a boy, made some clay sparrows; and when he touched them they came to life and flew into the sky. We await today that singular touch of power which shall give life to our clay souls and lift us up to God's blue heaven. It is such a liberation into freedom that we seek. For this true freedom is at once the way and the truth and the life. And it is the knowledge that in His will is both our peace and our power to make and to remake the world.

INDEX

INDEX

INDEX

Greek, 114, 206-13
theocentric, 230
true, 231
Humanist, Christian, 197, 202-31, 278
Humanists, 68, 138
Critical, 33
Humanitarians, 137
Humanity, notion of, 245
Humility, 207, 209
Humor, 239
Huss, John, 135
Hutten, von, 49

Idea, immanence of, 84, 303
Ideal, and actual, 124
Idealism, 87, 160, 161, 162, 165, 172, 249, 303
Ideas
innate, 74
Platonic, 261
Identity, principle of, 134, 294, 295
Ideologies, 203
Idolatry, 29, 35, 230
cultural, 199
Ignorance, 158, 159, 167, 259, 261, 262
Image of God, 173, 197, 199, 200, 224, 225, 229, 230, 240, 279, 286, 305, 315, 316
Incarnation, 136, 181, 186, 196, 200, 201, 219, 230, 301
Incontinence, 263, 264
Individual, suppression of, 132
Individualism, 128
Infinite, the, 237
Infinities, the false, 292
Inge, W R., 156
Innocence, 175
Inquiry, principle of free, 138
Intellectualism, 165
Interiority, 84
Introversion, pattern of, 118
Irenaeus, 130, 241, 311, 313, 314, 315
Irony, 99, 118, 119, 120, 121, 122, 123, 124, 125, 126, 205, 208, 209, 239, 249, 306
Irresponsibles, The, 39-40
Isaac, 134, 275
Isaiah, 220, 221, 222, 245

Jacob, 16, 134, 159, 275
Jacopone da Todi, 135
Jaeger, Werner, 217
Janaka, 237

Jaspers, Karl, 22, 24, 36, 43, 59, 61, 62, 63, 127, 189, 190, 191, 195, 199, 244
Jeremiah, 24, 152, 278, 306, 311
Joachim of Flores, 135
Job, 219
John of the Cross, St., 109, 271, 273
Joubert, Jacques, 81, 89, 106
Joyce, James, 170
Judaism, 219, 228
Judgment, 301, 309, 312
suspension of, 187
Justin Martyr, 309

Kant, Immanuel, 37, 81-83, 89, 114, 153, 190, 209, 228, 240, 297, 304
Kierkegaard, Sören, 36, 41, 46, 58, 74, 75, 77, 85, 88, 90, 92, 124, 130, 146, 158, 181, 182, 191, 200, 209, 210, 227, 243, 244, 247, 249, 251, 279, 282, 292
Kingdom, the, 314, 315
Knowledge
identification of virtue with, 263
practical, 46
scientific, 204
tree of, 265

Laforgue, Jules, 120
Lamennais, de, 188, 200
Laughter, 239
Law, the, 94, 95, 218, 228, 267, 300, 302, 303, 305, 308, 309
Lawrence, D. H., 43, 44
Lear, 100
Legalism, 228, 277
Leibnitz, 81
Lenin, Nicolai, 31, 87, 151
Lessing, 265
Litchtenberg, 184
Limit situation, 127, 192
Livy, 176
Locke, John, 61, 68, 81
Logic, 160
Logicism, 92, 133
Logos, the, 214, 238, 252
Longing for the infinite, 107, 108, 109, 223, 235, 236, 244, 275
Lotze, Hermann, 205
Love
of God, 245; *see also Agape and Eros*
theocentric, 93
Lucian, 42
Lucretius, 104

323

INDEX

325

Self-transcendence, 214, 233-36, 238-40,
242, 243-47, 248, 251, 272, 282,
287, 288, 290, 291, 292, 300, 306
Self-will, 306, 307, 314
Seneca, 218
Shakespeare, 97, 161, 162, 273, 287
    doubt in, 98
    irony in, 99
Shelley, 51, 52
Silesius, Angelus, 260
Simon, St., the Theologian, 269
Sin, 64, 93, 114, 119, 125, 130, 139, 176,
    186, 197, 218, 223, 224, 225, 226,
    227, 232, 233, 239, 241, 246, 247,
    251, 255, 259, 261, 264, 267, 271,
    273, 277, 280-81, 289, 292, 305, 307,
    313
    dialectical, 278
    original, 54, 105, 122, 311, 313
Sinner, 122
Skepticism, 16, 71-73, 88, 114, 216, 276
Socrates, 22, 71, 95, 109, 110, 138, 158,
    163, 191, 208, 209, 210, 211, 212,
    213, 218, 220, 227, 257, 258, 260,
    262, 263, 264, 266, 267, 268, 276,
    277, 279, 303, 304.
Socratic cross-questioning, 185
Socratism, 186
Solipsism, 79, 88, 114, 229
Solon, 207
Sophistication, 185
Sophistry, 43, 44, 102, 174, 297
Sophists, 209
Sophocles, 208
Sorokin, Pitirim, 59
Soul, the, 210, 211, 238, 241, 261
    care of, 212
Spencer, Herbert, 42
Spengler, Oswald, 8, 33, 52, 59, 100,
    104, 115, 116, 135, 166
Spinoza, 68, 81, 112
Spirit, 229, 240, 241, 242, 243, 245, 247,
    250, 251, 286, 305, 306, 309, 310,
    315, 316
    dichotomy of, 289, 290
    Holy, 245, 280, 300, 309, 311
    personal, 186, 188
    primacy of, 228
Staël, Mme de, 109
Standpoint, problem of the, 47
    Socratic, 303
Starting point, 285, 298
    Greek, 264

human, 204
    practical, 188
State, the, Hegel on, 87
Stoicism, 72, 105, 166, 228, 275
Strowski, 222
Subhuman, 208
Subjectivism, 114
Substance, 252
Symonds, J. A., 49, 50, 51, 101
Synthesis, 136
    medieval, 129, 130, 131
    Thomist, 131

Tacitus, 219
Tautology, 86, 88, 114, 295
Taylor, A. E., 211
Teacher, the true, 256, 279, 281, 282
Temperance, 264
Tennyson, Alfred, 51, 56
Terence, 228
Tertullian, 53
Thales, 88
Theaetetus, 163
Theism, 212
Theologia crucis, 139, 297, 309
Theology, 133
Theonomy, 196
Theresa, St., 109
Thielicke, Helmut, 196
Thought, validity of, 162
Time, 155, 157, 165, 182, 303
Titanism, 176, 199, 229, 275, 306, 307,
    309
Tiutchev, 15, 25
Tolstoi, 107
Totalitarianism, 128, 129, 135
Toynbee, Arnold, 116
Tragedy, 146, 175, 200, 208, 286, 303,
    309, 312, 314, 316
    Greek, 267
Tragic, the, 298
Tragic situation, 199
Transfiguration of the world, 159, 195,
    196, 198, 200, 315, 316
Trinity, the, 240
Truth
    practical nature of, 286
    as personal, 298
    as relational, 298
Turgenev, I, 204, 205

Unamuno y Jugo, Miguel de, 77, 79, 88,
    158